SCHOLASTIC

100 ENGLISH LESSONS

Terms and conditions

IMPORTANT – PERMITTED USE AND WARNINGS – READ CAREFULLY BEFORE USING

Recommended system requirements:

- Windows: XP (Service Pack 3), Vista (Service Pack 2), Windows 7 or Windows 8 with 2.33GHz processor
- Mac: OS 10.6 to 10.8 with Intel Core™ Duo processor
- 1GB RAM (recommended)
- 1024 x 768 Screen resolution
- CD-ROM drive (24x speed recommended)
- 16-bit sound card
- Adobe Reader (version 9 recommended for Mac users)
- Broadband internet connections (for installation and updates)

For all technical support queries, please phone Scholastic Customer Services on 0845 6039091.

SCHOLASTIC

Book End, Range Road, Witney, Oxfordshire, OX29 0YD
www.scholastic.co.uk

© 2014, Scholastic Ltd

1 2 3 4 5 6 7 8 9   4 5 6 7 8 9 0 1 2 3

British Library Cataloguing-in-Publication Data
A catalogue record for this book is available from the
British Library.

ISBN 978-1407-12762-0
Printed by Bell & Bain Ltd, Glasgow

Due to the nature of the web we cannot guarantee the
content or links of any site mentioned. We strongly
recommend that teachers check websites before using
them in the classroom.

Extracts from *The National Curriculum in English*, *English
Programme of Study* © Crown Copyright. Reproduced
under the terms of the Open Government Licence
(OGL). http://www.nationalarchives.gov.uk/doc/open-
government-licence/open-government-licence.htm

Author
Pam Dowson

Editorial team
Rachel Morgan, Melissa Somers, Marion Archer,
Suzanne Adams

Cover Design
Andrea Lewis

Design Team
Sarah Garbett, Shelley Best and Andrea Lewis

CD-ROM development
Hannah Barnett, Phil Crothers, MWA Technologies
Private Ltd

Typesetting
Ricky Capanni, International Book Management

Illustrations
Tomek.gr

Acknowledgements
The publishers gratefully acknowledge permission
to reproduce the following copyright material:

David Higham Associates for the use of an
illustration by Nick Sharratt from *Cliffhanger* by
Jacqueline Wilson. Illustration © 1995, Nick Sharratt
(1995, Corgi Yearling).
David Higham Associates for the use of extracts
from *Cliffhanger* by Jacqueline Wilson. Text © 1995,
Jacqueline Wilson (1995, Corgi Yearling).
David Higham Associates for the use of the poem
'Timothy Winters' by Charles Causley. Poem © 1975,
Charles Causley.
David Higham Associates for the use of extracts
from *How to Train Your Dragon* by Cressida Cowell.
Text © 2003, Cressida Cowell (2003, Hodder
Children's Books).
HarperCollins Publishers Ltd for the use of an
extract from *The Hobbit* by JRR Tolkien. Text ©
1937, 1965 The JRR Tolkien Estate.
David Heathfield for use of the story 'Deer
and Jaguar' retold by David Heathfield. www.
davidheathfield.co.uk, www.wordstories.org.uk
Carol Emery Phenix for the use of her painting of
Smaug the Impenetrable. Image © Carol Emery
Phenix.
Random House Group Limited for the use of
extracts from *Cliffhanger* by Jacqueline Wilson.
Text © 1995, Jacqueline Wilson. (1995, Corgi
Yearling).
Random House Group Limited for the use of text
from *Astrosaurs: Robot Raiders* by Steve Cole. Text
© 2010, Steve Cole (2010, Red Fox).
Brenda Williams for the use of the poem 'The
legend of Robin Hood' by Brenda Williams, first
published in *Child Education*. Poem © 2011, Brenda
Williams (2011, Scholastic Ltd).

Every effort has been made to trace copyright
holders for the works reproduced in this book,
and the publishers apologise for any inadvertent
omissions.

Contents

Introduction

About the series

The *100 English Lessons* series is designed to meet the requirements of the 2014 Curriculum, English Programmes of Study. There are six books in the series, Years 1–6, and each book contains lesson plans, resources and ideas matched to the new curriculum. It can be a complex task to ensure that a progressive and appropriate curriculum is followed in all year groups; this series has been carefully structured to ensure that a progressive and appropriate curriculum is followed throughout.

About the new curriculum

The curriculum documentation for English provides a single-year programme of study for Year 1 and Year 2, but joint programmes of study for Years 3–4 and Years 5–6.

There is a much greater focus on the technical aspects of language – including grammar, punctuation, spelling, handwriting and phonics. These are the building blocks to help children to read and write. It has been perceived that these aspects have to be taught discretely, however the approach encouraged in this series is to embed these elements into existing learning. For example, using a focus text to identify the use of punctuation and using that as a springboard to practise it.

There is a spoken language Programme of Study which outlines statutory requirements across Years 1–6. Within the English curriculum there are also attainment targets that involve 'discussion', 'talking', 'participating' and 'listening'. The aims of speaking and listening are below:

> *The National Curriculum for English reflects the importance of spoken language in children's development across the whole curriculum – cognitively, socially and linguistically. The quality and variety of language that children hear and speak are vital for developing their vocabulary, grammar and their understanding for reading and writing. Teachers should therefore ensure the continual development of children's confidence and competence in spoken language. Children should develop a capacity to explain their understanding of books and other reading, and to prepare their ideas before they write. They must be assisted in making their thinking clear to themselves as well as to others and teachers should ensure that children build secure foundations by using discussion to probe and remedy their misconceptions. Children should also be taught to understand and use the conventions for discussion and debate.*
>
> *Statutory requirements which underpin all aspects of speaking and listening across the six years of primary education form part of the National Curriculum. These are contextualised within the reading and writing domains which follow.*

Terminology

The curriculum terminology has changed; the main terms used are:

- **Domains:** The area of the subject, for English the domains are 'Reading' and 'Writing'.
- **Sub-domains:** The next level down to the domains. In English, Reading's sub-domains are 'Word reading' and 'Comprehension' and Writing's sub-domains are 'Transcription' and 'Composition'.
- **Curriculum objectives:** These are the statutory programme of study statements or objectives.
- **Appendix:** Any reference to an appendix refers to an appendix of the National Curriculum for English document. There are two appendices – one for spelling (Appendix 1) and one for vocabulary, grammar and punctuation (Appendix 2).

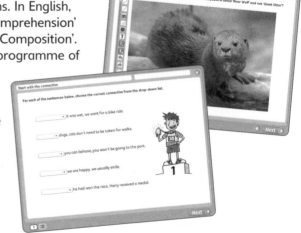

About the book

This book is divided into six chapters; each chapter contains a half-term's work and is based around a topic or theme. Each chapter follows the same structure:

Chapter introduction

At the start of each chapter there is a summary of what is covered. This includes:

- **Introduction:** A description of what is covered in the chapter.
- **Expected prior learning:** What the children are expected to know before starting the work in the chapter.
- **Overview of progression:** A brief explanation of how the children progress through the chapter.
- **Creative context:** How the chapter could link to other curriculum areas.
- **Preparation:** Any resources required for the teaching of the chapter, including things that need to be sourced or prepared and the content that can be located on the CD-ROM.
- **Chapter at a glance:** This is a table that summarises the content of each lesson, including: the curriculum objectives (using a code system, please see pages 8–10), a summary of the activities and the outcome.
- **Background knowledge:** A section explaining grammatical terms and suchlike to enhance your subject knowledge, where required.

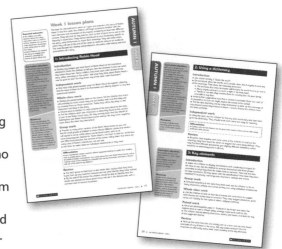

Lessons

Each chapter contains six weeks' of lessons, each week contains five lessons. At the start of each week there is an introduction about what is covered and the expected outcomes. The lesson plans then include the relevant combination of headings from below.

- **Curriculum objectives:** A list of the relevant objectives from the Programme of Study.
- **Resources:** What you require to teach the lesson.
- **Introduction:** A short and engaging activity to begin the lesson.
- **Whole-class work:** Working together as a class.
- **Group/Paired/Independent work:** Children working independently of the teacher in pairs, groups or alone.
- **Differentiation:** Ideas for how to support children who are struggling with a concept or how to extend those children who understand a concept without taking them onto new work.
- **Review:** A chance to review the children's learning and ensure the outcomes of the lesson have been achieved.

Assess and review

At the end of each chapter are activities for assessing and reviewing the children's understanding. These can be conducted during the course of the chapter's work or saved until the end of the chapter or done at a later date. There are four focuses for assess and review activities in each chapter:

- Grammar and punctuation
- Spelling
- Reading
- Writing

Elements of speaking and listening will be included where relevant within these four areas.

All four focuses follow the same format:

- **Curriculum objectives:** These are the areas of focus for the assess and review activity. There may be one focus or more than one depending on the activity.
- **Resources:** What you require to conduct the activities.
- **Revise:** A series of short activities or one longer activity to revise and consolidate the children's learning and ensure they understand the concept(s).
- **Assess:** An assessment activity to provide a chance for the children to demonstrate their understanding and for you to check this.
- **Further practice:** Ideas for further practice on the focus, whether children are insecure in their learning or you want to provide extra practice or challenge.

Photocopiable pages

At the end of each chapter are some photocopiable pages that will have been referred to in the lesson plans. These sheets are for the children to use; there is generally a title, an instruction, an activity and an 'I can' statement at the bottom. These sheets are also provided on the CD-ROM alongside additional pages as referenced in the lessons (see page 7 About the CD-ROM). The children should be encouraged to complete the 'I can' statements by colouring in the traffic lights to say how they think they have done (red – not very well, amber – ok, green – very well).

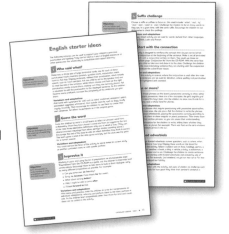

English starter activities

At the beginning of the book there is a bank of English starter activities (pages 11–14). These are games and activities that will help children familiarise and consolidate their knowledge of grammar, punctuation and spelling. The use of these will be suggested throughout the chapters, but they are also flexible and therefore could be used at any time.

⋓SCHOLASTIC

About the CD-ROM

The CD-ROM contains:

- Printable versions of the photocopiable sheets from the book and additional photocopiable sheets as referenced in the lesson plans.
- Interactive activities for children to complete or to use on the whiteboard.
- Media resources to display.
- Printable versions of the lesson plans.
- Digital versions of the lesson plans with the relevant resources linked to them.

Getting started

- Put the CD-ROM into your CD-ROM drive.
    - For Windows users, the install wizard should autorun, if it fails to do so then navigate to your CD-ROM drive. Then follow the installation process.
    - For Mac users, copy the disk image file to your hard drive. After it has finished copying double-click it to mount the disk image. Navigate to the mounted disk image and run the installer. After installation the disk image can be unmounted and the DMG can be deleted from the hard drive.
- To complete the installation of the program you need to open the program and click 'Update' in the pop-up. Please note – this CD-ROM is web-enabled and the content will be downloaded from the internet to your hard-drive to populate the CD-ROM with the relevant resources. This only needs to be done on first use, after this you will be able to use the CD-ROM without an internet connection. If at any point any content is updated you will receive another pop-up upon start up with an internet connection.

Navigating the CD-ROM

There are two options to navigate the CD-ROM either as a Child or as a Teacher.

Child

- Click on the 'Child' button on the first menu screen.
- In the second menu click on the relevant class (please note only the books installed on the machine or network will be accessible. You can also rename year groups to match your school's naming conventions via the Teacher > Settings > Rename books area).
- A list of interactive activities will be displayed, children need to locate the correct one and click 'Go' to launch it.
- There is the opportunity to print or save a PDF of the activity at the end.

Teacher

- Click on the 'Teacher' button on the first menu screen and you will be taken to a screen showing which of the *100 English* books you have purchased. From here, you can also access information about getting started and the credits.
- To enter the product click 'Next' in the bottom right.
- You then need to enter a password (the password is: login).
- On first use:

    - Enter as a Guest by clicking on the 'Guest' button.
    - If desired, create a profile for yourself by adding your name to the list of users. Profiles allow you to save favourites and to specify which year group(s) you wish to be able to view.
    - Go to 'Settings' to create a profile for yourself – click 'Add user' and enter your name. Then choose the year groups you wish to have access to (you can return to this screen to change this at any time). Click on 'Login' at the top of the screen to re-enter the disk under your new profile.
- On subsequent uses you can choose your name from the drop-down list. The 'Guest' option will always be available if you, or a colleague, wish to use this.
- You can search the CD-ROM using the tools or save favourites.

For more information about how to use the CD-ROM, please refer to the help file which can be found in the teacher area of the CD-ROM. It is a red button with a question mark on it on the right-hand side of the screen just underneath the 'Settings' tab.

Curriculum grid

This grid shows the full curriculum objectives for Year 4. The codes are referenced in the chapter introductions. Additional information is provided in italics, this includes the statutory information from the appendices and information about when certain objectives are introduced.

Domain	Code	Curriculum objective
Reading: Word reading	RWR1	To apply their growing knowledge of root words, prefixes and suffixes (etymology and morphology) as listed in English Appendix 1, both to read aloud and to understand the meaning of new words they meet.
Reading: Comprehension	RWR2	To read further exception words, noting the unusual correspondences between spelling and sound, and where these occur in the word.
	RC1	To develop positive attitudes to reading and understanding of what they read by listening to and discussing a wide range of fiction, poetry, plays, non-fiction and reference books or textbooks.
	RC2	To develop positive attitudes to reading and understanding of what they read by reading books that are structured in different ways and reading for a range of purposes.
	RC3	To develop positive attitudes to reading and understanding of what they read by using dictionaries to check the meaning of words that they have read.
	RC4	To develop positive attitudes to reading and understanding of what they read by increasing their familiarity with a wide range of books, including fairy stories, myths and legends, and retelling some of these orally.
	RC5	To develop positive attitudes to reading and understanding of what they read by identifying themes and conventions in a wide range of books.
	RC6	To develop positive attitudes to reading and understanding of what they read by preparing poems and playscripts to read aloud and to perform, showing understanding through intonation, tone, volume and action.
	RC7	To develop positive attitudes to reading and understanding of what they read by discussing words and phrases that capture the reader's interest and imagination.
	RC8	To develop positive attitudes to reading and understanding of what they read by recognising some different forms of poetry.
	RC9	To understand what they read, in books they can read independently, by checking that the text makes sense to them, discussing their understanding and explaining the meaning of words in context.
	RC10	To understand what they read, in books they can read independently, by asking questions to improve their understanding of a text.
	RC11	To understand what they read, in books they can read independently, by drawing inferences such as inferring characters' feelings, thoughts and motives from their actions, and justifying inferences with evidence.
	RC12	To understand what they read, in books they can read independently, by predicting what might happen from details stated and implied.
	RC13	To understand what they read, in books they can read independently, by identifying main ideas drawn from more than one paragraph and summarising these.
	RC14	To understand what they read, in books they can read independently, by identifying how language, structure, and presentation contribute to meaning.
	RC15	To retrieve and record information from non-fiction.
	RC16	To participate in discussion about both books that are read to them and those they can read for themselves, taking turns and listening to what others say.

■ SCHOLASTIC

Domain	Code	Curriculum objective
Writing: Transcription	WT1	To use further prefixes and suffixes and understand how to add them (English Appendix 1).
	WT2	To spell further homophones.
	WT3	To spell words that are often misspelled (English Appendix 1).
	WT4	To place the possessive apostrophe accurately in words with regular plurals and in words with irregular plurals.
	WT5	To use the first two or three letters of a word to check its spelling in a dictionary.
	WT6	To write from memory simple sentences, dictated by the teacher, that include words and punctuation taught so far.
	WT7	To use the diagonal and horizontal strokes that are needed to join letters and understand which letters, when adjacent to one another, are best left unjoined.
	WT8	To increase the legibility, consistency and quality of their handwriting.
Writing: Composition	WC1	To plan their writing by discussing writing similar to that which they are planning to write in order to understand and learn from its structure, grammar and vocabulary.
	WC2	To plan their writing by discussing and recording ideas.
	WC3	To draft and write by composing and rehearsing sentences orally (including dialogue), progressively building a varied and rich vocabulary and an increasing range of sentence structures (English Appendix 2).
	WC4	To draft and write by organising paragraphs around a theme.
	WC5	To draft and write by, in narratives, creating settings, characters and plot.
	WC6	To draft and write by, in non-narrative material, using simple organisational devices such as headings and subheadings.
	WC7	To evaluate and edit by assessing the effectiveness of their own and others' writing and suggesting improvements.
	WC8	To evaluate and edit by proposing changes to grammar and vocabulary to improve consistency and accuracy, including the accurate use of pronouns in sentences.
	WC9	To proofread for spelling and punctuation errors.
	WC10	To read aloud their own writing, to a group or the whole class, using appropriate intonation and controlling the tone and volume so that the meaning is clear.
	WC11	To develop their understanding of the concepts set out in English Appendix 2 by extending the range of sentences with more than one clause by using a wider range of conjunctions, including *when, if, because, although*.
	WC12	To develop their understanding of the concepts set out in English Appendix 2 by using the present perfect form of verbs in contrast to the past tense.

Domain	Code	Curriculum objective
Writing: Composition	WC13	To develop their understanding of the concepts set out in English Appendix 2 by choosing nouns or pronouns appropriately for clarity and cohesion and to avoid repetition. *Using pronouns for clarity and cohesion is a focus in Year 4 building on avoiding repetition focus of Year 3.*
	WC14	To develop their understanding of the concepts set out in English Appendix 2 by using conjunctions, adverbs and prepositions to express time and cause.
	WC15	To develop their understanding of the concepts set out in English Appendix 2 by using fronted adverbials. *This is introduced in Year 4.*
	WC16	To develop their understanding of the concepts set out in English Appendix 2 by learning the grammar for Years 3 and 4 in English Appendix 2.
	WC17	To indicate grammatical and other features by using commas after fronted adverbials. *This is introduced in Year 4.*
	WC18	To indicate grammatical and other features by indicating possession by using the possessive apostrophe with singular and plural nouns.
	WC19	To indicate grammatical and other features by using and punctuating direct speech.
	WC20	To use and understand the grammatical terminology in English Appendix 2 accurately and appropriately when discussing their writing and reading.

English starter ideas

The following activities can be used to support your children's grammar, punctuation and spelling. They can be used as a part of English lessons or at other points over the school day to consolidate and support learning.

1 Who said what?

Objectives
● To use inverted commas to punctuate direct speech.

Make two or three sets of large laminated cards, one for each of these punctuation marks: inverted commas, question mark, exclamation mark, comma, full stop. Display sentences, without their punctuation, which include speech, such as *I can't said Jack*. Ask one child to act as the speaker and one to read the rest of the sentence, while others choose and hold up the right punctuation marks around them, making sure they are correctly placed. Ask a volunteer to add the punctuation to the displayed sentence. As the children become more proficient, increase the complexity of the sentences you give them.

Variations and adaptations
Add cards with synonyms for *said*, such as *asked, exclaimed, whispered, yelled, demanded, suggested, whimpered*. Also include adverbs, such as *shyly, loudly, angrily, forcefully*. Then encourage the children to use these to create their own sentences, for others to punctuate as in the original game.

2 Guess the word

Objectives
● To use dictionaries to check the meanings of words they have read.

Invite the children to work in small teams to select an unusual word from a dictionary. Once they have chosen a word ask them to suggest to the rest of the class three alternative definitions, only one of which is true. (They can choose incorrect meanings from other, perhaps similar sounding words.) Encourage the rest of the class to vote on which definition they think is correct. The team gains a point if the class guess wrongly, but the class win the point for a correct answer.

Variations and adaptations
You could narrow the focus of the activity to words linked to current study in another curriculum area, or with specific prefixes.

3 Improvise it

Objectives
● To demonstrate an understanding of using prepositions expressing time and cause.

Working in pairs, and using the list of prepositions on photocopiable page 'Prepositions' from the CD-ROM as a guide, ask the children to improvise brief conversations. Encourage them to take turns to build a short dialogue, using as many different prepositions as possible. For example:
- *Can you come over **on** Saturday?*
- *Sorry, no, **because** I have tickets **for** the match.*
- *What about coming **before**?*
- *Well, I might be able to come **after**.*
- *I'll look **forward to** that.*

Variations and adaptations
After some oral practice, invite the children to write the conversations on individual whiteboards, rehearse and perform them to the class, perhaps in role. As the children learn prepositions other than those for time and cause, these can be added to the activity.

4 Suffix challenge

Objectives
● To use suffixes and understand how to add them.

Choose a suffix or suffixes to focus on, this could include: '-ation', '-ous', '-ly', '-tion', '-sion', '-ssion' or '-cian'. Challenge the children to list as many words as they can, in a given time, with the same suffix. Encourage the children to use dictionaries to check the spellings.

Variations and adaptations
A similar, timed activity can be used for words derived from other languages, such as Greek, Latin and French.

5 Start with the connection

Objectives
● To extend the range of sentences with more than one clause by using a wider range of conjunctions.

This activity is designed to reinforce the concept that clauses can be joined with the conjunction at the beginning of the sentence. Make a set of laminated cards, each with a conjunction written on them. You could use those on photocopiable page 'Conjunction list' from the CD-ROM. With the cards face down, ask a child to take one and show it to the class. Challenge the children to create the most interesting sentence they can starting with the conjunction which introduces the subordinate clause.

Variations and adaptations
Carry out this activity in reverse, where the conjunction is used after the main clause. The sentences can be used for dictation, where spelling and punctuation can also be highlighted and assessed.

6 One or more?

Objectives
● To reinforce difference between using the possessive apostrophe for singular and plural nouns.

Show some simple phrases on the board, punctuated correctly to show either singular or plural possession. Here are a few examples: *the girl's dog/the girls' dog; the boy's team/the boys' team*. Ask the children to show one thumb for a singular phrase, and a whole hand for plurals.

Variations and adaptations
Show the class phrases that require punctuating with possessive apostrophes, such as *the sheeps wool, the cats paws*. Ask the children to write the phrases on their individual whiteboards, placing the apostrophe correctly according to whether you ask them to show singular or plural possession. Then invite them to show you their written phrases, so you can assess their understanding.

Dictate short sentences for the children to write, telling them whether they should be singular or plural. For example: *There was frost on the car's windows; The soldiers' weapons glinted in the sun*.

7 Fronted adverbials

Objectives
● To use fronted adverbials.

Tell the class that fronted adverbials answer questions, such as *where, when, how, why, how often* or *how long*. Display these words on the board for reference during the activity. Select a subject such as food, holidays, games, a pet, a wild animal, weather, a book, a king, a vehicle, a baby, a policeman, a mermaid, an astronaut and so on. Challenge the children to create sentences on the given subject starting with fronted adverbials and answering one of the questions listed. For example, *Last weekend, we got our new car* or *For two whole weeks, we enjoyed our holiday*.

Variations and adaptations
Once they are familiar with the activity, ask pairs of children to challenge each other, awarding points for how good they think their partner's sentence is.

■SCHOLASTIC

8 Spot the pronoun

Objectives
● To choose nouns or pronouns appropriately for clarity and cohesion and to avoid repetition.

Slowly read aloud some short sentences including both nouns and pronouns. Invite the children to use a signal to show when they notice one or the other, or both. They could put up one thumb for a noun, and two for a pronoun. If the focus is on pronouns only, they could stand up when they hear the first and sit down for the next.

Variations and adaptations
Encourage the children to prepare for the session by writing their own sentences and the sharing those with the whole class.

9 Spellchecker

Objectives
● To learn to spell words correctly and have plenty of practice in spelling them.

One of the main ways we know if a word is spelled correctly is seeing if it looks right. This activity is designed to develop the children's visual discrimination skills in relation to spelling. Using any current spellings the children are working on, this could include the word list for Years 3 and 4 in Appendix 1 of the English Curriculum or spelling patterns such as /ai/ spelled 'ie', 'eigh' or 'ey' or /s/ spelled 'sc'. Write three alternatives for each word on the board, only one of which is correct. Number them 1, 2 and 3. Challenge the children to select the one they think is the correct spelling, showing their choice by voting, or writing their choice on individual whiteboards. This will allow you to informally assess their spelling knowledge. Let them know which spelling is correct. After several challenges, return to any words which seemed problematic, giving the children another chance to select the correct spelling. Finally, remove the words from view and ask the children to write the words on their whiteboards, showing you their results, allowing for further assessment.

10 Homophones

Objectives
● To learn to spell further homophones.

Spend some time making a class collection of homophones. This could be done as an ongoing home-learning activity, with the children contributing homophones they have found to a display or class reference book for all to share. Each homophone could have its meaning written alongside, or a sentence making its meaning clear. Use the collection to dictate sentences to the class for the children to write them down, using the correct homophone. These can be done quickly on whiteboards, or on paper for assessment.

Variations and adaptations
Encourage the children to compose their own sentences containing one or more homophones which they will read to the class themselves and ask for the correct spelling to be identified by the listeners. The child must then provide the correct answer for the class to check if they were right.

11 Show, don't tell

Objectives
● To identify and use inference in reading and writing.

From a selection of fiction or poetry, choose sentences or paragraphs to read aloud to the class which show, rather than tell, how characters are feeling. For example, *His fingers seemed not to belong to him as he fumbled to untie the knots* – which suggests nervousness, anxiety or suffering from extreme cold. Challenge the children to explain in simple language what the extracts are telling us about the characters.

Variations and adaptations
Use the activity in reverse by giving the children a simple, telling sentence which they must make more interesting by rephrasing it in a showing way. For example, *Jan was scared* or *Hannah felt angry*.

12 The perfect verb

Objectives
● To use the perfect form of verbs to mark relationships between time and cause.

Begin by asking the children to create a bank of verbs in both the present and past participles, such as *walked, talking, thrown, taken, helped, reading*. Each verb should be written in felt-tipped pen on pieces of card, so that they are easy to read. Once the set of cards has been produced, ask a child to select a card at random and show it to the class. The children should write on individual whiteboards all of the forms of the verb *to have* that can precede the selected verb, thereby putting it into the perfect tense. For example, *walked* could be preceded by *has, had* or *have*, whereas *talking* could only be preceded by *has been*. For each verb, invite suggestions for sentences containing it.

13 Blurb matching

Objectives
● To increase their familiarity with a wide range of books.
● To improve handwriting.

As part of a handwriting lesson, ask the children to copy the blurbs from a wide range of books. The blurbs must be numbered and ideally laminated. The book titles, authors and illustrators, if there are any, should also be copied. You should keep a central list of the titles against the numbered blurb that goes with each one. For instance, Title: *The Suitcase Kid* by Jacqueline Wilson matches with blurb number 4, and so on.

Put six of the blurbs and their titles into envelopes, creating several sets. Then use them for a matching activity, where children are invited to read the blurb and select the title they think it most closely fits. The answers the children provide can then be checked against your master list. After some time, rearrange the contents of the envelopes.

14 Edit it

Objectives
● To evaluate and edit by assessing their own and others' writing, and suggesting improvements.

Use a short piece of writing of the text type the class are familiar with, and display it on the board. You could write this yourself, or source it from elsewhere. It should be a piece that requires editing either for technical errors or to improve the composition, or both. Adapt this according to the particular current needs of the class. Read the text to the class or ask a child to read it aloud. Invite suggestions for where and how the text could be improved. Where alternative sentence structure or vocabulary changes are offered, consider all edits, debating as a class which would improve the text most before making a final decision. This will demonstrate to the children that it isn't necessarily their first idea that is the most appropriate, and that it is worth spending a little time considering their options. If spellings do need correcting, dictionaries could be used to check and make alterations.

15 Prefix game

Objectives
● To use prefixes and understand how to add them.

Produce cards with prefixes on, such as 'in-', 'ir-', 'il-', 'im-', 'super-', 'auto-', 'anti-' and also produce cards with sets of words that go with each prefix. Use the cards to play 'Pairs' or 'Snap' where the children have to match a prefix to its root word – the child with the most correctly matched cards wins.

Variations and adaptations
Using just the prefix cards, choose one at random and give the children a limited amount of time to write down as many words using the prefix as they can.

16 French spellings

Objectives
● To spell words of French origin.

Create a list of 'gue', 'que' and 'ch' words, for example *chef, unique, brochure, antique, league, cheque, parachute, plague, dialogue, chevron*. Read them aloud to the children and ask them to spell them on individual whiteboards. Review and discuss the spellings together.

Variations and adaptations
Use the words in sentences instead of on their own, for example:

● *The cheeky boy stuck out his tongue.*

● *We stayed in a chalet in Austria.*

● *The athlete had a fine physique.*

● *Chicago is a city in America.*

● *The monster was truly grotesque.*

● *He was a bit vague about where he had been.*

17 Getting technical

Objectives
● To learn grammatical terminology.

List the definitions, but not the words, that you want to focus on. For example, for the terms *conjunction* and *pronoun* you might write:

1. These words are used in place of nouns.

2. A word that links two words or phrases together.

Explain that you DO NOT want anyone to say the answer. Rather, you want them to give an example that might help others (such as *blue is one* or *slow plus '-ly' gives slowly is an example*), then facilitate class interaction around the words. Ensure you end the activity with clear explanations of the terms, concluding with writing the actual words next to each definition.

Terms you may wish to use include: *determiner, pronoun, possessive pronoun* and *adverbial*. Children may need a little practice with this activity, but will get the hang of it soon enough.

Robin Hood

In this chapter the children will define the key features of a legend and use this, together with the historical period in which it is set, to discuss, plan and write a character study, newspaper report, wanted poster, persuasive piece, dialogue from an adventure story and a ballad. They will perform pieces to an audience. Work on pronouns, inverted commas, spelling tricky words and using dictionaries included. They will read fiction, non-fiction and poems.

Expected prior learning
- Can make simple notes.
- Can use dictionaries to check meanings and spellings using the first two letters of a word.
- Can define a myth.
- Can understand the conventions of writing newspaper reports.
- Can use pronouns.
- Can discuss characters in stories.
- Can offer opinions in group discussions.
- Can understand and use sentences, clauses and connectives.
- Can discuss what makes a good plot.
- Can use inverted commas.
- Can understand that a story can be told in verse.

Overview of progression
- Comprehension and discussion skills will be developed through identifying key features of several text-types which will then be used to plan, perform and write a variety of pieces.
- The children will further develop their understanding of how characters can be defined by what they say, do and how they interact.

Creative context
- Character studies could lead to drama work, where use of particular language and speech patterns can be further developed.
- Children could make their own costumes for their performance of a ballad, which can be a form studied in music.
- Art work could incorporate portraits of key characters and depictions of settings, costume and architecture.
- The theme would fit in with history work on the Normans and Saxons.
- There are opportunities to discuss issues such as right and wrong in PSHE.
- Concepts of volume and tone when presenting work orally can be linked to the study of sound in science.

Preparation
There are many versions of the stories of Robin Hood for children. Marcia Williams' *The Adventures of Robin Hood* (Walker Books) is recommended, but any you prefer may be used. Aim to find a variety for both less and more experienced readers. It would be helpful to have some background knowledge of the period in history when the stories are set.

You will also need:
Various images of Robin Hood; individual whiteboards and pens; computers; internet access; dictionaries, including online and rhyming versions; highlighter pens; list of myths from Year 3 work; non-fiction texts relating to the late 12th century; images of archaeological artefacts and ancient writing; sample newpaper report; large sheets of paper; felt-tipped pens; examples of Wanted posters; glue sticks; scissors.

On the CD-ROM you will find:
Interactive activity 'Character interview'; photocopiable pages 'Conjunction list', 'The Ballad of Robin Hood and the Archery Contest', 'The Green Children of Woolpit'

Chapter at a glance

An overview of the chapter. For curriculum objective codes, please see pages 8–10.

Week	Lesson	Curriculum objectives	Summary of activities	Outcomes
1	1	RC: 1, 2, 4, 5, 13	Reading Robin Hood stories. Establishing prior knowledge, identifying main characters and overall themes.	• Can identify key characters and main themes.
	2	RWR: 1, 2 RC: 3, 9	Identify unknown words in Robin Hood stories and find their meanings in a dictionary.	• Can successfully identify and find meanings of new vocabulary.
	3	RC: 5, 13	Sorting characters, settings and themes in new version of the story.	• Can discuss and compare key elements of two versions of the story.
	4	RC: 4, 13 WC: 2, 10	Making notes to use to retell the story.	• Can make notes, practise and retell a version of the story.
	5	RWR: 1 WC: 10	Work in pairs to extend and enhance own version of story to include new vocabulary, and retell to a group.	• Can successfully retell own enhanced version of the story to an audience.
2	1	RC: 15, 16 WC: 2	Identifying factual and fictional elements in the Robin Hood legend and suggesting areas for further research.	• Can understand a legend is a story with fictional elements, based on historical fact and set in a historical period.
	2	RC: 15 WC: 2	Using books and the internet to research historical facts about the period in which Robin Hood is set.	• Can successfully find and record information from non-fiction texts.
	3	RWR: 1, 2 WT: 3, 6	Investigate and learn to spell words with a soft /ch/ and words ending in 'ue'.	• Can understand and spell some tricky words.
	4	WC: 2, 6	Plan a newspaper report about Robin Hood.	• Can create plans that include known characters, are set in the correct period and are organised into paragraphs.
	5	WT: 8 WC: 6	Use plans to write a newspaper report.	• Can create newspaper reports that include all key features and are in best handwriting.
3	1	RC: 11, 16 WC: 3, 5	Find details about a given character in the Robin Hood story, make notes and share as a role-on-the-wall.	• Can produce a role-on-the-wall for a given character, following research.
	2	RC: 10, 11 WC: 5	Write a study of a character from the Robin Hood legend, using information previously gathered.	• Can produce character studies that are appropriate, making reference to the role-on-the-wall information.
	3	WC: 1	Analyse and agree on key features of an effective 'Wanted' poster and make a rough draft of their own.	• Can identify key features and make drafts of their own posters.
	4	WC: 13, 20	Play 'Spot the pronoun' and demonstrate an understanding of their use by writing pairs of sentences.	• Can produce pairs of sentences that show understanding of the use of pronouns following given information.
	5	WC: 5, 13, 20	Create finished 'Wanted' posters, using role-on-the-wall information and identified key features.	• Can use drafts to create effective posters, including agreed key features. Pronouns show clarity and cohesion.
4	1	RC: 10, 16 WC: 2	Discuss whether Robin Hood was right or wrong to steal, and the effects of his actions on others.	• Can form and record opinions, based on discussion, about whether Robin Hood was right or wrong.
	2	RC: 10, 16	Courtroom scene of Robin on trial with children taking on a variety of roles, to decide whether Robin was a thief.	• Can consider different viewpoints before deciding their verdict.
	3	RC: 16 WC: 2	Weigh up information of key characters to discuss and decide on the true villain of the piece.	• Can participate in a discussion, following factual reading, leading to decision on the villain.
	4	WC: 11, 13	Investigate the use of subordinate clauses before and after the main clause, using conjunctions appropriate to arguments.	• Can demonstrate their understanding of subordinate clauses and use appropriate conjunctions.
	5	WC: 11, 13	Write a persuasive argument for the villain of their choice, with supporting evidence from reading and discussion.	• Can write effective persuasive pieces, including sentences with subordinate clauses, appropriate conjunctions and correct use of pronouns.

Chapter at a glance

Week	Lesson	Curriculum objectives	Summary of activities	Outcomes
5	1	WC: 1	Identify key features of an adventure story. Complete a cut-and-paste activity to create outlines of three Robin Hood adventures.	• Can demonstrate their understanding of the key features of an adventure story by correctly organising jumbled sections of three stories.
	2	WC: 2, 5	Identify key elements of settings appropriate to a Robin Hood adventure, with associated appropriate vocabulary.	• Can create spider diagrams with key features and appropriate vocabulary for a given setting.
	3	WC: 10, 19	Write speeches by four Robin Hood characters and punctuate them accurately. Read aloud to a partner.	• Can demonstrate ability to create speeches for particular characters and write them using accurate punctuation.
	4	WC: 3, 10	Select and plan a short scene from a Robin Hood story to act as a group.	• Can work in groups to create a short Robin Hood adventure scene and perform it to the class.
	5	WC: 5, 19	Use scenes acted the previous day as the basis for writing a short narrative piece, including dialogue.	• Can complete stories which tell a scene from a Robin Hood adventure, using correctly punctuated dialogue.
6	1	RC: 1, 8 WC: 1	Listen to and read examples of ballads and identify key features. Practise and read together a given ballad.	• Can identify key features of ballads and read a ballad with suitable intonation, taking note of punctuation.
	2	RC: 6	Groups rehearse a given section of the ballad practised previously, improving and assessing their delivery.	• Can rehearse a performance of a ballad and assess it against their own criteria.
	3	RC: 6	Rehearsed ballad is performed for an audience, in costume, if possible,	• Can perform the ballad and the class evaluate their performance.
	4	WC: 1, 3	Listen to further ballad examples, recap key features, select a Robin Hood story to write as a ballad and begin to draft ideas.	• Can understand the criteria for a ballad and make rough drafts of own versions.
	5	WC: 3, 10	Drafts are used to rehearse stories with a partner before composing ballads according to agreed key features, using correct punctuation.	• Can write their own versions of Robin Hood ballads that have rhyme and rhythm and are correctly punctuated.

Background knowledge

Ballad: A narrative poem or song, often of folk origin, telling a story in rhyming stanzas. There is often no known author, and they can be very long.

Clause: A special type of phrase, whose main word is a verb that describes an event or state of affairs. Clauses can sometimes be complete sentences.

Conjunction: A word which links two phrases or clauses together. One form of connective.

Direct speech: Written form of words said by a speaker, using speech, or quotation marks to indicate what was said.

Legend: A traditional story set in a particular historical period, often thought to be true but unauthenticated.

Pronoun: A word used in place of a noun to avoid repetition and to aid coherence and clarity.

Role-on-the-wall: Device for recording description and characteristics of characters. The outline of a person is drawn on a large sheet of paper; words and phrases are written inside and around it, defining aspects of that character.

Subordinate clause: Gives more information about the main clause. It does not make sense when written on its own as it is incomplete. Needs a conjunction to join it to the main clause, which may precede or follow.

■SCHOLASTIC

Week 1 lesson plans

The basis for this half-term's work on myths and legends is the story of Robin Hood. In this first week, the children will begin to become familiar with the main elements and characters of the legend, comparing at least two different versions. They will look for key themes, such as that of good versus evil or the disparity in social class. They will be introduced to new vocabulary specific to the story, using dictionaries to check their meanings. They will make notes which they will use at the end of the week to retell the story to an audience. The main focuses are reading comprehension, discussion, note-taking and oral presentation of a story.

1: Introducing Robin Hood

Introduction
● Display any images you have found of Robin Hood on the interactive whiteboard. Invite the children to tell you who the character is and ask what they know about him. Some children may have seen a film version of the story, either animated or live action. Ask what they think about Robin Hood – was he good or bad? Do they know any of the other main characters?

Independent work
● Give each child photocopiable page 40 'Robin Hood: the legend', allowing time for most of them to read it to themselves and offering support to any less experienced readers.

Whole-class work
● Display the photocopiable sheet on the board. Tell the children that there will probably be some words they are not familiar with and that they will be working more on those tomorrow. Today they will be focusing on the characters and ideas in the story.
● Choose several children to read sections of the story aloud to the class.
● Ask the children what new characters or ideas they found in this version of part of the Robin Hood story. Do they already know that the Sheriff of Nottingham was Robin Hood's best-known enemy? Do they know anything more about the other key characters?

Group work
● Provide as many other versions of the Robin Hood stories as you can find for small groups of children to share. Marcia Williams' comic-strip version will appeal to some, while others can be found online, such as at: www.storynory.com (search for 'Robin Hood'). Ask them to look for similarities and differences between the versions of the stories, telling them that there are many tales of Robin's adventures, not just one.
● Ask them to make notes on individual whiteboards as they read.

Differentiation
● Less experienced readers could be offered suggested headings to guide their reading, such as *people, places, events*.
● Confident readers and internet users could source their own Robin Hood stories online, making a note of the websites for potential later use by themselves and others. (Ensure safe use of the internet by children.)

Review
● Ask each group to feed back to the whole class, saying what they have found. Sum up any common features and ask what themes they have noticed.
● By the end of the lesson the children should be able to identify that the stories are adventures about good versus evil, set in the distant past, with a common cast of named characters.

Expected outcomes
● All children can offer opinions about the story, using their notes to retell it.
● Most children can use and understand new vocabulary when using notes to retell the story.
● Some children can extend the story to engage their audience, stressing the theme of good versus evil.

Curriculum objectives
● To increase their familiarity with a wide range of books, including fairy stories, myths and legends, and retell some of these orally.
● To identify themes and conventions in a wide range of books.
● To identify main ideas drawn from more than one paragraph and summarise these.
● To listen to and discuss a wide range of fiction, poetry, plays, non-fiction and reference books or textbooks.
● To read books that are structured in different ways and read for a range of purposes.

Resources
Photocopiable page 40 'Robin Hood: the legend'; a range of versions of the Robin Hood story (including Marcia Williams' *The Adventures of Robin Hood*); various images of Robin Hood to display on the interactive whiteboard; individual whiteboards and pens; computers available for some children to access the internet (optional)

Curriculum objectives
- To use a dictionary to check the meanings of words that they have read.
- To apply their growing knowledge of root words, prefixes and suffixes (etymology and morphology) as listed in Appendix 1, both to read aloud and to understand the meaning of new words they meet.
- To check that the text makes sense to them, discussing their understanding and explaining the meaning of words in context.
- To read further exception words, noting the unusual correspondences between spelling and sound, and where these occur in the word.

Resources
A range of dictionaries, including online versions; copies of the texts used in lesson 1

2: Using a dictionary

Introduction
- Use starter activity 2 'Guess the word'.
- On the board, show the words: *serf, crusade, alms*. Ask if anyone knows any of the meanings. Then show the following sentences:
  - *The serf knew that when his master sold the land, he would have to go with it.*
  - *Many knights went on a crusade to fight in the Holy Land.*
  - *Thanks to the alms they received from the wealthy lord, the poor family were able to buy food.*
- Invite further suggestions now that a context is provided. Note 'cru' and 'al' as exceptions to how we might expect the words to be spelled.
- Tell the class that they will be using dictionaries to look up the meanings of any unusual words they noticed in lesson 1's texts. Ensure the children have the texts available.

Independent work
- Using the texts, ask the children to find any new vocabulary and look them up in the dictionary. They should write each word and copy its meaning.

> **Differentiation**
> - Children who are fast finishers can be given extra words to find, such as *coffer, bailey, garderobe, kirtle, parapet*.

Review
- Bring the class together and invite some of the children to read out the meanings they have found for others to suggest the word being defined. They may find that different dictionaries give slightly different definitions, which would be an interesting point to discuss.

Curriculum objectives
- To identify themes and conventions in a wide range of books.
- To identify main ideas drawn from more than one paragraph and summarise these.

Resources
Copies of the stories used previously; cards with the following labels: *Robin Hood, Little John, Maid Marian, Greenwood, Sherwood, castle, robbery, fighting, helping the poor*; individual whiteboards; photocopiable page 41 'Ambush in the forest'

3: Key elements

Introduction
- Select nine children to display the labelled cards, randomly arranged, for the class to see. Ask the children to arrange themselves into three groups according to what they think the labels have in common. Then ask the class for their comments. Do they agree with the classification? How have they been classified? If necessary, rearrange into characters, settings and events.

Group work
- Grouped according to the texts they have read, ask the children to list as many characters, settings and events as they can, using individual whiteboards.

Whole-class work
- Ask the children to look at their list of events and invite them to suggest what themes the stories have in common. They may suggest adventure, good versus evil, fighting for the rights of others, defying authority.

Paired work
- Hand out photocopiable page 41 'Ambush in the forest' and allow the children time to read it. Mixed ability pairings might work well for this.
- The children should identify characters, setting and events, and look for any of the suggested themes.

Review
- Hold up the cards from the first activity one at a time and ask who found examples of any of them in the story. Did any others emerge? Use the responses to informally assess their understanding of the key elements.

Curriculum objectives
● To identify main ideas drawn from more than one paragraph and summarise them.
● To increase their familiarity with a wide range of books, including fairy stories, myths and legends, and retell some of these orally.
● To discuss and record ideas.
● To read aloud their own writing, to a group or the whole class, using appropriate intonation and controlling the tone and volume so that the meaning is clear.

Resources
Photocopiable page 40 'Robin Hood: the legend'; photocopiable page 41 'Ambush in the forest'; any books about Robin Hood used previously

4: Note-taking and storytelling

Introduction
● Display the following notes: *R. Hood, outlaw, Sherwood forest; Merry Men – L. John, Will S., and so on – outlaws; ambushed rich, gave to poor; enemy Sheriff of Nott.*
● Tell the children these are notes to help them retell the story so far, and then use them to demonstrate.

Independent work
● Using the texts they have been reading, ask the children to make their own brief notes on paper, so that they can retell part of the story of Robin Hood.

Paired work
● In pairs, ask the children to practise using their notes to retell their version of the story. Encourage listening partners to make positive and helpful comments. Explain that their retellings will improve if they repeat them.

Differentiation
● Pair children according to their oral skills. Very confident speakers and listeners could benefit each other, but less experienced speakers, particularly those for whom English is not their first language, could be overwhelmed by a particularly fluent partner.

Review
● Invite some of the children to use their notes to share their retelling with the rest of the class. Have a brief follow-up discussion about the similarities and differences that the children found in the versions of the stories they read. Ask: *Do the same themes and key features appear?*

Curriculum objectives
● To read aloud their own writing, to a group or the whole class, using appropriate intonation and controlling the tone and volume so that the meaning is clear.
● To apply their growing knowledge of root words, prefixes and suffixes (etymology and morphology) as listed in Appendix 1, both to read aloud and to understand the meaning of new words they meet.

Resources
Children's own notes; copies of any texts used during the week, for reference to vocabulary

5: Story performance

Introduction
● Using your notes from lesson 4, demonstrate two retellings – first a basic version, told in an uninteresting way, then an enhanced version including some of the newly acquired vocabulary, using appropriate intonation, pace and tone.
● Ask the class to point out the differences between the two retellings, agreeing on what makes the second version better.
● Explain to them that they will be using their retellings from lesson 4 to extend and enhance their versions of the story, so they should include new and interesting vocabulary. They could blend elements from more than one story.

Paired work
● In the same pairs as lesson 4, the children should talk about ways in which their retelling of the story could be extended and enhanced before rehearsing a few times. They may refer to the texts to select appropriate vocabulary.

Group work
● Arrange the pairs into groups of four or six to present their retelling of the story to each other. Encourage the listeners to offer positive feedback.

Differentiation
● Non-native English speakers may need support.

Review
● Ask the class to explain what they found easy or difficult about today's activities. How successful do they think they were in both enhancing and delivering their own retellings? Is there anything they would change to improve their performance?

Expected outcomes
● All children can use a legend as a basis for writing a newspaper report.
● Most children can create their own story based on what they already know, using a given headline.
● Some children can include further historical information in their newspaper reports following personal research.

Curriculum objectives
● To participate in discussion about both books that are read to them and those they can read for themselves, taking turns and listening to what others say.
● To discuss and record ideas.
● To retrieve and record information from non-fiction.

Resources
Photocopiable page 40 'Robin Hood: the legend'; photocopiable page 41 'Ambush in the forest'; highlighter pens; list of myths from Year 3 work

Week 2 lesson plans

The children will start to develop their understanding of what a legend is and how it differs from myths. They will link the legend to the time of the Crusades in the 12th century and discuss the differences between fiction and historical fact in the stories. They will plan and write a fictional newspaper report based on their developing knowledge of the stories of Robin Hood, following research and discussion. Attention will be given to the quality of handwriting in the finished reports and during the week the children will learn tricky spellings derived from French, to link with the influence of the Normans at the time of the Robin Hood legend.

1: What is a legend?

Introduction

● On the interactive whiteboard, display a list of myths the children are familiar with, from their work in Year 3. These might include 'Theseus and the Minotaur', stories about unicorns or mermaids, Odysseus, Norse myths and so on.
● Ask the children what type of story these are (myths) and how they differ from the legend of Robin Hood. (Legends may have some basis in historical fact and are set in particular historical periods.) Ensure that the children understand the terms *legend*, *fiction*, *non-fiction* and *fact*. Define a fact as something for which we have evidence in some form.

Paired work

● Using photocopiable page 40 'Robin Hood: the legend' and photocopiable page 41 'Ambush in the forest', ask the children to highlight anything they think is a fact that could be supported by evidence. They should find more in 'The legend of Robin Hood' as this is more factual in nature.

Whole-class work

● Invite the children to share their suggestions, asking them to provide reasons for their selections.
● Open a discussion about the fictional elements of the two texts. Ask: *How do we know they are fiction?* The children may suggest that there could not be any specific evidence for particular stories, that no-one could know what words were spoken, or what the characters were thinking.
● Ask the class which parts of the texts could be researched to see if evidence exists. They may suggest looking for character or place names, finding out about the Crusades, trying to discover if Robin was recorded as winning any archery competitions or if there was such a cloth as Lincoln Green.

Independent work

● Ask the children to refer to the photocopiable sheets to create two lists on a sheet of paper, headed *Fiction* and *Fact*.
● In note form, they should record which parts of the texts they think are fact and which fiction, under the appropriate heading.

Differentiation
● If any children have problems understanding the difference between fact and fiction, talk with them further about things they know to be real, and fiction-based stories they are familiar with.

Review

● Select a few children to share their lists with the rest of the class and then invite comments from others. Did everyone agree on what was fact and what was fiction?

Curriculum objectives
● To retrieve and record information from non-fiction.
● To discuss and record ideas.

Resources
Non-fiction texts (from books and online) relating to the late 12th century, including information on King Richard the Lionheart, the Crusades and the tensions between the Saxons and ruling Normans; the children's lists of facts from lesson 1; images of archaeological artefacts and ancient writing

2: Is it true?

Introduction
● Display images of archaeological artefacts and ancient writing. Explain that these items give us evidence about the past. Today they will be history detectives, searching for evidence to discover what truths are in the Robin Hood legend. Ask the class to refer to their lists of facts from lesson 1.

Paired work
● Using books and online resources, ask the children to search for information about things on their list, and any others they think may be relevant, to provide evidence for historical fact in the stories.
● They should make brief notes of their findings, to include their sources, such as book title, page number or web address.

> **Differentiation**
> ● Allocate research material according to the reading ability of pairs of children. Experienced computer users may be able to work independently, but you may wish to pre-select suitable internet sites to save research time.

Review
● Bring the class together and ask some of the children to share their findings. Summarise the evidence and remind the children about the fictional elements they found in the stories. Finish with a vote on whether Robin Hood existed.

Curriculum objectives
● To spell words that are often misspelled (Appendix 1).
● To read further exception words, noting the unusual correspondences between spelling and sound, and where these occur in the word.
● To apply their growing knowledge of suffixes, both to read aloud and to understand the meaning of new words they meet.
● To write from memory simple sentences, dictated by the teacher, that include words taught so far.

Resources
Following list of spellings: *chef, chalet, machine, brochure, league, tongue, antique, unique*; individual whiteboards

3: French derivations

Introduction
● Say in French: *'Bonjour la classe! Comment ça va aujourd'hui? Bien, oui?'*
● Can anyone translate? Tell the children that because of the Norman invasion many words we use today originated in France, which is why some of our spellings can be tricky. Today they will be learning to spell some of these words.

Whole-class work
● Display these eight words: *chef, chalet, machine, brochure, league, tongue, antique, unique*. Ask the children which they recognise. Can they pronounce any of them? Do they know the meanings? Supply these as necessary.
● Ask: *Can anyone suggest two ways the words could be pronounced?* (Such as the hard and soft /ch/, pronouncing the final /ue/.) *How would we know which is correct?* (It would sound right – we would recognise it.)
● Read the words together several times. Hide the words and choose some examples. Write the words in two or three different ways, only one of which is correct and ask the children vote for the correct spelling.

Paired work
● Invite the children to help each other learn the words in two ways. Firstly, one gives a meaning and the other writes the word on their whiteboard. Secondly, one asks the other to spell a word. For both, partners need to agree on the correct spelling.

Independent work
● Display the words and ask the children to record them in their spelling logs.

Review
● Use starter activity 16 'French spellings', asking the children to spell the words on whiteboards to show you.

Curriculum objectives
● In non-narrative material, to use simple organisational devices.
● To discuss and record ideas.

Resources
Board showing the newspaper-type headlines: *Hood strikes again!, People's champion wins battle, Robin Hood escapes!*

4: Robin in the news (1)

Introduction
● Display the prepared headlines and ask the children what they remind them of (news headlines). Ask what stories they might suggest.

Whole-class work
● Remind the class about key features in newspaper reports, such as opening with the ending (for example, *Yesterday two men robbed...*), including the five Ws – *who, why, what, where* and *when.*
● Discuss the headlines and explain that the children will create a newspaper report about Robin Hood to go with them. They will be planning it today. Remind them they should aim to make it sound like a real event based in the correct historical period. It could be based on a known story, or one they create.

Independent work
● Encourage the children to select a headline and plan the events in their newspaper story, noting which characters will appear, when and where the incident happened, what the outcome was and why Robin Hood was involved. They should organise their notes into paragraphs, with appropriate subheadings.

Paired work
● Invite the children to use their plan to tell a partner their story. Ask the partners to provide positive critical feedback.

Differentiation
● Some of the children may need to refer to texts used in earlier lessons for ideas.

Review
● Ask the children which headlines they chose and select a few volunteers to briefly outline their story ideas.

Curriculum objectives
● To use simple organisational devices.
● To increase the legibility, consistency and quality of their handwriting.

Resources
Children's own plans from lesson 4; sample newspaper report of your choice, suitable for sharing with the class

5: Robin in the news (2)

Introduction
● Read the newspaper report you have chosen, asking the children to listen for key aspects of its structure. Make them aware of where subheadings are used.

Whole-class work
● Discuss with the class the way the sample newspaper report has been written – use of language, structure, use of subheadings, names and other details, inclusion of the five Ws. There may also be quotes from those involved.
● Remind the children they should aim to include these features in their own report, as well as their best joined handwriting.

Independent work
● Allow the children to write their newspaper reports, using their plans.
● If time, a partner could listen to the report and offer constructive feedback.

Differentiation
● Encourage more experienced writers to include quotes in their report.

Review
● Ask the children to consider their writing. Does it fit the headline? Does it sound like a newspaper report? Did they include all of the five Ws? If not, which were missing and why? Ask for some examples to be shared. Did they write in paragraphs? How would they rate their handwriting out of ten?

Week 3 lesson plans

Now that the children are more familiar with the Robin Hood legend, this week they will be looking in more detail at each of the key characters. They will read about them and work in a group to gather information in order to write a study of a given character. They will use this information later in the week to create a 'Wanted' poster for a character of their choice, having first identified the key elements of such a poster. Following on from work in Year 3, they will further develop their knowledge of how to use pronouns to aid cohesion and clarity.

1: Character studies (1)

Introduction

● Show the images of characters from the Robin Hood story on the interactive whiteboard. Ask the children to suggest who each one is, giving reasons for their choices.
● Explain that no one knows what they might really have looked like (if they existed at all), but the stories do give fairly consistent ideas about their physical descriptions and characteristics.

Group work

● Explain to the children that this week they will be looking at individual characters in the Robin Hood legend, starting today with gathering information to write a character study. To do this they will need to find out as much as they can about their particular character. They will be working in groups to help each other gather the information and presenting it as a role-on-the-wall for all to share later in the week.
● Allocate one key character to each group of 4–6 children, perhaps Robin Hood, Maid Marian, the Sheriff of Nottingham, Friar Tuck, Little John and Will Scarlet. Each group will need access to suitable books and the internet, if available.
● Tell the children to make brief notes on anything they find out about their character, including their physical description, any skills they have, their good and bad points. Explain that the things characters do in the stories can give clues about what they were like.
● Allow the children sufficient time to make their notes before they transfer key points, on which they agree, to a role-on-the-wall sheet. This is a large outline of a person with aspects of their character written in and around it. Physical descriptions could be written outside the outline, with characteristics written inside.

> **Differentiation**
> ● The group activity would probably work best if the groups are of mixed abilities.

Review

● Pin the role-on-the-wall sheets to a space on the classroom wall for one or two representatives of each group to talk through with the rest of the class. Encourage the listeners to ask questions, which the presenters should be prepared to answer. Leave the sheets in place for reference throughout the week.

Expected outcomes

● All children can plan and design a 'Wanted' poster for one of the Robin Hood characters.
● Most children can decide on the key features of a 'Wanted' poster and use these to create their own, using pronouns where appropriate.
● Some children can create a highly effective poster using a variety of print sizes and including extra detail.

Curriculum objectives

● To participate in discussion about both books that are read to them and those they can read for themselves, taking turns and listening to what others say.
● To draw inferences such as inferring characters' feelings, thoughts and motives from their actions, and justify inferences with evidence.
● To compose and rehearse sentences orally (including dialogue), progressively building a varied and rich vocabulary and an increasing range of sentence structures (See Appendix 2).
● In narratives, to create settings, characters and plot.

Resources

Interactive whiteboard display showing a variety of different images of the key characters in the Robin Hood story; books about Robin Hood at different reading levels; role-on-the-wall sheets – a large outline of a person on a piece of paper; individual whiteboards and pens; large sheets of paper and felt-tipped pens

Curriculum objectives
● In narratives, to create settings, characters and plot.
● To ask questions to improve their understanding of a text.
● To draw inferences such as inferring characters' feelings, thoughts and motives from their actions, and justify inferences with evidence.

Resources
Board display containing the words: *strong, gentle, tall, fearless, determined, holy, musical, talented, bold, caring*; interactive activity 'Character interview' on the CD-ROM

2: Character studies (2)

Introduction
● Show the words on the board and read them together. Ask the children which of the characters in the Robin Hood legend each of the words could describe and to justify their choices. (There will be many possibilities.)

Whole-class work
● Explain to the children they will be writing a study of a character of their choice from the legend. Using interactive activity 'Character interview' on the CD-ROM, select one character from the story and work through the interview questions with the class, inviting them to provide the answers.

Independent work
● Provide time for the children write their character studies, referring to the roles-on-the-wall and the displayed words as necessary.
● Remind them to include in their writing both a physical description and what their character was like. This should be organised into at least two paragraphs.

> **Differentiation**
> ● It might be beneficial for some children to read through the roles-on-the-wall with an adult before starting to write. Encourage confident writers to create more paragraphs.

Review
● Select another character from the story of Robin Hood and interview them using the interactive activity 'Character interview' on the CD-ROM. The children may wish to change some of the interview questions.

Curriculum objectives
● To discuss writing similar to that which they are planning to write in order to understand and learn from its structure, grammar and vocabulary.

Resources
Images of 'Wanted' posters; photocopied examples of 'Wanted' posters

3: Wanted posters (1)

Introduction
● Show the class several 'Wanted' posters (old Wild West examples are good).
● Inform them that they will be making one later in the week, about one of the Robin Hood characters.

Whole-class work
● Briefly look together at key features of the posters that the children will need to use for their own versions. Explain to the class that they will work in groups to make their own lists of key features for use later.

Group work
● Using examples of 'Wanted' posters, the children should agree on the key features and annotate the posters. They should notice names, reward, description, crime, use of language, varieties of font style and size. Sometimes pictures are included, but not always, so descriptions become more important.
● Each group's final agreed features should be written on paper for later use.

Independent work
● Invite the children to independently choose their character and make a rough draft of their 'Wanted' poster to use later in the week.

> **Differentiation**
> ● You may wish to appoint a leader for each group to oversee the discussion.

Review
● Ask representatives from each group to report back to the class on the key features they agreed. Ask the class which they have included in their drafts.

Curriculum objectives
● To choose nouns or pronouns appropriately for clarity and cohesion and to avoid repetition.
● To use and understand the grammatical terminology in Appendix 2 accurately and appropriately when discussing their writing and reading.

Resources
Display the words: he, she, we, it, him, her, they, us, this, that, these, who, which

4: Pronouns

Introduction
● Remind the class that pronouns are used in place of nouns, before playing starter activity 8 'Spot the pronoun'.

Whole-class work
● Show the class the pronouns: he, she, we, it, him, her, they, us, this, that, these, who, which. Read the pronouns together. Remind them that pronouns can refer to people, things or ideas that the reader already knows something about.
● Say the following sentences twice: Joe played for the school team. He often scored for them. Ask them to identify the pronoun. Explain that the first sentence is needed for the second to be understood.
● Provide a few other examples. Can anyone in the class suggest others?

Independent work
● Ask the children to write their own pairs of sentences, similar to the examples.

> **Differentiation**
> ● It may benefit some children to be given subjects on which to write, such as an animal, house, school, farm, castle, forest, burglar, king, monster and so on.

Review
● Play 'Spot the pronoun' again with the class in order to reinforce the concept of pronouns, and to have the opportunity for informal assessment.

Curriculum objectives
● In narratives, to create settings, characters and plot.
● To choose nouns or pronouns appropriately for clarity and cohesion and to avoid repetition.
● To use and understand the grammatical terminology in Appendix 2 accurately and appropriately when discussing their writing and reading.

Resources
'Wanted' poster to display; Bon Jovi's 'Wanted Dead or Alive' (optional); children's draft posters (from lesson 3); key features list made earlier in the week

5: Wanted posters (2)

Introduction
● Display the 'Wanted' poster and play an excerpt of Bon Jovi's song 'Dead or Alive'. Briefly discuss with the class the purpose of this type of poster.

Whole-class work
● Remind the children that they will be creating their own 'Wanted' poster today, using the drafts they made earlier. Recap the key features of a 'Wanted' poster agreed earlier in the week. Display the list on the board.
● Remind the children of their work on pronouns and encourage them to use these where appropriate.

Paired work
● Give the children a few minutes to explain to a partner what they will include in their 'Wanted' poster. Then they should make any amendments necessary after brief comparison and discussion.

Independent work
● Ask the children to use their drafts to create a finished version of their 'Wanted' poster, using the key features as a checklist.

> **Differentiation**
> ● It may benefit some of the children to have their own copy of the key features checklist, so they can tick off each item as they include it. Encourage more experienced writers not to include a picture of the wanted person, but to write a more detailed description instead.

Review
● Select a few children to read out narrative sections of their posters. The rest of the class should listen out for where pronouns have been used successfully. Invite positive comments on the use of vocabulary in the descriptions.

Week 4 lesson plans

This week's focus is mainly on non-fiction, where the children consider and debate the rights and wrongs of Robin Hood's actions, asking the question: Is theft ever right? They will find out more about the historical characters of the Sheriff of Nottingham, King John and King Richard, discussing their roles in the legend to decide for themselves who is the villain. This will culminate in them producing a piece of persuasive writing, presenting their views about the biggest villain and justifying their opinion. They will also work on developing their use of connectives, particularly those used in argument and debate.

1: Right or wrong?

Introduction

- Display the tick and cross on the interactive whiteboard. Ask: *How do these make you feel when you see them on your work?* Listen to all responses and be aware that some children may be particularly sensitive on this issue.
- Explain that while it may be easy to say, for example, that a sum is right or wrong, in some real-life situations it isn't always that easy. Stealing is against the law and is wrong, but what if a very poor person steals a loaf of bread to feed their starving family? Is it still wrong? Are there degrees of right and wrong? Tell them that during the 18th and 19th centuries people of all ages could be imprisoned in some countries for up to seven years for doing just that. Discuss these issues.
- Explain to the class how this links to the story of Robin Hood. (Stealing from the rich to give to the poor.)
- What theme is suggested here? Potential themes could be: Is stealing ever right? What is right and wrong? What is our responsibility to those less fortunate than ourselves?
- Talk briefly about how our actions, both good and bad, have an impact on others. Point out that this was the case with Robin Hood.

Independent work

- Hand out photocopiable page 42 'Right or wrong?'
- Ask the children to think about what they know of Robin Hood, what they consider to be the good and bad things he did and how his actions affected different people. Allow them enough time to complete the sheet based on their own opinions.

Paired work

- When the sheets have been completed, invite the children to work in pairs to share their thoughts. Do they have similar views? Are there any areas where they disagree?

Group work

- Encourage the pairs to join together to form groups of four or six and to take turns to share their opinions. Remind the children of the importance of being a good listener, and encourage them to ask each other relevant questions about their decisions.

Differentiation
- Adult support may be needed for less experienced writers to complete the photocopiable sheet. Encourage more confident learners to give several reasons for their opinions.

Review

- Draw the class together and ask representatives to summarise each group's opinions. Ask: *Was Robin Hood a hero or a crook?* Encourage the children to think and contribute their own opinions, briefly giving their reasons for their ideas. Conclude by holding a class vote on the issue.

Expected outcomes

- All children can contribute to a class discussion and write a persuasive piece using appropriate connectives.
- Most children can ask questions to improve their understanding and use the discussion effectively in their persuasive writing.
- Some children can include more complex sentences with sub-clauses and present a more effective persuasive piece, using a wider range of connectives.

Curriculum objectives

- To ask questions to improve their understanding of a text.
- To participate in discussion about both books that are read to them and those they can read for themselves, taking turns and listening to what others say.
- To discuss and record ideas.

Resources

A large tick and cross displayed; photocopiable page 42 'Right or wrong?'

■SCHOLASTIC

2: Robin on trial

Introduction
● Arrange the classroom to represent a simple version of a courtroom with tables for the prisoner, defence and prosecution, as well as chairs for the jury and onlookers. Tell the children that today Robin Hood is to be put on trial for being a thief and they will decide the outcome.

Group work
● Allocate roles to the children – Robin, jury, defence, prosecution, witnesses (such as Sheriff, the robbed, local villagers). Others can be onlookers, whose opinions will be needed later.
● Allow the children time to talk about their roles, considering what each might have to say in the trial. Robin can speak with the defence and prosecution. They can use lesson 1's work on photocopiable page 42 'Right or wrong?' to guide their discussions.

Whole-class work
● Before starting the trial ensure everyone knows to listen carefully to each other. With the teacher in role as judge or court usher to control the proceedings, begin the trial and call on each character to speak in turn.
● After Robin and the witnesses have been questioned, onlookers may also be asked for their opinion. Finally, the jury should discuss and give their verdict.

Differentiation
● Confident speakers are required for the main roles (Robin, defence, prosecution, key witnesses), as they need to speak clearly to ask and answer questions.

Review
● With the children out of role, ask for their comments on the trial. Do they think it was fairly conducted? Were there enough witnesses on each side? Did they believe people were telling the truth? Did they all agree with the verdict?

3: Who is the villain?

Introduction
● Tell the children there's something you think they should know – as if sharing a confidence – Robin Hood was not the only one thought to be a villain. Can they suggest others? Ask the class what they know about the Sheriff, King Richard and King John that might make them villains.

Independent work
● Hand out photocopiable page 43 'Who is the villain?' for the children to read by themselves. (Some may need support for this.) The information on the sheet may help them decide on the true villain.

Paired work
● Encourage pairs to talk about the relative merits and shortcomings of the characters on the photocopiable sheet (the Sheriff, King John and King Richard), comparing them with what they know about Robin. They should aim to come to a decision about which they feel is the true villain. They could highlight parts of the text to support their views.

Review
● Bring the class together for a discussion about the villainy of the four characters. The children should justify their opinions with evidence from the texts and their wider knowledge. Conclude by having a vote to see which of the potential villains gets the most 'villain points'.

Curriculum objectives
● To extend the range of sentences with more than one clause by using a wider range of conjunctions.
● To choose nouns or pronouns appropriately for clarity and cohesion and to avoid repetition.

Resources
Four large word cards containing the conjunctions: *but, however, or, although*; photocopiable page 44 'Clauses and conjunctions'; photocopiable page 'Conjunction list' from the CD-ROM

4: Conjunctions and subordinate clauses

Introduction
● Choose four children to display the word cards. Say a one-clause sentence, for example *The cake was delicious*. Invite the children to extend it by using one of the cards, thus adding a sub-clause, such as *but I ate too much*. Repeat with other sentences. Can anyone begin a sentence with *although*? For example: *Although he was ill, Bill went to school.*

Whole-class work
● Explain to the class that the first sentences began with a main clause and you added subordinate clauses. When the sentence began with the conjunction, the main clause came second. A clause can stand alone as a sentence and it makes sense. A subordinate clause is not complete on its own, but gives more information about the main clause. A conjunction is needed to join them together. Point out that the conjunctions you used are useful when presenting an argument. As a class, make a list of five more sentences.

Independent work
● Provide photocopiable page 44 'Clauses and conjunctions' for the children to complete and photocopiable page 'Conjunctions list' from the CD-ROM to help them when writing their own sentences. Note that they will also be using pronouns, which they worked on last week.
● Ask pairs to share and compare their answers to the photocopiable sheet.

Differentiation
● Extend the learning by asking some children to create further sentences, using more of the conjunctions that appear on photocopiable page 'Conjunction list' from the CD-ROM.

Review
● Play a sentence completion game, based on the four original conjunctions. Read out the beginning of a sentence for the children to complete orally.

Curriculum objectives
● To extend the range of sentences with more than one clause by using a wider range of conjunctions.
● To choose nouns or pronouns appropriately for clarity and cohesion and to avoid repetition.

Resources
Large display cards with the names: *Robin Hood, King John, King Richard, Sheriff of Nottingham*; photocopiable page 43 'Who is the villain?'

5: Persuasive writing

Introduction
● Give four children a name card to take on the roles of the four 'villains'. Ask confident learners to summarise why they think their choice is the true villain.

Whole-class work
● Explain that the children will be writing to persuade readers that their character choice is the true villain in the Robin Hood legend. Remind them of the work done earlier in the week.
● To make their writing effective, they should include a range of sentence types, including subordinate clauses, using interesting conjunctions and use pronouns appropriately. Read an example to ensure they understand the task.

Independent work
● Provide time for the children to write their persuasive pieces of writing.

Differentiation
● Confident writers could compare other potential villains, to strengthen their argument.

Review
● Invite some children to read their persuasive pieces. Select examples for each of the four characters, and ask for comments on the strength of the arguments. Did anyone notice if conjunctions for arguments were being used?

Week 5 lesson plans

This week the children will look at Robin Hood as an adventure story, ordering scrambled elements of three stories about him. They will create spider diagrams of appropriate settings for a Robin Hood adventure, along with suitable vocabulary. Also, they will work on inverted commas in the context of the stories, as well as devising, planning and performing a new Robin Hood adventure. This will culminate in them writing their acted scenes as a correctly punctuated narrative.

1: What makes an adventure?

Introduction
- Show the class a short trailer of a suitable adventure film from an internet site such as: www.viewster.com.
- Ask what kind of story this is (an adventure).
- Explain that trailers are designed to whet the appetite and give a brief overview of the story. Story plans are a little like this in that they do not tell the whole story, but summarise the key elements.

Whole-class work
- Remind the children that they have written adventure stories in Year 3, and ask them what are the key features of such stories. You may wish to remind them that there are three basic parts – the beginning, middle and end.
- Scribe their answers on the whiteboard, or reveal your previously prepared version of them:
    - *Beginning: Something happens to propel the hero into a quest or adventure; a danger is announced or an enemy met.*
    - *Middle: the hero goes on an adventure to solve the problem and overcome the threat. There will be a series of events and obstacles in his way, but he generally finds ways to overcome them. This will be the biggest part of the story.*
    - *Ending: All problems are resolved and the hero is victorious.*
- Ask for one or two examples from the Robin Hood stories the children know, to illustrate this structure.

Independent work
- Hand out photocopiable page 45 'What makes an adventure?', glue, scissors and paper.
- Tell the children they will complete the activity on their own. They should cut out the nine boxes and rearrange them into three Robin Hood adventures. They should only stick them down when they are happy that they have the story sections correctly organised.
- Allow the children enough time to complete the activity.

Paired work
- Once the children complete the activity, they should find a partner and compare their results. Do they agree?

Differentiation
- If children finish early ask them to devise their own three-part adventure plan, or use a section of one of the stories on the photocopiable sheet to expand and tell orally to a partner.

Review
- Ask the children if they had arranged their stories in the same way as their partner. What strategies did they used to decide which parts fitted together, and in what order? Read out the correct order for each story so the children can check their own work.

Curriculum objectives
● In narratives, to create settings.
● To discuss and record ideas.

Resources
Interactive whiteboard screen with images of appropriate and inappropriate settings for a Robin Hood adventure; large sheets of plain paper

2: Settings

Introduction
● Show the class the images of settings, such as a *forest, castle, airport, supermarket* and a *medieval market*. Ask the children which would be suitable settings for a Robin Hood adventure.

Whole-class work
● Explain to the class that to describe a setting effectively we use as many of our senses as we can.
● Demonstrate how to note features of one setting by using a spider diagram and writing the setting in the centre. (Choose one that the children will not be working on later.) Ask for suggestions under headings for what might be seen, heard, felt, smelled and possibly tasted in the setting and list these on the spider diagram. Create further links, with suggestions for vocabulary that might be used to describe each element.

Group work
● Give each group a setting for a Robin Hood adventure, such as *dungeon, forest, outlaws' camp, castle, market*. They should work together, using large sheets of paper, to create a spider diagram similar to the one demonstrated.

> **Differentiation**
> ● This would be an appropriate task for mixed-ability groups, with a more experienced writer as the chief scribe.

Review
● Ask the class which sense was easiest to find examples for, and which was the most difficult. Choose representatives from each group to share and explain their spider diagrams to the class, and then display them for later use.

Curriculum objectives
● To use and punctuate direct speech.
● To read aloud their own writing, using appropriate intonation, tone and volume so that the meaning is clear.

Resources
Large speech bubbles made of paper with something written in them that one of the Robin Hood characters might say, for example the Sheriff might say *Those outlaws are a menace. I'll catch them whatever I have to do*; photocopiable page 46 'Inverted commas'; individual whiteboards and pens

3: Inverted commas

Introduction
● Invite children to hold up the prepared speech bubbles and say the words in role.

Whole-class work
● Demonstrate how one of the speeches would be written down as a narrative, using punctuation correctly. Ask the children to write the other speeches, correctly punctuated, on their own whiteboards.
● Use starter activity I 'Who said what?'.

Independent work
● Hand out photocopiable page 46 'Inverted commas' for children to complete. Remind them that they should use appropriate verbs and/or adverbs to describe the way in which the speech was said. For example, *Robin whispered conspiratorially, the Sheriff snarled menacingly*.

Paired work
● After completing the photocopiable sheet, ask pairs to compare their work. They should enjoy reading each other's speeches in role, using appropriate tone, pace and intonation as well as checking each other's punctuation.

Review
● Invite some of the children to read out, in role, one of their speeches for the class to guess the speaker. Finish by using the starter activity I 'Who said what?' again and ask the children if they feel confident using inverted commas.

4: Robin's new adventure (I)

Curriculum objectives
● To compose and rehearse sentences orally (including dialogue), progressively building a varied and rich vocabulary and an increasing range of sentence structures.
● To read aloud their own writing, to a group or the whole class, using appropriate intonation and controlling the tone and volume so that the meaning is clear.

Resources
Individual whiteboards and pens

Introduction
● Offer the class several scenarios for a new Robin Hood adventure, some that are possible and some not. For example, *robbing a bank, taking part in an archery contest* and so on. Ask the children which would work and ask for other suitable ideas.

Whole-class work
● Inform the class that they will be planning a new adventure for Robin and ask them to recap on which characters could be included. Explain that they will be acting a scene from their story, so it will need to be quite short and they should select a section from the start, middle or end. It will be a bit like the film trailer watched earlier in the week.
● Together, briefly recap the key features of adventure stories.

Paired work
● Give pairs 5–10 minutes to think of an idea for a new adventure.

Group work
● Arrange the pairs into groups and assign one child in each group to be the leader. The children should share their ideas for a new adventure and vote to decide which one they will use to create a scene to act out.
● They will need to allocate parts to each group member. One could be the narrator. The group leader could also act as director, if appropriate. Each group should rehearse their scenes, which should be 2–3 minutes in length.

Review
● Bring the class together so each group can perform their short scene. Encourage the rest of the class to offer positive feedback on the scenes.

5: Robin's new adventure (2)

Curriculum objectives
● In narratives, to create settings, characters and plot.
● To use and punctuate direct speech.

Resources
Any notes the children made the previous day

Introduction
● Select one of yesterday's groups to re-enact the scene they created together. Ask the rest of the class to listen carefully to the dialogue.

Whole-class work
● Explain that the children will be writing their short scenes as though they are a chapter from a book, rather than a playscript.
● Take a few lines from the scene the group performed and demonstrate how to write it as a narrative, including correct punctuation and text to support the dialogue; in other words, to tell the story.
● Explain that even though group members will be telling the same story, they will be doing so in their own way, so the retellings will not be identical. It is not vital to have the dialogue exactly the same as it was spoken, as long as the main ideas are included.

Independent work
● Provide time for the children to write their short scenes as narratives.

Differentiation
● Encourage more confident writers to start a new line for each speaker and to use a wider range of interesting vocabulary.

Review
● Ask a few volunteers to share their narratives, while the rest of the class review if the scene is effective and includes correctly punctuated dialogue.

Week 6 lesson plans

In this final week of the unit, the children will look at how the legend of Robin Hood has been told in the poetic form of a ballad. They will listen to Brian Patten reading a modern-day ballad, demonstrating the form before reading a traditional version about Robin. They will discuss this ballad before rehearsing it in groups, evaluating their performance and performing it as a class to a wider audience. Then they will read and listen to further examples of ballads before using their knowledge to draft and write their own ballads about another of the Robin Hood stories.

1: Reading a ballad

Introduction
● Play the class an audio clip of a modern ballad, such as Brian Patten reading his poem 'Geography lesson' (this can be found at: www.poetryarchive.org search for 'Geography lesson').
● Explain that this type of poem is called a *ballad*. Play the clip again, asking the children to make notes on their whiteboards of anything they notice about the poem.
● Ask them to share their observations. They may have noticed that the poem tells a story, that it has a rhyme scheme and that there is a definite rhythm to it. Some may pick up on lines that follow on from each other with no obvious pauses, suggesting that punctuation has been used in some places and not others.

Whole-class work
● Hand out photocopiable page 47 'The legend of Robin Hood' and read it to the class.
● Ask the children if the features they noticed from the first ballad also occur in this ballad.
● Do they notice any extra features? They may spot that some rhyming words have different spellings or that it is organised in rhyming couplets.
● Read two or three couplets of the ballad aloud to the class, firstly in a monotone, ignoring punctuation, then accurately in a well-modulated voice. Ask what differences they notice and why the second version was better. Remind them of their performances the previous week and what made them good.
● Look particularly at the lines:
  ● *Throughout Sherwood Forest, his bold band of men*
  ● *Would swoop on the Normans, then hide in their den.*
● Draw the children's attention to the punctuation in these lines, where commas mark the pauses, causing the first line to run on into the beginning of the second. Practise reading the lines as a class.

Paired work
● Encourage the children to work in pairs to practise reading part or all of the ballad, helping each other to achieve a good delivery.

Review
● Bring the class back together and ask for volunteers to read a couplet each to the rest of the class. Practise reading the whole ballad aloud as a whole class. Conclude by agreeing a list of key features for a ballad, which the children can write down for reference later in the week when they will be composing their own.

Curriculum objectives
● To prepare poems and playscripts to read aloud and to perform, showing understanding through intonation, tone, volume and action.

Resources
Photocopiable page 47 'The legend of Robin Hood' (with couplets numbered)

2: Rehearsing a ballad performance

Introduction

● Allow the children to see you quietly reading a newspaper at the front of the class.
● After a minute or two, tell them that in Robin Hood's time few people could read, so public performances of stories and ballads were common – it was often how news was communicated, but as with most stories told orally, it was often embellished. A larger-than-life performance would be much enjoyed.

Whole-class work

● Tell the children that they will be performing the ballad they practised in lesson 1, for others in the school. (Another class or perhaps as part of an assembly.)
● Spend time together in order to recap and agree the criteria for a good oral performance.

Group work

● Arrange the children into groups of three or four, giving each group one or two couplets of the ballad to read and rehearse.
● Encourage them to learn their lines by heart and allow time for them to practise, which can include suitable actions.

Review

● Organise the groups to stand in order and perform their couplets, from memory where possible. Remind them to listen out for the preceding line, so they are ready to perform their own. After practising two or three times, ask the class to judge their own performance according to the previously agreed criteria.

Curriculum objectives
● To perform a poem showing understanding through intonation, tone, volume and action.

Resources
If possible, some simple minstrel-style costumes (optional); photocopiable page 47 'The legend of Robin Hood'

3: Performing a ballad

Introduction

● If costumes are to be worn, the children should get ready.
● Before the performance, go through the performance checklist from the rehearsal and then rehearse for a final time.
● Remind the children about keeping together when delivering lines, speaking loudly without shouting, being clear and good intonation.

Whole-class work

● When the audience are in place, you or one of the children should announce the performance.
● Then invite the class to perform the ballad.

> **Differentiation**
> ● Some children may feel more confident if they have the written text available to refer to, although memorisation of the text should be encouraged.

Review

● Afterwards, discuss the performance with the class. Ask the children what they thought went well and if there was any way they could improve on another occasion. What advice would they give to others doing the same thing?

Curriculum objectives
● To discuss writing similar to that which they are planning to write in order to understand and learn from its structure, grammar and vocabulary.
● To compose sentences orally, including dialogue, progressively building a varied and rich vocabulary and an increasing range of sentence structures.

Resources
Photocopiable page 'The Ballad of Robin Hood and the Archery Contest' from the CD-ROM; brief versions of some stories from the Robin Hood legend (such as those in Marcia Williams' *The Adventures of Robin Hood* or online sources); rhyming dictionaries

4: Composing a ballad (1)

Introduction
● Allow the children to listen to a song that tells a story in ballad style (such as the video of Jonathan Kelly's 'Ballad of Cursed Anna', which can be found at www.youtube.com).

Whole-class work
● Recall the key features of a ballad. Ask: *How does this song fit the criteria?*
● Inform the class that over the next two days they will be composing their own ballad, to tell of an incident from the Robin Hood legend.
● Use photocopiable page 'The Ballad of Robin Hood and the Archery Contest' from the CD-ROM as a model of a typical ballad, once again highlighting the key features. Ask the class how this ballad differs from the ballad they performed. They may notice the different rhyme scheme and how some of the language is structured differently. For example *his long bow he would use* or *laughed when they did hear* give it a period feel.

Independent work
● Ask the children to research and select a Robin Hood story to turn into a ballad. Allow sufficient time for them to read around the stories and make their decision. Encourage the children to begin to draft ideas for their ballads. They must decide on their rhyme scheme and aim to write at least four verses.

Differentiation
● Some children may find it difficult to use rhyme and keep the sense of the piece, as well as maintain the rhythm. Offering possible rhyming words, rhyming dictionaries and practising syllable counting may help children when drafting their ballads.

Review
● Make a list of words the children may use for line ends for which rhymes would be needed, such as *hood, forest, men, bow, castle*. What suitable rhymes can the children find? Demonstrate to the class that it may be better to choose different words where suitable rhymes cannot be found.

Curriculum objectives
● To compose sentences orally, including dialogue, progressively building a varied and rich vocabulary and an increasing range of sentence structures.
● To read aloud their own writing, to a group or the whole class, using appropriate intonation and controlling the tone and volume so that the meaning is clear.

Resources
The children's drafts from lesson 4

5: Composing a ballad (2)

Introduction
● Allow the children a few minutes to share their ideas from lesson 4 with a partner. Draw the class together and ask if they have any problems with their ballads, which others may be able to suggest solutions to.
● Remind the children to take care with punctuation, particularly dialogue and where lines lead into one another.

Independent work
● Provide time for the children to work quietly to complete their ballads.
● Once they have completed their ballads, ask pairs to read them to each other.

Differentiation
● Invite more experienced writers to write quatrains, while those less experienced may feel more comfortable writing couplets. All of the children should be encouraged to use language and structure appropriate to the period.

Review
● Conclude by inviting some of the children to read their work aloud to the rest of the class. Remind them to take careful note of the punctuation they used. Assess their use of rhyme and rhythm as they read. Finished ballads could be displayed for all to read, or be collected in and placed into a book of ballads.

Curriculum objectives

● To use and punctuate direct speech.
● To choose nouns or pronouns appropriately for clarity and cohesion and to avoid repetition.
● To use and understand the grammatical terminology in Appendix 2 accurately and appropriately when discussing their writing and reading.

Resources

Individual whiteboards and pens; fiction books of the children's choice

Grammar and punctuation: Inverted commas and pronouns

Revise

● Use starter activity 8 'Spot the pronouns' and starter activity 1 'Who said what?'.
● Ask the children to use a book to look at how the dialogue is punctuated and to find pronouns. Invite them to share their findings with a small group.
● Dictate pieces of dialogue and ask the children to write them correctly. For example: *'Greetings, Robin,' said Little John in his unique way.; Friar Tuck might have been chef for the band, but he was a poor cook.; Although the brochure said it was antique, the lady had her doubts.; 'Because the chalet is beautiful, I will buy it,' said Tom.* Write the correct versions of the sentences on the board for the class to check their own work.

Assess

● Challenge the children to rehearse orally a conversation between three people. Then ask them to write it down, correctly punctuated, using pronouns for clarity and avoiding repetition.

Further practice

● Encourage the children to practice writing down more conversations.

Curriculum objectives

● To spell words that are often misspelled (Appendix 1).
● To read further exception words, noting the unusual correspondences between spelling and sound, and where these occur in the word.

Resources

Individual whiteboards and pens; 'Snap cards' (sets of tricky words)

Spelling: Words with soft /ch/ and words ending in 'gue' and 'que'

Revise

● Use the variation of starter activity 4 'Suffix challenge' with the class.
● Recap some of the spellings the children have learned by using starter activity 16 'French spellings'.
● Ask the children to try and spell the following words (they include the same sounds as those learned in lesson 3, week 2): *parachute, Charlotte, Chicago, chevron, chivalry, cheque, mosque, plaque, physique, grotesque, analogue, dialogue, intrigue, plague, vague.*
● Collect in their work and check the children's spellings.

Assess

● Provide the children with sets of sentences containing gaps where there are missing words and ask the children to write the correct spellings in the space.

Further practice

● To check the children can spell tricky words, make a set of cards with the words on them for the children to play 'Snap' and 'Kim's game' (where the children are shown the word cards for a short time before writing them from memory), to encourage instant recognition.
● Invite the children to read the words on the cards for others to write them on their whiteboards.

Curriculum objectives
● To check that the text makes sense to them, discussing their understanding and explaining the meaning of words in context.
● To ask questions to improve their understanding of a text.
● To draw inferences such as inferring characters' feelings, thoughts and motives from their actions, and justify inferences with evidence.
● To identify main ideas drawn from more than one paragraph and summarise these.
● To identify how language, structure, and presentation contribute to meaning.

Resources
Photocopiable page 'The Green Children of Woolpit' from the CD-ROM; quantity of randomly selected fiction books for further practice; highlighter pens

Reading: Legends

Revise
● Give each of the children photocopiable page 'The Green Children of Woolpit' from the CD-ROM, and a highlighter pen. Allow them time to read the story. Ask: *What kind of story would you say this is?* They should identify it as a legend, and be able to give reasons, such as that is a historically-based story with some elements that would appear to be fact, but others fiction.
● Ask the children to highlight those parts of the text that they think might be fact, and that could be researched to discover if this is correct. They should notice names of people and places, the reign of King Stephen, the foods available and whether there is a Woolpit village sign as described. Allow the children time to carry out some research to ascertain the facts.
● Briefly discuss their findings and then ask which elements of the story they consider to be fiction.
● To recap on performance features, invite children to read aloud part of the story to others in a group.
● Also, use the text as a reminder about the use of punctuation and elements of grammar and vocabulary. Where was punctuation used for direct speech? How were paragraphs organised? Did they notice any sentences beginning with a subordinate clause? Did they notice any unusual words? Were any sentences written in such a way as to suggest a period feel to the writing? Can anyone spot one of the tricky spellings they learned?

Assess
● Ask the children to write their own 'Guide to legends' in order to show their understanding of the genre. Explain that this will take the form of a guide for readers wishing to choose legends, so that they do not confuse it with other types of story. They should write in the form of a question-and-answer scenario, such as: *What is a legend? What will a legend contain? What is the difference between a legend and a myth? What will not usually be in a legend? Can you name some examples of legends?*
● You should encourage the children to form their own questions as well as giving them one or two as starters. Where children are finding difficulty in devising their own questions, you can provide some, noting this as part of your assessment. The children will be able to use their guides when they carry out the Writing assessment that follows.

Further practice
● To consolidate the children's understanding of both legend and adventure, as well as other genres, provide groups of children with randomly chosen piles of fiction books. Invite them to sort the books according to their own criteria into generic sets.
● When the books are sorted, ask them how they decided which books went together. How much help were the titles? Were some books already known to any of the group? Did they read the blurbs and examine the cover illustration? Did they read any of the text? Which type of book did they find most of? Were any books particularly difficult to define?

Curriculum objectives

● To draft and write by composing and rehearsing sentences orally, progressively building a varied and rich vocabulary and an increasing range of sentence structures, correctly punctuated.
● In narratives, to create characters and settings and plot.
● To extend the range of sentences with more than one clause by using a wider range of conjunctions.
● To choose nouns or pronouns appropriately for clarity and cohesion and to avoid repetition.
● To read aloud their own writing, to a group or the whole class, using appropriate intonation and controlling the tone and volume so that the meaning is clear.

Resources

Highlighter pens; children's 'Guide to legends' work (from the Reading assessment)

Writing: Legends

Revise

● Discuss the following aspects with the children: legend features; adventure features; vocabulary; punctuation; performance.
● Invite the children to examine the structure of stories, noting that they have a beginning, middle and end, and that most of the action usually takes place in the middle.

Assess

● Explain to the children that they are going to plan and write an adventure story based on the legend of Robin Hood by using an existing plot or creating one of their own, part of which they will relate to a partner.
● To begin, ask the children to use their 'Guide to legends' work (written for the Reading assessment) to and create their own checklist to cover:
  ● the key features of an adventure story
  ● vocabulary choices
  ● essential punctuation features of a narrative
  ● key features of a good oral performance.
● These all link to the headings revised previously. You may wish to offer some guidance here, by discussing what might be included with the class, so that no important aspects (such as paragraphing, inclusion of correctly punctuated dialogue, choice of varied and interesting vocabulary) are missed.
● Explain to the class that they will use their checklist for two purposes. Firstly, as a guide while they are writing and secondly, to use in order to evaluate their own and others' performances.
● Inform the class that this will be an extended piece of writing; a complete story with a beginning, middle and ending.
● For the second part of the assessment task, allow the children time to devise and plan their stories, referring to their personal checklists as they do so.
● For children stuck for ideas, allow them access to the texts they have been using throughout the unit to find a story which they have not yet used as the basis for their own adventure. Modern narrative retellings of the original ballads may be useful here.
● When plans are complete, invite the children to use these to briefly tell their story to a partner. They should use their performance checklist to evaluate their own and each others' storytelling. If you wish to assess this element of their work more formally, yourself and other adults could listen to extracts from each child's story, although this would be time-consuming and would not be ideal to do as a whole-class activity from the other children's point of view.
● Provide the children with sufficient time to write their stories. It may be necessary to allow two sessions for this to be done, particularly if you wish to give the children the opportunity to read, edit and redraft parts of their writing.

Further practice

● Examine with the class the types of criteria the children included in their checklists. Which were used by most children? Which elements were the most difficult to include? Would they alter their lists now that they have used them? How useful did they find them for planning and for evaluating?

Robin Hood: the legend

If you were to venture deep into the greenwood of long ago England, you would be wise to keep a watchful eye open for the outlaw Robin Hood, especially if you were wealthy. But Robin and his band of Merry Men would be hard to spot; wearing their clothes of Lincoln Green they would be well camouflaged. If you had little money you would have nothing to fear, for the legend tells us that Robin robbed from the rich to give to the poor, and that his sworn enemy was the Sheriff of Nottingham, who lived in a huge stone castle.

As a champion archer and accomplished swordsman, Robin might have gone to fight in the Crusades with King Richard the Lionheart, but he chose to wage war against the rich and greedy instead. He was not alone in his hideout in Sherwood Forest – he gathered a band of men to help him, such as Little John (who was not so little!), Will Scarlet, Mutch the Miller's Son, Allan-a-Dale who would entertain the company with his singing and Friar Tuck who was well-known for enjoying his food. And stories also tell of Robin's love for the fair Maid Marian, a noblewoman who helped him in many an escapade.

Robin and his Merry Men would do all they could to help the poor and needy, even if it meant breaking the law, which was why they were hunted by the Sheriff's men. Many were the battles fought in forest, marketplace and castle and many were the wounds inflicted on both sides.

But did he really exist? We will probably never know the truth. Some say that he was a nobleman, Robin of Loxley, or maybe the Earl of Huntingdon, others that he was just a forester's son. There are claims that he lived in Nottinghamshire and in Yorkshire. But what is certain is that stories of this dashing and daring renegade have been told for over 800 years and look set to be a favourite for generations to come.

■SCHOLASTIC
www.scholastic.co.uk

Ambush in the forest

It was early morning deep in the forest of Sherwood. All that could be heard were the calls of birds and the occasional snap of a twig as the two companions trod their way carefully along the greenwood track. Whooosh! As if from nowhere, an arrow shot past them, thudding into a nearby tree trunk, stopping the men instantly. Looking around they could see no sign of anyone, but a voice called out "Stay where you are. Throw down your weapons." A small dagger and a sling-shot were thrown to the ground, then from the shadows there appeared four figures clad in green.

"Name yourselves, strangers, and tell of your business," demanded the leader of the band.

"Thomas and Edwin, of the next county, on our way to Nottingham market," one replied nervously.

"What money have you?"

"Little, sire, just enough for a day's food. We are seeking work, for our families are in great need."

"Then you are fortunate, Thomas and Edwin. Welcome to the Greenwood. I am Robin Hood, and my Merry Men here are John, Will and Allan. Come to our camp where Friar Tuck and Maid Marian are preparing breakfast. We will see how we can help you."

"Robin Hood?" said Edwin. "Folk say you rob from the rich to give to the poor. It seems the stories I've heard about you are indeed true."

"As you say," Robin replied, "but the Sheriff does not make our task an easy one. His archers lay in wait wherever we go and there is a high price on our heads."

"Aye Robin," said Little John, "but there is no finer archer in the land than you, and pity the man who takes me on with the quarter staff."

The outlaws blindfolded the bemused pair and guided them further into the forest where the smell of cooking reminded them how long it had been since they last ate. The Sheriff's venison was not their usual fare for breakfast.

Right or wrong?

■ Write in the boxes the things Robin Hood did that you think were either bad or good.

Bad things	Good things

■ How would different people feel about his actions? Write your thoughts below.

People he robbed

_____

_____

People he gave money to

_____

_____

The Sheriff of Nottingham

_____

_____

His fellow outlaws

_____

_____

I can identify key features of a character and say what effect
I think these have on others.

How did you do?

PHOTOCOPIABLE   **■SCHOLASTIC**
www.scholastic.co.uk

Who is the villain?

- Read the text below. Who do you think is the villain?

The Sheriff of Nottingham

Appointed by the King, his job was to enforce the law and bring criminals to justice. This included capturing outlaws to ensure the safety of trade routes through Sherwood Forest, or to stop them poaching the King's deer. He is usually thought of as Robin's greatest enemy.

He also collected taxes from the people and as he was not paid by the King he often kept some of the money for himself. When Robin Hood and his men took from the rich, there was less money for him to collect in taxes, so he schemed and plotted to find ways to capture Robin and his Merry Men. Fortunately for him, he had many soldiers to call upon to fight Robin and his fellow outlaws.

King John

As king, it was John who allowed the Sheriff so much power. He was keen to gather taxes from the people, whether they were rich or poor, to buy back lands he had lost in a war with France. Many of his barons did not agree with the way he ruled the land, especially the way he dealt with the country's money.

Some people think he was a hard-working king, but others say he was spiteful and cruel. He was certainly disloyal to his brother Richard, as while he was king and away fighting in the Crusades, John tried to take over, but failed and fled the country for a time. He only became king after Richard died.

King Richard, the Lionheart

Richard is often seen as a good man who fought for England, but in fact he only visited the country twice in his reign, for a total of six months. He couldn't speak English, as his first language was French, and he used English money, collected from taxes, to pay for the years he spent fighting in the Crusades in the Holy Land.

Richard had rebelled against his father and while on the Crusades ordered 2,600 prisoners to be executed.

Clauses and conjunctions

■ Add a subordinate clause to these main clauses, using a suitable conjunction. The first ones start with the main clause.

Josh didn't go to the party _____

_____

Nadia was so excited _____

_____

Mr Patel had been learning to water-ski _____

_____

■ In these examples, the subordinate clause will come first. Notice the comma after the subordinate clause.

Even though it was a cold day, _____

_____

Unless Olly finds his missing sock, _____

_____

While the twins were sleeping, _____

_____

■ Now write two sentences of your own, one starting with the main clause and one starting with the subordinate clause. In each sentence, underline the conjunction you have used.

I. _____

_____

_____

2. _____

_____

I can use conjunctions to write sentences with subordinate clauses.

How did you do?

PHOTOCOPIABLE   **SCHOLASTIC**
www.scholastic.co.uk

Name: _____   Date: _____

What makes an adventure?

■ Here are some mixed-up plots for three Robin Hood adventures. Cut them out, then rearrange and stick them onto a sheet of paper, to form outlines of the stories. There is a beginning, middle and ending for each story.

✂

Robin hears of a village where all the farm animals have been taken in place of money for taxes. He is outraged and is determined to do what he can for the poor villagers.	The ransom is reluctantly paid and the spy put in prison.	Robin Hood moves into the forest, builds up a band of men and starts to steal from the rich to give to the poor. The Sheriff hears of this.
Fortunately, not all the Merry Men are taken prisoner. They storm Nottingham Castle and everyone is saved. Robin and his men go back to the forest.	Robin and his men sneak into the castle in disguise, fool the guards and release their friend.	A new recruit to the Merry Men is found to be a spy for the Sheriff of Nottingham.
Maid Marian is able to let Robin know where the livestock is being kept. He and his men release the animals at the dead of night, and return them to their owners, but Little John is captured and imprisoned.	He sends his henchmen to seek out the band of outlaws. After a fierce battle in Sherwood forest, Robin and some of the others are captured and imprisoned.	Robin discovers this when he follows the man to the market and overhears a suspicious conversation. Robin hatches a plot to give him false information, which leads the Sheriff's men into a trap. The soldiers are held captive and a message is sent to the Sheriff of Nottingham for a ransom to get his men back.

Inverted commas

■ Write something in each of the speech bubbles that these characters from the Robin Hood legend might say. Then rewrite their speech as a sentence below, using the correct punctuation.

Robin Hood

Little John

_____

_____

Friar Tuck

Sheriff of Nottingham

_____

_____

I can write appropriate dialogue for different characters and use the correct punctuation for writing direct speech.

How did you do?

Name: _____   Date: _____

The legend of Robin Hood

There once was an outlaw, in a time long ago
Who was swift with a sword and great with a bow.

With a hood round his face and a tunic of green
His skill with a longbow had to be seen.

Throughout Sherwood Forest, his bold band of men
Would swoop on the Normans, then hide in their den.

He robbed from the rich, to give to the poor.
Robin Hood was a brave man, of that we are sure.

The Sheriff of Nottingham wanted him caught
But his courage and daring beat all who he fought.

Will Scarlet, Friar Tuck and big Little John
Were all at his side in battles he won.

With the flight of an arrow or clash of broad swords
These outlaws would bring down their cruel Norman lords.

As a hero to Saxons, it wasn't too long
Before minstrels and poets put his deeds into song.

His life is a legend. Who he was, still unsure
But he robbed from the rich and he gave to the poor.

by Brenda Williams

PHOTOCOPIABLE

Science fiction

This half term uses the science-fiction genre to generate use of the imagination in creating settings, characters and invented technological objects which the children will weave together into their own science-fiction story. They will write a newspaper report on an alien invasion and read several forms of poetry, which they will use to create calligrams. Throughout, the children will draft, edit and redraft their writing, sharing it with others, working collaboratively and offering each other constructive criticism. They will be introduced to fronted adverbials, use the possessive apostrophe for singular and plural nouns, use dictionaries to check spellings and work on prefixes and suffixes in spelling.

Expected prior learning
- Can understand what a prefix is.
- Can use the apostrophe for possession for singular and plural.
- Can understand what an adverb is and be able to give examples.
- Can use inverted commas, apostrophes, pronouns and connectives.
- Can describe characters and develop a setting.
- Can participate in class discussions.
- Can write in paragraphs.

Overview of progression
- Through analysing several text-types and discussing their own work, the children will further develop their listening and speaking skills as well as deepening their knowledge about the structure of the texts. They will become increasingly adept at gathering ideas to write first drafts, which the children know they will edit in order to improve their work ready for a final draft. An integral part of this process will be the sharing and discussing of their writing with others.

Creative context
- The science-fiction genre lends itself well to interpretation in music as children can create sound effects for space and alien creatures.
- Dance and drama activities could include representing movements of spacemen, planets or aliens. Role-play activities can be extended into presenting dramatic performances to a wider audience.
- The written work the children produce can be collected in to form a large display used along with any associated art work they are asked to create.
- There are clear links with science, including further investigation of scientific inventions which have an impact on our daily lives.

Preparation
Gather together as many appropriate examples of science-fiction stories as you can. The *Astrosaurs* series is popular and an extract from one title is included. The children will need to browse through several science-fiction extracts themselves and you may wish to select examples from books you are familiar with and to share them with the class. Familiarise yourself with film and TV examples of the genre that the children may recognise.

You will also need:
Clips of film and TV soundtracks; large sheets of paper; individual whiteboards and pens; examples of science fiction texts; sticky notes; art and/or collage materials; a range of dictionaries; scissors; glue sticks; images of science-fiction characters; coloured pencils; books for display and research; internet access; a book on inventions, such as *Until I Met Dudley* by Roger McGough and Chris Riddell; highlighter pens; examples of calligrams.

On the CD-ROM you will find:
Media resources 'Ambient space music', 'Science-fiction settings', 'Old technological objects'; interactive activities 'Get the apostrophe right!', 'Automatically super!'; photocopiable pages 'City of the future', 'The Engineer', 'Prepositions'

Chapter at a glance

An overview of the chapter. For curriculum objective codes, please see pages 8–10.

Week	Lesson	Curriculum objectives	Summary of activities	Outcomes
1	1	RC: 1, 16 WC: 2	Identify and record for later use, common settings, characters and plots found in science-fiction stories	• Can contribute to wall displays with ideas for settings, characters and plots for science-fiction stories.
	2	WT: 4 WC: 16, 18	Use starter activity 6 'One or more?' and complete the sheet 'Hooray for the apostrophe', comparing results with a partner.	• Can demonstrate understanding of the use of the possessive apostrophe with singular and plural nouns.
	3	RC: 1, 16	Read science-fiction texts as a class and in groups, to identify elements of the genre.	• Can understand settings, characters and plots in science-fiction stories.
	4	WC: 5	Look at a variety of images of possible settings for science-fiction stories. Select one and write a brief description of it.	• Can select appropriate settings and children's own versions created, with descriptive captions.
	5	WT: 1, 5	Investigate spellings with the prefixes 'in-', 'im-', 'il-', 'ir-'. Find a spelling rule for when double consonants are used and find meanings in a dictionary.	• Can discover a spelling rule and find definitions.
2	1	WC: 15, 17, 20	Play adverb game, learn about fronted adverbials, use activity sheet and write sentences in books.	• Can demonstrate understanding of fronted adverbials and their punctuation.
	2	WC: 5	List generic science-fiction character types and create three characters to fit settings already made.	• Can discuss character types, select three main characters and describe orally and in writing.
	3	WC: 5, 19	Improvise conversations between two invented science-fiction characters, then write versions of these using correct punctuation.	• Can develop characters by creating conversations orally and in correctly punctuated written form.
	4	WC: 2, 5, 11, 13, 19, 20	Read extended character profile and discuss, identify grammatical and information features. Write draft of extended profile for one of the characters described previously.	• Can write first drafts of extended character profiles.
	5	WC: 11, 13, 19	Discuss and use drafts to edit and write completed character profiles.	• Can read and discuss drafts and then edit before writing a final version.
3	1	RC: 15, 16 WC: 2, 4	Consider and discuss the use of technology now and in the future. Research particular objects, making notes.	• Can research and make notes on technological objects.
	2	RC: 13	Groups discuss notes from previous lesson, plan, rehearse and deliver presentation of their findings.	• Can use notes from research to plan, rehearse and deliver presentation to whole class.
	3	WT: 1, 3	Investigate words with the given prefixes, using dictionaries to find meanings. Learn to spell the words.	• Can understand words with the prefixes and spellings learned.
	4	RC: 1, 2	Watch short film clip and discuss effects of future technological breakthroughs.	• Can consider and discuss positive and negative effects of possible future invented objects.
	5	WC: 2	Consideration of possible newly invented objects, leading to creating a labelled diagram.	• Can discuss and select new objects and then create labelled diagrams.
4	1	WC: 1, 5	Discuss how to weave setting, character and new object into a plot. Create and discuss plan.	• Can plan, discuss and adapt stories as necessary.
	2	WC: 14	Learn some prepositions of time and cause. Use starter activity 3 'Improvise it' and write simple sentences involving prepositions.	• Can begin to identify prepositions expressing time and cause and demonstrate a growing understanding of them.
	3	RC: 1 WC: 3, 15, 17	Check over story plans, adjusting if necessary then use them to write a first draft of their stories.	• Can use plans successfully to write first drafts of science-fiction stories including all required elements of narrative, grammar and punctuation.
	4	WC: 7, 8, 9	Work as a class to suggest improvements to a text. Use checklist to edit and improve stories. Share and comment on a partner's work.	• Can use checklists to edit drafts, which are shared, with any further changes being made.
	5	WT: 7, 8 WC: 5	Remind children of aspects of good handwriting before rewriting edited drafts of stories in a clear, legible hand.	• Can write final, edited version of their science fiction stories, using best handwriting for display.

Chapter at a glance

Week	Lesson	Curriculum objectives	Summary of activities	Outcomes
5	1	WC: 1	Analyse newspaper reports, identifying key features, sharing findings and creating a checklist for reference.	• Can identify and understand key features of newspaper reports.
	2	WC: 2, 3	Talk about the Roswell incident. Groups develop own ideas for a story of aliens landing locally and act them out in role.	• Can create stories of an alien landing, with question and answer role plays used to develop them.
	3	WC: 4, 13, 19	Listen to openings of stories, recap on key features and write first draft of opening paragraphs. Share with groups and edit.	• Can draft, share and edit opening paragraphs of alien stories.
	4	WC: 4, 7, 8, 9, 11, 13, 19	Teacher-in-role requires class as reporters to write final drafts of their opening paragraphs from previous day. Share some with the class.	• Can recap key features of a news report and work independently to write first drafts of opening paragraphs.
	5	WT: 7, 8 WC: 4, 13, 19	Teacher-in-role requires class to complete their aliens report. When complete, children act as editors to read and comment on partner's report.	• Can write and share final reports, with comments being given and received from a partner.
6	1	RC: 8, 14 WC: 1	Read three science fiction calligrams and identify poetic forms.	• Can choose two or three subjects and a range of words and phrases noted for possible use in poems. • Can check spellings using dictionaries.
	2	WT: 1	Identify, investigate, learn and test words with the suffix '-ous'.	• Can group adjectives with the suffix '-ous' according to spellings.
	3	RC: 7	Complete common similes and devise their own, more interesting ones with the science fiction theme. Class guess object from similes read out.	• Can gather ideas for a collection of similes that may be used in science fiction poems.
	4	WC: 3, 7	Consider the week's work and write a first draft of two poems. Work with a partner to experiment and decide on shapes for poems.	• Can attempt first drafts which are shared with a partner for comments. • Can select appropriate shapes for final drafts.
	5	WT: 8 WC: 7	Review drafts and edit before final calligrams are created. Some are shared with the class and all are put on display.	• Can produce their final drafts of calligrams.

Background knowledge

Calligram: Sometimes known as a shape poem, a calligram is a poem of any form, written inside an appropriate shape.

Character profile: A detailed description of a character, giving a physical description as well as information about their personality and characteristics.

Draft: A version of a piece of writing using first ideas, the writer knowing that it will not be the finished version.

Edit: Reading through a piece of writing with the intention of changing it in order to improve the quality in a variety of ways.

Fronted adverbials: An adverbial is a word or phrase that makes the meaning of a verb more specific. When it is fronted, it occurs at the start of the sentence.

Possessive apostrophes: The position of the apostrophe shows whether the owners or possessors are singular or plural.

Prefix: A group of letters added to the front of a word to create another word.

Prepositions: A preposition links a noun or pronoun to some other word in the sentence. Prepositions often describe locations or directions, but can describe other things, such as relations of time.

Science fiction: A genre of writing where the narrative is imaginary, based on scientific possibilities, usually set in the future.

Week 1 lesson plans

This half term begins with the children identifying setting, character and plot features of science fiction stories. They go on to find these features in a particular text. Then they use this knowledge to focus on science-fiction settings, creating their own artistically and adding descriptive captions. They will use the settings later in the term when they write their own science-fiction stories. A lesson on using the possessive apostrophe for singular and plural nouns is a reminder of work first covered in Year 3, and children also learn to spell words with prefixes indicating negatives.

1: Introducing science fiction

Introduction

- Play the class one or more audio clips from popular science-fiction based films or television series that they are likely to be familiar with. (These can be found online.)
- Ask the children what type of stories the music is linked to. They may suggest space, or adventure. If they are not familiar with the term *science fiction*, introduce it to them.
- Ask what work they did in Year 3 that might fit into the science-fiction genre. (Aliens and Robots.)

Whole-class work

- Write *science fiction* on the board and ask what we mean by each of the words individually, scribing the children's suggestions.
- Use their responses to help formulate a definition of science-fiction stories. They may suggest that such stories are a little like predicting the future, or imagining life on other planets or in another world. They may link science fiction to the development of new technologies, or perhaps a society on earth which has had to adapt because of the impact of global warming.
- Ask: *What science-fiction stories do you know?*
- Remind the class that stories have a setting, characters and plot, and display the sheets with these headings. Pin the sheets to a wall, not too close together as the children will be using them in the next part of the lesson and will need easy access.

Group work

- Organise the class into groups of 4–6 and give them sticky notes and pens. You may wish to appoint a leader in each group.
- In their groups, ask the children to suggest suitable settings, types of character and plots that might be used in science-fiction stories.
- Explain to the children that they should write their suggestions on the sticky notes and attach them to the appropriate ideas sheet.

> **Differentiation**
> - Mixed-ability groups would work well, perhaps allowing experienced writers to scribe, while giving everyone the opportunity to contribute orally.

Review

- When the children have made their suggestions, go over each ideas sheet with the class, summarising their thoughts. There will be some ideas that are duplicated, which is fine as this suggests well-used and well-known tropes. Look also for more unusual ideas that perhaps only one or two groups have thought of.
- Inform the children that they will find these ideas sheets useful in future lessons, and leave them on display for reference. You may wish to make a sheet summarising the main ideas, so the children can have their own copies later.

Expected outcomes

- All children can identify and discuss common features of sci-fi stories and create an illustrated setting; they begin to use the possessive apostrophe for singular and plural; and spell some words with the prefixes 'ir-', 'in-', 'im-', 'il-'.
- Most children can discuss in detail common features of sci-fi stories; they are reasonably confident with the possessive apostrophe; and can spell most words with the prefixes 'ir-', 'in-', 'im-', 'il-'.
- Some children can link character and plot to particular types of sci-fi setting and include detail in their illustrations; they can confidently use the possessive apostrophe for both singular and plural; and have learned to spell words with the prefixes 'ir-', 'in-', 'im-', 'il-'.

Curriculum objectives

- To participate in discussion about both books that are read to them and those they can read for themselves, taking turns and listening to what others say.
- To discuss and record ideas.
- To listen to and discuss a wide range of fiction, poetry, plays, non-fiction and reference books or textbooks.

Resources

Various audio clips of well-known soundtracks of film and television science-fiction stories; three large ideas sheets of paper with the headings: *Setting*, *Characters*, *Plot*; sticky notes

---

Curriculum objectives
● To indicate possession by using the possessive apostrophe for singular and plural nouns.
● To learn the grammar for Year 4 in Appendix 2.
● To place the possessive apostrophe accurately in words with regular plurals and in words with irregular plurals.

Resources
Photocopiable page 72 'Hooray for the apostrophe!'; individual whiteboards and pens; interactive activity 'Get the apostrophe right!' on the CD-ROM

2: Possessive apostrophes

Introduction
● Use starter activity 6 'One or more?' including your choice of variation.

Whole-class work
● Recall use of the possessive apostrophe and remind the children that without the it we could easily be confused when reading. For example, we wouldn't be sure whether one or more than one person or thing is being referred to.
● Reinforce the fact that plural nouns where there is no possession indicated do not require any apostrophe, for example *There were many trees in the garden.*
● Suggest the mnemonic: *Before the s it's singular, after the s there's many more*, noting exceptions such as *men's, children's* or *sheep's.* Can anyone spot why there is an anomaly?
● Use screen 1 of the interactive activity 'Get the apostrophe right!' on the CD-ROM. Ask children to put up a hand for each sentence they think is correct.

Independent work
● Hand out photocopiable page 72 'Hooray for the apostrophe!' for the children to complete on their own.
● Allow pairs of children time to compare their answers, noting differences.

> **Differentiation**
> ● Some of the children may benefit from concentrating separately on singular and plural use of the apostrophe.

Review
● Examine the photocopiable sheet together, ask where any pairs disagreed. Use the remaining two screens of interactive activity 'Get the apostrophe right!' on the CD-ROM, to check if the children can identify where the possessive apostrophe is used correctly. (Or, the children could complete it independently.)

Curriculum objectives
● To participate in discussion about both books that are read to them and those they can read for themselves, taking turns and listening to what others say.
● To listen to and discuss a wide range of fiction, poetry, plays, non-fiction and reference books or textbooks.

Resources
Photocopiable page 'City of the future' from the CD-ROM; examples of science fiction texts; media resource 'Ambient space music' on the CD-ROM; ideas sheets (created in lesson 1); sticky notes

3: Identifying science-fiction elements

Introduction
● Read the extract on photocopiable page 'City of the future' from the CD-ROM, with the audio 'Ambient space music' on the CD-ROM to provide atmosphere.

Whole-class work
● Share the text extract with the class. Ask them to tell you which elements of the extract are clues to this being a science-fiction story, and highlight them.
● Ask the children which elements are to do with setting, which with characters and which with plot (to link to lesson 1).
● Point out the apostrophes in the text and ask the children what sort of apostrophe it is in each case. Also, note the punctuation used for direct speech.

Group work
● Arrange the children into groups and provide them with several different science-fiction stories to browse through.
● Refer to the three ideas sheets (from lesson 1) and ask them to look through the books, working together to search for examples of settings, characters and plots that match their original suggestions. They should also note any new ideas. These can be written on sticky notes and added to the ideas sheets.

Review
● Encourage each group to summarise their findings for the whole class. Which common features did they find? Were there any other useful points that they discovered? Were they able to add to the ideas sheets?

Curriculum objectives
● In narratives, to create settings.

Resources
Art and/or collage materials; media resource 'Science-fiction settings'

4: Creating settings

Introduction
● Show the class the photographs from 'Science-fiction settings' on the CD-ROM.
● Invite them to identify the types of setting and suggest descriptive vocabulary to go with each, including as many of their senses as possible.
● Ask the children to select one type of setting to draw, paint or make a collage of. They can use any ideas generated earlier in the week as well as those you have shown them, but they should make it their own version.
● Emphasise to the class that as they are focusing on settings alone, they should not include characters at this point.

Independent work
● Encourage the children to select their art materials and create their setting.
● Invite them to add a descriptive caption, using interesting and appropriate vocabulary. They may wish to give their setting a name.

Review
● Select some of the children to show and explain their settings to the rest of the class. Have they named their setting? Ask the class to suggest vocabulary suitable for describing the settings displayed.

Curriculum objectives
● To use the first two or three letters of a word to check its spelling in a dictionary.
● To use further prefixes and suffixes and understand how to add them (Appendix 1).

Resources
A range of dictionaries; photocopiable page 73 'Not that!'; individual whiteboards and pens

5: Prefixes that mean 'not'

Introduction
● Display the following text on the board: *I'm getting impatient with this illegible writing. It's impossible to see if the spelling is incorrect, especially the irregular words.*
● Read the sentences aloud, and then highlight the words *impatient, illegible, impossible, incorrect, irregular*.

Whole-class work
● Ask the children what the highlighted words have in common. They may notice that all the words start with 'i', that two have double consonants after the 'i' and that all the words have a meaning referring to opposites, for example *impatient* means *not patient*.

Paired work
● Hand out photocopiable page 73 'Not that!', asking them to investigate the words to find a rule for when to use double consonants, such as the letters 'l', 'm' and 'r' are doubled when the root word begins with the same letter.

Independent work
● Using appropriate dictionaries ask the children to now work independently to find and copy the meanings of the words on the sheet. Remind them to look for the first three letters of the words when using the dictionaries, as the first two letters are the same in each set because they share the same two-letter prefix.

Differentiation
● To extend the learning, invite the children to look up other words starting with the same pairs of letters, listing any others with the same prefix. They will need to check meanings, so they do not include words where the letters are not used as prefixes
---

Review
● Select some of the words from the lesson and ask the children to write them on their whiteboards, showing you their results for informal assessment.
● Use starter activity 15 'Prefix game'.

Week 2 lesson plans

The children start the week with an introduction to fronted adverbials, building on the knowledge they already have about adverbs. They will make use of this grammatical form throughout their writing this year. Following their work on science-fiction settings last week, the children look this week at appropriate science-fiction characters to inhabit them, considering language that matches their creations. With characters created, the children will draft and write extended profiles for one of their main protagonists.

1: Fronted adverbials

Introduction
● To remind children about adverbs from Year 3, play the game 'In the manner of' by giving volunteers a verb to act, such as *walking, looking, reading, thinking* or *laughing*. Then whisper to them the manner in which you want them to perform, for example *thoughtfully, stupidly, quietly, slowly, seriously* and so on. The class should suggest which adverb the actor is portraying.

Whole-class work
● Ask the children what adverbs do, such as provide more information about the verb.
● Introduce them to the phrase *fronted adverbial* and explain that these are usually phrases that provide even more information than adverbs alone.
● Invite them to suggest where in a sentence they think fronted adverbials will come, such as at the start.
● Explain that adverbials occur at any point in the sentence, but writers often put them at the start to create dramatic effect or add emphasis. We don't often use them in our spoken language.
● Tell the class that fronted adverbials answer questions such as *where, when, how, why, how often* or *how long*.
● With the class, use starter activity 7 'Fronted adverbials'.
● Demonstrate on the interactive whiteboard by moving an adverbial from the end of a sentence to the beginning, altering the punctuation accordingly. For example, change *We went to the beach on Sunday* to *On Sunday, we went to the beach*. Repeat with one or two other sentences.
● Point out the adverbial and the comma you have placed after it.

Paired work
● Hand out photocopiable page 74 'Fronted adverbials puzzle' for pairs of children to solve together.
● Remind them of the questions that fronted adverbials answer, telling them that this is a clue as to which part of the sentences on the sheet will come at the beginning of the sentence. For example, it will have information about time, place, frequency and so on.
● Advise them to arrange the cut-out boxes on the table until they are happy with their results, before sticking any of them down.

Independent work
● When the cut-and-paste activity is complete, ask the children to write the re-formed sentences in their books, correctly punctuated, using capital letters and full stops, as well as placing commas after the fronted adverbials.

Review
● Invite volunteers to read out their sentences, pausing at the comma. Ask the children to suggest sentences with fronted adverbials for a given subject, such as spaceships, moons, aliens and journeys.

Curriculum objectives
● In narratives, to create characters.

Resources
Various images of science-fiction characters (both well-known and generic) from science-fiction stories, including films (live and animated), television programmes and books; photocopiable page 75 'My science-fiction characters'; coloured pencils

2: Science-fiction characters (1)

Introduction
● Show the class the images characters from science-fiction stories. Do the children recognise any, and what do they know about them? Make a list.

Whole-class work
● Explain that the children will be creating some science-fiction characters to fit in with the settings they made last week. Start a list of character types on the board by writing *warriors, robots, computer experts.*
● Ask the class for suggestions of others, but stress you are looking for types and not named characters (such as: *scientists, astronauts, aliens* and so on).

Independent work
● Ask children to select three main characters, each of a different type, to fit their settings. Hand out photocopiable page 75 'My science-fiction characters' to complete. They may draw a simple picture of each character in the box, but they should give most attention to the written information.

Paired work
● Ask children to use their photocopiable sheets as notes to describe one or more of their characters to a partner. They can add further information from their discussion and should be prepared to answer and ask questions.

Review
● Ask some children to describe a partner's character to the rest of the class. Does the creator of the character agree that they have given a fair description?

Curriculum objectives
● In narratives, to create settings and characters.
● To use and punctuate direct speech.

Resources
Children's photocopiable sheets (from lesson 2)

3: Science-fiction characters (2)

Introduction
● Choose two science-fiction characters, from different stories. Imagine they meet and improvise and model a brief conversation between them.

Whole-class work
● Ask the class to explain what sort of questions the two characters asked each other. What other things might two such strangers have to say to one another when they first meet?
● Encourage them to make suggestions of unlikely pairings of science-fiction characters and what they might ask or say to each other.

Paired work
● Using yesterday's photocopiable sheets, invite the children to improvise conversations between one of their characters and a partner's. They should briefly introduce themselves, in role, and follow up with questions and answers.
● After a short time, call out 'Change!' and ask the children to move on to a different partner and to start a new conversation. Repeat this a few times.

Independent work
● Encourage the children to write a brief conversation between two of their own science-fiction characters, using correct punctuation for direct speech.

Differentiation
● Challenging children to involve all three characters in their written conversation.

Review
● With a partner, invite children to use the written conversation and to read the dialogue alone, as with a playscript. The punctuation should help them.

Curriculum objectives
● To discuss and record ideas.
● In narratives, to create settings, characters and plot.
● To choose nouns or pronouns appropriately for clarity and cohesion and to avoid repetition.
● To extend the range of sentences with more than one clause by using a wider range of conjunctions.
● To use and punctuate direct speech.
● To use and understand the grammatical terminology in Appendix 2 accurately and appropriately when discussing their writing and reading.

Resources
Children's character sheets (from lesson 3); photocopiable page 'The Engineer' from the CD-ROM

4: Drafting extended character profiles

Introduction
● Read aloud to the class the text on photocopiable page 'The Engineer' from the CD-ROM. You may wish to display it on the interactive whiteboard or give them their own copies to follow.

Whole-class work
● Tell the children that this is an extended character profile of one of the main characters in a science-fiction story.
● Ask them what sorts of information are given about the character – both explicit and implicit. What do we know about him from other characters in the extract as well as what we are told directly?
● Can the children spot any examples of fronted adverbials, connectives and direct speech being used? How have the paragraphs been organised? Can they spot the pronouns?
● Explain to the class that they will use the work they have already done on characters to select one to write their own extended character profile about. Today they will write a first draft.

Independent work
● Using their work from lessons 2 and 3 to guide them, invite the children to choose one of their characters and then write a first draft of their extended character profile. They should aim to include some fronted adverbials and direct speech.

Review
● Ask volunteers for examples of sentences they have written that include fronted adverbials, and also some of the direct speech they have included. Encourage the rest of the class to provide comments on the characters.

Curriculum objectives
● To choose nouns or pronouns appropriately for clarity and cohesion and to avoid repetition.
● To extend the range of sentences with more than one clause by using a wider range of conjunctions.
● To use and punctuate direct speech.

Resources
Children's drafts (from lesson 4); a small selection of any books for display purposes

5: Writing extended character profiles

Introduction
● Flick through a selection of books and ask the class if they think the authors made any changes as they were writing them.
● Explain that all writers re-read their work, looking for technical errors like spelling or punctuation, but mainly to see how they might improve their work. This might be by choosing better words, deleting some parts or noticing where they have repeated a word, so they will find a synonym to replace one of them.

Whole-class work
● Ask the class what they found easy and what was more difficult while writing their own drafts.
● Explain to them that they now have an opportunity to work in the same way as the writers whose books are on the school bookshelves, by reading through their first drafts to look for ways of improving their work.

Independent work
● Allow the children time to read and edit their drafts. Some may find it helpful to ask a partner for advice on particular points in their writing.
● When they are happy with their editing, ask the children to write finished copies of their character profiles in their best handwriting.

Review
● Ask the class what sort of changes they made to their first drafts. Who corrected technical errors, such as spelling, grammar or punctuation? Did anyone change words? Were any deletions or additions made? Ask the children to provide examples.

Week 3 lesson plans

The focus this week is on new technology, its effects on our lives and possibilities for inventions of the future. The children will first consider the technology they use themselves and work in groups to research particular objects. Having gathered information, the groups will work together to plan, rehearse and present their findings to the class. They will follow this up by considering what technology might offer us in the future and consider the effects this might have on our lives. They will end the week by having fun inventing an object of the future and describing it in a labelled diagram. To support their work, they will look at the prefixes 'inter-', 'super-' and 'auto-' in relation to the language of technology and science fiction.

1: Research into new technology

Introduction
● Show the children the media resource 'Old technological objects' on the CD-ROM, along with other images, such as an old computer, record player, radio, cassette player, old model car, torch and light bulb.
● You may also wish to bring in real objects as they could have a greater impact because the children can hold and perhaps try them.
● Explain that when these were first invented they were technological breakthroughs that amazed and fascinated people. They changed peoples' lives.

Whole-class work
● Explain that technology often features in science-fiction stories, with new inventions that might be around in the future. For example, light sabres in *Star Wars*, hoverboards in *Back to the Future* and teleportation machines in *Star Trek*.
● Can the children think of any other examples?
● Ask the class what current technology they use, such as mobile phones, MP3 players, game consoles, computers, music players, HD or 3D televisions.
● Inform the children that they will be working in groups, researching one of these new forms of technology to see how much they can find out about it and then later they will present their findings to the class.
● Today they will concentrate on gathering their information.

Group work
● Organise the children into mixed-ability groups. Give each group one of the above forms of technology to research using books and the internet, if possible. While the children may be able to find their own books and internet sites, it will save time if you have sourced these previously.
● Ask the children to make notes about what they find, including references to their sources so that they can find them again if necessary. Explain that they should not copy large pieces of information, but organise their findings into paragraphs, to refer to when making their oral presentation.
● Helpful headings for their searches might be: *Who invented it? When was it first used? What did early examples look like? What size were they? How much did they cost and what is the cost now?* These questions could also be used as internet search terms, with the name of the object included.

> **Differentiation**
> ● Confident internet users could be encouraged to search online, while other group members concentrate on using the books provided.

Review
● Rearrange the children into new groupings for them to briefly share their findings with each other. This task should help them when they rehearse and give their presentations later.

Expected outcomes
● All children can discuss and find information on recently invented objects. They can learn prefixes applicable to technological words. They can draw and label a new object and write a simple paragraph about its purpose.
● Most children can learn to spell new words with the prefixes 'inter-', 'super-', 'auto-'. They can provide more information in their paragraph about their new object.
● Some children can use a greater range of sources for their research and present it confidently to the whole class.

Curriculum objectives
● To retrieve and record information from non-fiction.
● To discuss and record ideas.
● To participate in discussion about both books that are read to them and those they can read for themselves, taking turns and listening to what others say.
● To organise paragraphs around a theme.

Resources
Media resource 'Old technological objects' on the CD-ROM; range of books for children's research into modern technology, such as Some titles could be: *How Things Work* First Library of Knowledge series (Blackbirch Press), *Popular Science Almanac for Kids: Brain Pop* (Time Home Entertainment), or *1000 Inventions and Discoveries* (DK); internet access (if possible)

Curriculum objectives
● To identify main ideas from more than one paragraph and summarise these.

Resources
You may wish to prepare a PowerPoint presentation, show books or have large drawings to be annotated for the Introduction; children's research notes (from lesson 1); any resources the children may need to make their presentations

2: Presenting research

Introduction
● In front of the class model your own brief presentation about one of the items you used to illustrate technology of the past.

Whole-class work
● Inform the children that they can choose their own method of presentation, suggesting those listed above.
● Explain that they should first discuss in their groups how they will organise their presentation and what will be each member's role. They could have one person introducing their piece, one person showing illustrations or operating the computer and another providing the explanations.
● Their presentations should last 3–4 minutes, depending upon how much time you have available. Remind them to check on the length of time they are taking.

Group work
● Encourage the children to work in their groups to discuss and rehearse their presentations. You may wish to appoint a leader for each group.
● Allow the groups time to plan and rehearse, before they give their presentations to the rest of the class.

Review
● After each presentation, ensure you make a few positive comments on what the children managed to find out and how well they performed, also offering constructive advice where appropriate.

Curriculum objectives
● To use further prefixes and suffixes and understand how to add them (Appendix 1).
● To spell words that are often misspelled (Appendix 1).

Resources
Dictionaries; individual whiteboards and pens; the following words displayed: *internet, international, intergalactic, interstellar, automatic, automobile, autopilot, supermarket, superstore, supercity, supersonic*; interactive activity 'Automatically super!' on the CD-ROM; internet access (if possible)

3: Prefixes and technological words

Introduction
● Write on the board the words *web, mouse, keyboard*.
● Ask the class for definitions – there is more than one.
● Explain that with new technology words can gain new meanings such as these, while new words are being coined for new ideas and inventions.

Whole-class work
● Write the prefixes 'inter-', 'auto-' and 'super-' on the board.
● Say they are prefixes and ask the children for a reminder of what a prefix is.
● Explain to the children the meanings. Point out that 'inter-' means between or among; 'auto-' means self or own; 'super-' means above or better.
● Now ask the class for examples of words for each prefix, and for explanations of their meanings.
● Explain that these letter strings are not always prefixes, for example in the words *interesting* or *superb*.

Independent work
● Show the children the words displayed. Invite them to use dictionaries to find the words, check their meanings and write them down.

Differentiation
● Note those children finding difficulty with the spellings and spend time revising the words with them.

Review
● Ask some of the children to share with the class the meanings they have found. Were there any words not in the dictionaries? Invite the children to independently use interactive activity 'Automatically super!' on the CD-ROM, in order to consolidate their learning of prefixes.

Curriculum objectives
● To listen to and discuss a wide range of fiction, poetry, plays, non-fiction and reference books or textbooks.
● To read books that are structured in different ways and read for a range of purposes.

Resources
Film clip of opening titles to the TV cartoon *The Jetsons* (from internet search)

4: Future ideas

Introduction
● Play the short (1 minute) film clip of the opening titles of the 1960's TV cartoon *The Jetsons* (available online).
● Ask: *What examples of space-age technology did you spot?* Play the clip again for children to have a second chance to find them. Explain that this was how the cartoon creators saw the 21st century world.

Whole-class work
● Discuss with the class what new things they think might be around in the future. What would they like to see? What effects do they think these new things might have on our lives? Do they think we'll ever get teleportation? Will we ever live on the moon or other planets? The children may suggest ideas about renewable energy sources or medical breakthroughs that make us live longer.

Paired work
● Allow time for the children to talk to a partner about the points raised in the class discussion, giving everyone a chance to air their views. Ask them to consider the following questions: *Would the new ideas be good or bad? What benefits or problems might they cause? How would they affect our lives?*

Review
● Bring the class together and initiate a class discussion on the above points. The children should demonstrate that they have considered and discussed possible inventions in the future and the positive and negative effects these might have on our lives.

Curriculum objectives
● To discuss and record ideas.

Resources
A book on inventions, such as *Until I Met Dudley* by Roger McGough and Chris Riddell

5: New inventions

Introduction
● Remind the children about the objects from lesson 1 and have them available again, if possible. Explain that new inventions can change people's lives. For example, can they imagine living without telephones or electric light?
● Following on from lesson 4's discussion, ask the class what new objects or machines might there be in the future.

Paired work
● Working with a partner, invite the children to discuss their ideas for future inventions, drawing on discussions from the previous lesson and today.

Whole-class work
● Gather the class together and ensure the children understand labelled diagrams. Draw a simple example on the board, perhaps of an object they are familiar with. The labels should include brief explanations, for example *screen, to show information, see other people and what you are writing*.

Independent work
● Invite the children to create a labelled diagram of their own new object.

> **Differentiation**
> ● While some of the children may only be able to provide simple labels, encourage others to write more detailed explanations on their diagrams.

Review
● Share one or two pages from a book on inventions, such as *Until I Met Dudley*, showing them fun, alternative ideas as well as real information about how particular machines work.

Week 4 lesson plans

The main focus for the week is the drafting, editing and writing of a science-fiction story. Using what they have learned about the genre, the children will consider how to link their settings, characters and object into a story. The process is modelled for them with the text on photocopiable page 'The Engineer'. They will discuss their plans with a partner who will also comment later on their first drafts. The children have the opportunity to edit their work, using an editing checklist, and their final version will be in their best joined handwriting. They will also work on the use of prepositions of time and cause.

1: Fitting story elements together

Introduction

● Read out a short descriptive sentence using a 'Cluedo style' scenario linking setting, character and object to the science-fiction theme. For instance, *The Engineer was in his laboratory on Z27, tinkering with his invention, the futuroscanner.*
● Point out the three elements.

Whole-class work

● Remind the class about the settings, characters and objects they have created, explaining that they will bring these elements together in a science-fiction story. They will plan, draft and write them over several days.
● Hand out photocopiable page 76 'My Science fiction story' and go through it with the children, explaining each section and modelling it with your own ideas, based on *The Engineer.*
● Explain that they need to blend setting, characters and object together when they create their plots. Ask them to think about:
   ● the relationships between the characters. (Do they know each other, or will they meet in the story? How do they get on? Are other, minor characters involved? Remember the roles they were given will affect what they do in the story. The things they are given to say and how they say them should reflect their personalities.)
   ● how the settings are important. It will have some effect on what happens, or the story could be set anywhere. (For example, is special clothing or equipment required to survive there? Is it very isolated so that help is a long way away, or is it crowded so it's easy to get lost or to hide? Is it hot, dark, permanently light?)
   ● how the object should play a central role in the plot. (Does someone want to steal it? Does it malfunction? Does it have an amazing effect on others? Does it make possible things that previously were impossible?)

Independent work

● Invite the children to use photocopiable page 76 to plan their story and to refer to their previous work if they wish.

Paired work

● When the plans are complete, ask the children to use their planning sheets to briefly outline their story to a partner. Each child should be prepared to both ask and answer questions, about their plan.
● They do not have to agree with or accept their partner's criticisms or ideas, if they are happier with their own. However, the children do have the opportunity to take new suggestions on board and make changes to their plan.

Review

● Explain that there will be a day between planning and writing, so the children will have a period of thinking time in which to consider any further changes to their stories. Ask if anyone has already made some changes following their paired work. Encourage volunteers to offer examples as these may be useful to others.

Expected outcomes
● All children can use their previous work to plan and discuss their science fiction stories.
● Most children can devise a coherent plot in which setting, characters and object fit well.
● Some children can be very clear how their characters and invented objects will fit in with their setting.

Curriculum objectives
● In narratives, to create settings, characters and plot.
● To discuss writing similar to that which they are planning to write in order to understand and learn from its structure, grammar and vocabulary.

Resources
Children's previous work on setting, character and object (for reference); photocopiable page 76 'My science-fiction story'; photocopiable page 'The Engineer' from the CD-ROM

Curriculum objectives
● To use conjunctions, adverbs and prepositions to express time and cause.

Resources
The following words displayed: *adventurous, inter-galactic, whimpered, suspicious, supercharged* and *on, at, in, for, by, from, to*; photocopiable page 'Prepositions' from the CD-ROM; individual whiteboards and pens; a selection of fiction books from the class library

2: Prepositions to express time and cause

Introduction

● Look at the words displayed, ask the class which words might be called boring and which exciting. Explain that we need the so-called boring words. They are important because we use them much more often.
● Remind the class of how they also use conjunctions and adverbs such as *after, before, until, when, as, because*, when constructing sentences with more than one clause. Ask for examples.

Whole-class work

● Remind the children of the work they did in Year 3 on prepositions. Ask what they remember. Remind them that prepositions link nouns, pronouns or phrases to another word in the sentence, and give them photocopiable page 'Prepositions' from the CD-ROM.
● Display on the interactive whiteboard these examples of prepositions of time:
   ● *He got up at six o'clock.*
   ● *Tom hadn't seen Suzie for ages.*
● Then add these examples of cause:
   ● *He gave some flowers to her.*
   ● *Helen smiled at the baby.*
● Highlight the nouns and pronouns one colour and the prepositions (*at, for, to*) another.

Paired work

● Invite the children to do starter activity 3 'Improvise it', including the variation.

Review

● This can be a difficult concept to understand. Offer further practice by asking the children to find examples of prepositions in fiction books.

Curriculum objectives
● To listen to and discuss a wide range of fiction.
● To compose and rehearse sentences orally (including dialogue), progressively building a varied and rich vocabulary and an increasing range of sentence structures (See Appendix 2).
● To use fronted adverbials.
● To use commas after fronted adverbials.

Resources
Children's story plans (from lesson 1); prepared displayable editable text containing text that needs to be put into paragraphs (ideally a sci-fi piece of dialogue)

3: Drafting science-fiction stories

Introduction

● Choose three or four science-fiction books with a variety of good openings and read them aloud to the class.
● Ask for comments, such as *varied, interesting, grabs your attention, mysterious, good vocabulary choices*.

Whole-class work

● Explain to the children that they will use their plans to write first drafts of their science-fiction stories. Also, point out that their thinking time might have made them change some things about their first ideas, which is fine.
● Make them aware that they will be given a chance to edit their drafts before writing a final draft, so their best handwriting is not vital at this stage, though it still needs to be legible.
● Remind them to paragraph their work and include fronted adverbials with commas, and direct speech, and to be aware of how they use pronouns, conjunctions and prepositions.

Independent work

● Provide time for children to work independently, checking their plans, adjusting them if they wish and using them to write a first draft.

Review

● To further reinforce paragraphing, show the class a text you have previously typed up with the paragraphing removed. Work together to talk through the text, deciding where the paragraphs should go.

Curriculum objectives
● To assess the effectiveness of their own and others' writing and suggest improvements.
● To propose changes to grammar and vocabulary to improve consistency.
● To proofread for spelling and punctuation errors.

Resources
Prepare text to display and edit of the following: *The Engineer went into his laboratory. It was on Z27. I wonder what he's up to? said Sotor. Who knows? said Anja. It was almost midnight when The Engineer finally came out.*; children's drafts of their science-fiction stories; photocopiable page 77 'Editing checklist'

Curriculum objectives
● In narratives, to create settings, characters and plot.
● To use the diagonal and horizontal strokes that are needed to join letters and understand which letters, when adjacent to one another, are best left unjoined.
● To increase the legibility, consistency and quality of their handwriting.

Resources
Children's edited drafts of their science-fiction stories

4: Editing stories

Introduction

● Read the prepared text aloud to the class. Tell them that this is your first draft and you aren't happy with it, so it needs editing to improve it and you are asking for their help.

Whole-class work

● Ask the children for their suggestions of how to edit the text, such as using connectives, adding inverted commas, changing the final sentence to have a fronted adverbial, choosing more interesting vocabulary or extending some sentences to provide more information.
● Hand out photocopiable page 77 'Editing checklist' and explain its use.

Independent work

● Using the checklist on the photocopiable sheet, encourage the children to read through their drafts and edit them as necessary.

Review

● Ask the children to work in pairs and share their edited drafts. Using the checklists to guide them, invite the children to comment, discuss and make any further changes to improve their writing.

5: The final version

Introduction

● On the interactive whiteboard, quickly write the edited opening sentence to the paragraph you worked on previously with the class. Use poor handwriting.
● Discuss the advice the children would give you if this was your final written version. Agree that your handwriting needs improvement.
● Rewrite the sentence in good handwriting.

Whole-class work

● In today's lesson they will be writing their edited stories. Explain that because they have done all their thinking, planning, checking and editing, they can now concentrate on using their best handwriting.
● Remind them that good joined handwriting should be even in size and spacing, have letters joined with clear, parallel strokes and no ascenders crossing over descenders. Ask them to practise together with a few words.
● Tell them that their stories will be displayed for others to read, so their handwriting is important.
● Explain that as they write, occasional improvements may occur to them. Reassure them that it is fine if they do wish to make any final changes to improve their story even more.

Independent work

● Ask the children to work quietly, writing the final versions of their stories.

> **Differentiation**
> ● If rewriting is particularly difficult for some of the children, then allow them to concentrate on writing just one or two paragraphs.

Review

● Ask the children to reflect on the drafting, editing and redrafting process. Do they think their stories would have been as good without it? Ask the class for examples of improvements that were made.

Week 5 lesson plans

The children are familiar with newspaper reports, but this week they will look at the key features in greater detail than previously. Using the real-life Roswell incident as a basis, they will work in groups to plan a scenario of aliens landing in the locality which they, as reporters, must write about. They will act out interviews between a reporter and key witnesses which they will use as the basis for drafting the first paragraphs of their reports, comparing their various versions. They will then go on to redraft and complete their final full reports, which they will share and evaluate.

1: Analysing newspaper reports

Introduction
- Display the newspaper report on photocopiable page 78 'School's treasure trove!'.
- Ask the children if they know what type of writing this is (a newspaper report) and read it aloud to the class. Ask for their reactions to the story. How would they feel if this had happened at their school? What might their comments to the reporter have been?

Independent work
- Hand out the photocopiable sheet, telling the class that they will be writing a newspaper report later in the week. Although they have written newspaper reports before, today they will be looking in greater depth in order to write even better ones. They will be focusing particularly on how such reports are organised.
- Allow time for the children to read the story themselves and to think about the structure.

Whole-class work
- Ask the class the following questions: *What does the opening statement do? What job do the subheadings do? How is the content of each paragraph organised? How are the paragraphs divided up according to their content? How well do the subheadings match them? What do the quotes add to the story? What sort of people are quoted and how were they involved in the story? What information is given about them?* Discuss their responses to these questions.

Paired work
- Give pairs copies of other suitable stories you have sourced from local or national newspapers. Ensure they include at least paragraphs and quotes.
- Allow time for the children to analyse their news cuttings, highlighting the points you have discussed with them, and any others they may notice. For instance, some may contain photographs with captions.

> **Differentiation**
> - Select newspaper reports suitable for the range of reading abilities in your class.

Review
- Invite some of the children to feed back their findings to the class. Ask for examples of any of the features you discussed earlier, including hearing some of the opening statements or paragraphs. Did all the articles include subheadings? If they did, were they effective?
- Summarise by asking the children to contribute their suggestions for a list of key features that they would expect to find in a well-written newspaper report. Scribe this on the board for the children to copy for reference later in the week.
- By the end of the lesson, the children will have discussed key features of a newspaper report, analysed a second report according to those key features and drawn up a list of them for future reference.

Expected outcomes
- All children can analyse key features of a newspaper report and use these to write one of their own.
- Most children can include direct speech, appropriate subheadings for paragraphs and pronouns for cohesion and clarity.
- Some children can use a wider range of vocabulary and extend their ideas beyond the basic story.

Curriculum objectives
- To discuss writing similar to that which they are planning to write in order to understand and learn from its structure, grammar and vocabulary.

Resources
Photocopiable page 78 'School's treasure trove!'; news stories cut from local newspapers, one per pair of children; highlighter pens or coloured pencils

Curriculum objectives
● To compose and rehearse sentences orally (including dialogue), progressively building a varied and rich vocabulary and an increasing range of sentence structures (see Appendix 2).
● To discuss and record ideas.

Resources
Images of the alleged aliens from the Roswell incident; copies of newspaper reports of the above incident (available online)

2: Aliens have landed

Introduction
● Show the children the images of the Roswell incident aliens that you have sourced from the internet. Ask: *If you saw them, what would you think?*
● Explain that this really happened in 1947, showing them an image of a news report of the incident, but point out some people still don't believe it.

Group work
● Explain to the children that they need to imagine they are reporters for the local paper when news comes through that aliens have landed and it is now their job to cover the story.
● Arrange the class into groups of three or four and ask them to work together to create the story, by sharing and discussing ideas. They should think of what happened, where and when. They need to make notes as reminders and for reference.
● Assign roles to group members, so one is the reporter, one or two are witnesses and another is an expert. In role, the children should act out a question-and-answer scenario, with the reporter asking the questions.

Differentiation
● Assign the role of reporter to a more experienced speaker, who is able to formulate more open-ended questions, requiring the responses to have more explanation.

Review
● Choose some of the groups to share their role plays with the class. Check that the children have clearly considered their responses to the scenario of aliens landing and used these to discuss and formulate a storyline, which they have acted in their groups as a role play.

Curriculum objectives
● To organise paragraphs around a theme.
● To use and punctuate direct speech.
● To choose nouns or pronouns appropriately for clarity and cohesion and to avoid repetition.

Resources
Children's notes (from lesson 2); opening paragraphs from two or three news stories of your choice

3: Drafting the opening paragraph

Introduction
● Read to the class two or three opening paragraphs from news stories you have chosen, in order to remind them of the previous lesson.

Whole-class work
● Refer to the previous lesson, asking the children to recall and summarise the stories they created in their groups, including the gist of who said what in the reporter interviews.
● Today they will plan and share their opening paragraphs. Explain that they must think of an attention-grabbing title, and write a few examples on the board. Remind them of what is included in an opening statement and that they should include some direct speech, remembering what this adds to the story – directness, authenticity and credibility, which makes readers more likely to believe it. Ask them to list the 5 Ws – *when, where, why, what* (and maybe add *how*). Then write them on the board for reference.

Independent work
● Provide time for children to plan and draft their opening paragraphs.

Review
● Arrange the children into the groups they initially worked in when they created their story idea (in lesson 2). Invite each child to read the first draft of their paragraph to their group, to compare versions of the same story and discuss the differences. Afterwards, ask what differences they found. Did people start the story in different ways? Did they choose different speeches to quote? Did they still tell the beginnings of the same basic story?

Curriculum objectives
● To organise paragraphs around a theme.
● To use and punctuate direct speech.
● To choose nouns or pronouns appropriately for clarity and cohesion and to avoid repetition.
● To assess the effectiveness of their own and others' writing and suggest improvements.
● To propose changes to grammar and vocabulary to improve consistency.
● To proofread for spelling and punctuation errors.
● To extend the range of sentences with more than one clause by using a wider range of conjunctions.

Resources
The children's draft opening paragraphs (from lesson 3)

4: Paragraph deadline!

Introduction

● Act in role as the editor of the newspaper that the children write for. Remind your reporters that this is an important story. They must do a good job, by getting the facts and thinking of their readers.

● Say to them: *You all know what I expect, but let's just be sure and have a little reminder. What do I need to have in your reports?* Encourage the children to recap the points covered earlier in the week, then say: *OK, I need to have your opening paragraphs by the editorial deadline. So get your notes and get writing!* Set a time to allow for review at the end of the lesson.

Independent work

● Allow the children time to write the final drafts of their opening paragraphs, before asking them to assess the effectiveness of others' writing.

Review

● As they near the end of their writing time, circulate round the class, and in your editorial role ask some of the reporters to let you read the first sentences of their opening paragraphs. This will allow you to begin some assessment. When your appointed deadline arrives, select a few of the children to read out their openings to the class. Invite comments, particularly from others in the same group as the readers, who may have chosen to tell the story differently.

Curriculum objectives
● To organise paragraphs around a theme.
● To use and punctuate direct speech.
● To choose nouns or pronouns appropriately for clarity and cohesion and to avoid repetition.
● To use the diagonal and horizontal strokes that are needed to join letters and understand which letters, when adjacent to one another, are best left unjoined.
● To increase the legibility, consistency and quality of their handwriting.

Resources
The children's draft opening paragraphs

5: Publication day – completing the report

Introduction

● In editorial role again, say to your reporters: *OK, your opening paragraphs were good. You can go ahead and finish your reports. Remember to keep up the good work. I'm enjoying your great language – those direct quotes and accurate use of pronouns really lift your pieces. Your deadline is...? Any final questions?*

● Allow for children's queries, before saying: *OK, off you go.*

● Again, choose an appropriate time, allowing time for review at the end of the lesson.

Independent work

● Provide time for the children to quietly complete the writing of their news stories.

> **Differentiation**
> ● Children with good keyboard skills can be encouraged to work on the computer to make their work look more like a newspaper story.

Review

● Out of role, explain to the children that they are now to become the editors. Pair them up to swap stories, each reading the other's report with an editorial eye. Tell them their main focus is on the clarity and interest in the story, not the technical aspects. Ask them to offer each other positive critical feedback, suggesting one or two improvements if appropriate.

● Finally, have a brief class discussion about the children's own future critical reading of newspaper reports. How will they judge news stories with their new knowledge and skills?

Expected outcomes
● All children can talk about different poetic forms, choose appropriate words for and write their own calligram.
● Most children can write more than one calligram, also using alliteration and at least one simile.
● Some children can use a wider range of adjectives and more than one simile.

Curriculum objectives
● To recognise some different forms of poetry.
● To identify how language, structure, and presentation contribute to meaning.
● To discuss writing similar to that which they are planning to write in order to understand and learn from its structure, grammar and vocabulary.

Resources
Photocopiable page 79 'Space poems'; dictionaries

Week 6 lesson plans

The science-fiction half term concludes with a week's work on poetry. The children will read and compare three calligrams about space, written in different poetic forms, identifying the differences between how they are composed. They will choose their own subject and poetic form to draft, discuss, edit and write their own space poem, which they will produce as a calligram. In order to help select the best vocabulary for their poems, they will look at and learn to spell words ending with the suffix '-ous', and work on similes, seeing how they can capture the reader's interest and imagination.

1: Let's look at some poems

Introduction
● Draw a few shapes on the board such as a star, rocket, moon, robot.
● Explain to the children they are waiting to have poems written in them to make them into shape poems. Introduce the name *calligram*.

Whole-class work
● Explain to the children that they need to think about the science-fiction knowledge they have to gather ideas for some calligrams. The shapes let us know what the poem is about – its subject – but it is the poems themselves that are important. Once they have their subject, it is the poem that they begin with, not the shape.
● Hand out photocopiable page 79 'Space poems' and give the class time to read the poems quietly before reading them aloud yourself.
● Ask what differences they notice about the three types of poem. They should identify a haiku, a rhyming poem and one in free verse. Do they have a favourite, and why? Can they think of any other types of poem? They may recall the ballads from the Robin Hood unit, or suggest rhyming couplets, limericks or list poems.
● Explain that later the children will be writing science-fiction calligrams and today they will choose their subjects. What suggestions can they make? List the children's ideas on the board.
● Invite them to select two or three subjects for their poems.

Independent work
● Encourage the children to begin to list possible vocabulary for each of their subjects.
● Explain that they should think of adjectives, adverbs and adverbial phrases for description, a range of possible nouns and powerful verbs that might fit. They should use a dictionary to check any spellings they are unsure of. If they are thinking of writing a rhyming poem, they should also list possible rhyming words.

Paired work
● Allow the children time to share their first ideas with a partner, comparing their subjects and potential vocabulary.

Differentiation
● Rhyming poems are more difficult for children to compose as they limit their word choices and the rhythms can be hard to maintain. While they don't have to choose their poetic forms at this stage, you may wish to point this out either as a challenge or a gentle warning.

Review
● Invite some of the children to read out a selection of the words they have chosen, for the class to guess what subject they might refer to. Explain to the class that they will have some thinking time to carry on gathering their ideas and other words or phrases, which they should make a note of to add to their lists.

Curriculum objectives
● To use further prefixes and suffixes and understand how to add them (Appendix 1).

Resources
Individual whiteboards and pens; dictionaries

2: The suffix '-ous'

Introduction

● Write on the board the following words: *poison, danger, courage, mountain*.
● Ask the children which of the suffixes ('-tion', '-ate', '-ous', '-sion') can be added to all the words listed.
● When they have chosen '-ous', ask what the suffix means ('full of' as in *courageous* means *full of courage*).
● Explain that with these words, the suffix is just added to the root, but it isn't always that simple.

Paired work

● On the board, write: *humorous, serious, glorious, hideous, glamorous, spontaneous, famous, tremendous, curious, various*.
● Then challenge the children to work in pairs and group the words according to a pattern or rule they can discover, writing the words on their whiteboards.
● Invite them to try and think of other words that could fit into their groups, using a dictionary to check the spellings.
● Partners should test each other, taking turns to write a given word on the reverse of their whiteboards. Allow them to check their own spellings.

Review

● Ask the class what type of words these are (adjectives) and suggest they could use some in their poems. Give them several phrases with a science-fiction theme to write on paper for you to check later, including a selection of the target words, for example *a courageous astronaut, a hideous alien, a tremendous journey, a dangerous mission, a famous engineer*.

Curriculum objectives
● To discuss words and phrases that capture the reader's interest and imagination.

3: Science-fiction similes

Introduction

● Challenge the class to complete several well-known similes. For example: *As cold as...* (*ice*); *as quiet as...* (*a mouse*); *as warm as...* (*toast*); *as dry as...* (*a bone*); *as thin as...* (*a rake*).

Whole-class work

● Explain that similes such as these are often used in poetry to add interest and excite the imagination. Challenge the children to devise more original examples, inviting suggestions for: *a rocket as fast as...; a star as twinkly as...; a computer as clever as...*.
● Ask for examples of similes that use the word *like*, for example: *It glows like a huge white light bulb in the sky*, which could describe the moon.
● When several ideas have been shared, ask the children to think of some similes they could use in their poems.

Independent work

● Allow time for the children to gather ideas for similes they could use in their calligrams, noting them on paper, using different elements of the subjects they have already chosen.

Review

● Bring the class together and invite some of the children to read out a simile for the rest of the class to suggest what it might be referring to. For example, *It is something that is as white hot as a furnace* could refer to a meteorite or the sun, or *Its three green eyes shone like emeralds* might refer to an alien.

Curriculum objectives
• To compose and rehearse sentences orally (including dialogue), progressively building a varied and rich vocabulary and an increasing range of sentence structures (See Appendix 2).
• To assess the effectiveness of their own and others' writing and suggest improvements.

Resources
Children's work from earlier in the week; individual whiteboards

4: Drafting science-fiction calligrams

Independent work
• Allow the children time to draft at least two poems, each of a different type, using the work from earlier in the week.

Paired work
• Inform the class that they are now ready to think about how their poems will fit into appropriate shapes for their calligrams. They should begin to experiment, considering how line length will fit into different versions of possible shapes.
• Arrange the children into pairs and encourage them to share their first drafts, offering each other comments and advice, while also trying out ideas for shapes on their whiteboards.

Review
• Ask the children what types of poem they have decided upon. How easy or tricky was it to choose the right shapes? Did they have any problems to overcome and how did they do it?

Curriculum objectives
• To assess the effectiveness of their own and others' writing and suggest improvements.
• To increase the legibility, consistency and quality of their handwriting.

Resources
Children's drafts (created in lesson 4); coloured pens or pencils; examples of calligrams

5: Creating calligrams

Introduction
• Show the children several examples of calligrams, giving an overall impression, rather than a close look at the poetry. Invite comments from the class.
• Remind them that today they should enjoy creating their own calligrams for display. They need to use their best handwriting as well as considering use of colour. They should also consider the size of their finished pieces, as they will be displayed for others to read.

Independent work
• Before beginning their final versions, encourage the children to revisit their drafts, considering the comments from their partner in the previous lesson, and making any final changes they feel would improve their poems.
• Provide time for the children to have fun creating their calligrams, using colour for the shape outline and perhaps extra illustration outside the shape, to enhance their work.

Differentiation
• Allow some of the children to concentrate on creating just one calligram, while others can be encouraged to produce more than one.

Review
• Select several of the children to share their completed calligrams with the class, reading them out as well as showing the shapes themselves. The finished work should be used to create a wall display in the classroom.

Curriculum objectives
● To indicate possession by using the possessive apostrophe with plural nouns.
● To use fronted adverbials.
● To use commas after fronted adverbials.
● To use and understand the grammatical terminology in Appendix 2 accurately and appropriately when discussing their writing and reading.
● To place the possessive apostrophe accurately in words with regular plurals and in words with irregular plurals.

Resources
Individual whiteboards

Grammar and punctuation: Possessive apostrophe and fronted adverbials

Revise
● Use starter activities 6 'One or more?' and 7 'Fronted adverbials'.
● Remind the children of the mnemonic: *Before the s it's singular, after the s there's many more.* Can they remember the few exceptions to this?
● Read out sentences with and without fronted adverbials, asking the children to identify when one is used.

Assess
● Encourage the children to compose a paragraph with a science-fiction theme, such as observing events in an inventor's laboratory or reporting on a spacecraft landing on a distant planet.
● Explain that they must demonstrate their understanding of both possessive apostrophes and fronted adverbials by including at least two examples of each, underlining where they have been used.
● Allow the children time to think and plan their paragraphs before they start to write.

Further practice
● Invite the children to write a word with a possessive apostrophe on the board for the class to say whether it is singular or plural.
● Challenge the children to see how many examples of sentences using fronted adverbials they can find in books.

Curriculum objectives
● To use further prefixes and suffixes and understand how to add them (Appendix 1).
● To use the first two or three letters of a word to check its spelling in a dictionary.

Resources
Dictionaries; individual whiteboards and pens

Spelling: Prefixes, suffixes and dictionary work

Revise
● Use starter activities 2 'Guess the word', 4 'Suffix challenge', 9 'Spellchecker' and 15 'Prefix game'.
● Recap the meaning of the prefixes 'il-', 'in-', 'im-', and 'ir-'; make sure they know that they indicate *not*.
● Recap the meaning of words with the suffix 'ous'; make sure they know that they indicate being *full of*.

Assess
● Ask the children to write words from those they have learned by giving them the meaning and not the actual word. For example, say to them *Write the word that means not legal*, or *Write the word that means full of glory*.
● Encourage the children to look up the following words in a dictionary: *inattentive, illustrated, important, immeasurable, irrational, irritating.* Ask them to copy the words from the board, find their meanings in a dictionary and write whether the words use a prefix or not.

Further practice
● Invite the children to collect further examples of words with these prefixes and suffixes to make their own useful word list that can be used in their writing. They need to include the meanings of the words.
● As an additional fun activity, perhaps as a home-learning task, challenge the children to create a sentence with as many of the target words in as possible.

Curriculum objectives
● To understand what they read by checking that the text makes sense to them, discussing their understanding and explaining the meaning of words in context.
● To ask questions to improve their understanding of a text.

Resources
Photocopiable page 'City of the future' from the CD-ROM; photocopiable page 'The Engineer' from the CD-ROM

Reading: Science fiction

Revise

● Ask the children to recall the key elements in a science-fiction story, including generic settings, characters and plots.

● Hand out photocopiable page 'City of the Future' from the CD-ROM. Ask the children to read through the extract and pick out elements that indicate that this is a science-fiction story. Discuss these as a class.

● Work with the class to devise comprehension questions that might be asked about the extract, scribing them on the board. They should cover as many aspects of the story as possible. For example, can they suggest questions about setting, characters and plot? Can they devise questions that are not directly answered in the text, but are inferred? An example might be *Does Rennia Botblast have any enemies?* and the answer might be she has because she has installed security systems and some of her robots have gone missing. Also, the other characters talk about robot raiders.

● Encourage them to include questions about grammar, punctuation and sentence structure.

● Talk to the class about answering the comprehension questions in full sentences. For example, if the question was *What is special about Mekta city?*, it would not be fully correct for them just to write *It would be computer-controlled*. Discuss and decide together on what you will accept as a full answer, written as a complete sentence, such as *Mekta City was special because...*, and give your reasons.

Assess

● Ask the children to devise their own comprehension questions and provide their own answers, using the photocopiable page 'The Engineer' from the CD-ROM.

● Hand out the photocopiable sheets and explain that they will devise a series of questions to cover setting, characters and plot. Remind them to also include at least one question that involves grammar, vocabulary, punctuation or sentence structure. They should write their questions, remembering to use question marks, and follow each question with their answers, written in complete sentences.

Further practice

● Follow up the assessment session by asking the children your own comprehension questions for them to answer orally or in writing. This would allow you to assess the understanding of those children who found difficulty in framing their own questions, but who have nevertheless understood the text.

● As the children become more proficient in devising their own comprehension questions, invite them to choose books from the classroom shelves that they have enjoyed reading, and to create questions for other children. Answers can be stored elsewhere for the readers to check.

Writing: Science fiction

Revise

● Provide groups of children with a selection of science-fiction books. Ask them to read the blurbs on the back covers of the books and talk about them in their groups. As pointers for their discussion, write these questions on the board for them to refer to as they work:
  ● *What kind of language is used?*
  ● *Is it obvious that they are science-fiction stories? How is that achieved?*
  ● *What do you notice about the lengths of the sentences?*
  ● *What punctuation is there?*
  ● *How does the writer try to persuade you to read the book?*
  ● *Is there any mention of settings, characters or plot?*
  ● *What tense or tenses are used?*
  ● *How much of the story is given away?*
  ● *Are there any comments from reviews?*
● Draw the class together and ask for their observations. Did every group find the same things? If not, what differences were there? How successful do the children think the blurbs were in persuading them to want to read the book? What made the most successful blurbs work?

Assess

● Ask the children to complete the story of 'The Engineer' and then write their own blurb for it. Two lessons will be needed for this, more if you wish the children to draft, edit and redraft their work. Explain that as this is just the beginning of the story, they will need to flesh out the outline of the whole story before writing. Encourage them to do this by talking and planning orally with a partner.
● Explain to the children that they should concentrate on planning the main events of the plot, creating one or two other main characters and deciding how the story will end. They should also decide whether the whole story will take place on the spaceship or if they will land somewhere and so create another setting. Explain that there are clues in the extract that they can follow and develop, and they must keep true to what we already know of the character of the Engineer. However, they must decide is he good or evil. Is he working alone or with others?
● Allow the children time to talk, plan and make notes for their continuation of the story. They may decide to use the same story idea as their partner or have a different one – either way is fine, as they will be writing independently, so it is inevitable that their finished versions will differ.
● Before they start writing, remind the children that they need to include some dialogue in their story, which must be correctly punctuated. They should also aim to include fronted adverbials, and use pronouns for clarity and cohesion.
● When the stories are finished, invite the children to create their blurbs. Give them access to the original questions that they used when they were discussing book blurbs earlier, as these can act as a guide for their own writing.

Further practice

● Many of the children are likely to be curious about how others have completed the story, so organise a story-swap session, where the children can read each others' work. Follow this up with a class discussion on the different ideas the children came up with.
● Read out some of the blurbs to the class and ask for comments on them. Use the questions from the Revise session as a checklist and guide. How effective were the blurbs? Would they suggest any changes?
● When choosing books to read in the future, encourage the children to read the blurbs to help them decide if they think they will enjoy the book.

Hooray for the apostrophe!

■ Under each example below, write either 's' (for singular) or 'p' (for plural) according to what the apostrophe is telling you.

boy's	boys'	girls'	girl's	dads'	dad's
____	____	____	____	____	____

car's	cars'	cloud's	clouds'	mugs'	mug's
____	____	____	____	____	____

■ Rewrite each word and put the possessive apostrophes in the right place.

Singular	Plural
boats	boats
socks	socks
tables	tables
computers	computers

■ After each sentence, write 'singular' or 'plural'.

The dog was in the goats' field. _____

The chair's legs were broken. _____

The audience enjoyed the dancers' performance. _____

■ Now put the apostrophe in the right place in the sentences below.

The teachers books were on the desk. (singular)

The boys surprise was wonderful. (plural)

The kittens milk was warm. (plural)

Lots of ladies entered the mums race. (plural)

I can recognise and use possessive apostrophes for singular and plural nouns.

How did you do?

PHOTOCOPIABLE   **SCHOLASTIC**
www.scholastic.co.uk

Not that!

■ The prefixes 'in-', 'il-', 'ir-', 'im-' all mean 'not'. For example, 'imperfect' means 'not perfect'. Below are some words for you to investigate. Write the rule for the words and use a dictionary to write their definitions.

Word	Definition
inactive	
incorrect	
incapable	
Rule for above words	
illegal	
illegible	
Rule for above words	
immature	
immortal	
Rule for above words	
irregular	
irrelevant	
Rule for above words	

I can use a rule to help me spell words and I can find their meanings in a dictionary.

How did you do?

Fronted adverbials puzzle

■ Cut out the boxes below then rearrange them to make sensible sentences with fronted adverbials. When you are sure they are all correct, paste them onto another sheet of paper. (The capital letters and full stops are missing to give you a bigger puzzle to solve!)

■ After you have pasted the sentences, write them in your book, correctly punctuated, remembering to use a comma after the fronted adverbial.

✂-----------------

when our friends arrived
for three years
it was late at night
by practising every day
we built our den
every Saturday
Mrs Smith made her chocolate cake
the pirates sailed the seas
before Sami finished work
the aliens came to earth
the puppy jumped on to the sofa
in the garden
we ate our meal
the boy learned to swim
every time her owners weren't looking
because they wanted to make new friends

My science-fiction characters

- Create three science-fiction characters by drawing what they look like and completing the following details about them.

Name	Name	Name
_____	_____	_____

Physical description	Physical description	Physical description
_____ _____	_____ _____	_____ _____
Characteristics	Characteristics	Characteristics
_____ _____	_____ _____	_____ _____
Role	Role	Role
_____ _____	_____ _____	_____ _____
They might say...	They might say...	They might say...
_____ _____	_____ _____	_____ _____

I can create my own science-fiction characters to use in a story.

How did you do?

My science-fiction story

■ Complete the sections below.

Title: _____

Where is it set? _____

The main characters are

_____   _____   _____

My new object is _____

How will my characters fit into my setting?

_____

_____

How will my object fit into the story?

_____

_____

How will the setting affect the story?

_____

_____

How will my story start?

_____

_____

What will be the main events?

_____

_____

How will my story end?

_____

_____

I can plan my science-fiction story, using the ideas I already have.

How did you do?

Editing checklist

■ Use this list to help you check that you have included all of the important things that your story needs.

In my story, I have included:

☐ fronted adverbials with commas after them

☐ a range of connectives

☐ pronouns to make my meaning clear

☐ full stops

☐ capital letters

☐ direct speech, correctly punctuated

☐ prepositions of time and cause

My story:

☐ makes sense

☐ uses my main characters

☐ has a good opening paragraph to grab the reader's attention

☐ is written in paragraphs

☐ uses interesting and varied vocabulary

☐ has a description of my setting

☐ has enough information for the reader

☐ is good to read, with an interesting plot

☐ has a beginning, a middle (where most of the story takes place) and an ending

I can use a checklist to make sure I have included all of the key elements my story needs.

How did you do?

School's treasure trove!

School's treasure trove!

Staff and pupils at Jubilee Primary School, in Little Walton, were amazed earlier this week to learn that a Roman coin hoard worth thousands of pounds was unearthed. The coins were found during excavations for a new extension that is being added to their school building.

What's it worth?

Of the many questions they have about the fantastic find, probably the main one is "How much is it worth?" Head teacher Mr Parkinson said, "Even though we knew Romans had lived in this area, it was still a total surprise. We don't yet know the value of the hoard, or if we will receive any money."

Finds such as these do not automatically belong to the finder or the person on whose land they are found. The hoard is what is known as 'treasure trove' and has been reported to the police. Early reports suggest the value may be as high as £100,000, but that might be shared between the Crown, the school and the finder.

Digger driver's discovery

Jimmy Craig, 32, the digger driver who unearthed the hoard said, "I don't know if I'll get any reward or not. After all, I was just doing my job." When asked how he discovered the coins, Mr Craig told us "They were in a big old pot that my bucket scraped against. The pot broke and I could see round things inside, but I didn't know at first that they were coins. They were covered in dirt."

Project Romans!

The discovery has sparked off a big interest in the Romans and their time spent in the area. Children from Years 1 to 6 are all finding out more about these ancient invaders. "I think the Romans were very interesting," said Rachel, aged 7. If some of the reward money comes their way, she and her schoolmates may have a lot to thank those Romans for. Mr Parkinson told us "We could afford an even bigger extension if we get a portion of the reward, and I'm sure there will be lots of ideas for how to spend any money that might be left over."

Space poems

The red rocket

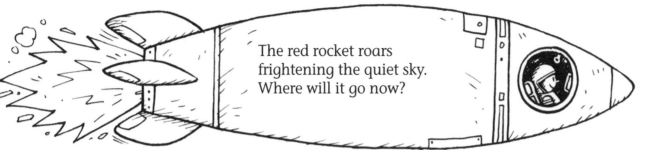

The red rocket roars
frightening the quiet sky.
Where will it go now?

A thing like a nose

An alien came,
he told us his name
but we didn't understand.
He had heads made of cheese,
and dozens of knees,
that he scratched with his hundreds of hands.
We offered him food,
and we thought it was rude
when he squashed it quite flat with his feet.
Then out from his toes,
came a thing like a nose,
which swallowed it whole and complete.
What a treat!

Faster than the speed of light

If I could,
I'd go faster than the speed
of light.
Quicker than time,
from some place in space,
on and on,
in the dark,
leaving all light behind.
Until I remembered Mum had packed
my torch.

Dragons

The rich theme of dragons is explored in several contexts in this half term. The children will discover myths and legends about dragons, those that play a role in Chinese culture and Viking dragon boats. They will look at dragon-themed poetry and enjoy the full-length story *How to Train Your Dragon*. They will study vocabulary and language structure to write information and explanation texts, a diary entry in role, a playscript and free-verse poem. They will develop their understanding of conjunctions, possessive apostrophes and homophones. Through discussion and paired work the children will further develop drafting, editing and performance skills.

Expected prior learning
- Can recall the features of a myth and are familiar with some myths.
- Can combine clauses using connectives and can suggest a number of connectives.
- Can use headings to structure text and paragraphs.
- Can understand that characters can be created through what they do and what they say and can provide examples from previous reading.
- Can understand playscript conventions.
- Can punctuate direct speech.
- Can punctuate with apostrophes correctly.
- Can discuss what makes a poem and talk about favourite poems.

Overview of progression
- By close reading and discussion, the children will gain greater insight into characterisation and drawing inference from the ways in which characters interact and through what they say.
- They will be introduced to the notion of creative non-fiction, where elements of fiction can engage the reader with factual information.
- The grammatical knowledge they have gained will be put to further use, with expectations that they can confidently use pronouns, prepositions and fronted adverbials in their writing.

Creative context
- The dragon theme lends itself to artistic interpretation in many ways, particularly when studying the Chinese New Year celebrations which can lead to a full themed day of activities incorporating music, dance and food.
- The Viking theme would fit into historical work on invaders and settlers.
- Dragon stories from Poland, China and Bohemia are included and can link to stories from other cultures in a wider context.

Preparation
A key text in the unit is Cressida Cowell's *How to Train Your Dragon* (Hodder), which you should read beforehand. It would be beneficial to have multiple copies of the book, although the unit can be delivered without it. Audio and film versions are also available and would be useful, though not essential, additions.

You will also need:
Images of dragons; large sheets of paper; felt-tipped pens; individual whiteboards and pens; books and online sources for finding out about the Chinese New Year; highlighter pens; sticky notes; dictionaries; copy of 'Not My Best Side' by UA Fanthorpe; images of the painting 'St George and the Dragon' by Paolo Uccello; selection of poetry books; internet access

On the CD-ROM you will find:
Media resources 'Chinese dragon', 'Chinese dragon dance', 'Viking dragon ship', 'Smaug by Carol Emery Phenix'; interactive activities 'Hiccup', 'Start with the connective'; photocopiable pages 'How the Dragon came to be', 'The Dragon of Krakow', 'St George and the Dragon', 'Horrendous descriptions'

Chapter at a glance

An overview of the chapter. For curriculum objective codes, please see pages 8–10.

Week	Lesson	Curriculum objectives	Summary of activities	Outcomes
1	1	RC: 5	Think and talk about what they already know about dragons. Complete the 'Dragonfile' sheet as a basis for think, pair and share.	• Can share with the class knowledge and ideas about dragons for comparison and discussion.
	2	RC: 4 WC: 2	Listen to 'How the Dragon came to be'. Identify it as a myth and list mythical characters. Use 'Dragon words' sheet to start gathering vocabulary for later writing.	• Can recall features of myths, mythical beasts listed and words and information written for later reference.
	3	RC: 4, 13	One half of class read 'The Dragon of Krakow' the other 'St George and the Dragon'. Groups share observations. New words added to 'Dragon words' sheets.	• Can identify stories as legends with similar key elements in the plots.
	4	WC: 2	Use 'Dragon words' sheets to share with a group, selecting words, phrases and information with the rest of the class.	• Can select and share vocabulary and information about dragons.
	5	WC: 3, 4	Use the week's work to write a guide for authors on the characteristics of a dragon, using paragraphs.	• Can write information texts, incorporating vocabulary and ideas gathered in the week.
2	1	WC: 11	Identify verbs, connectives and clauses in sentences; list and classify connectives and use them to create their own sentences.	• Can create sentences with two or more clauses, using a wider variety of connectives and some fronted adverbials.
	2	RC: 10, 15	Look at images of Chinese dragon dances. Use books and the internet to research Chinese New Year.	• Can gather information about Chinese New Year celebrations and the part played by dragons.
	3	RC: 13	Work with a partner to create a list of possible activities for a Chinese New Year celebration party.	• Can list possible activities, including necessary resources to share with others.
	4	WC: 4, 6, 15, 17	Recap on explanation texts, suggest ideas for what could be explained in Chinese New Year celebrations. Write explanation text.	• Can write explanation texts in paragraphs with headings, to include compound sentences and a range of connectives.
	5	WC: 7, 8, 9, 16	Discuss things to be considered when editing writing, including technical aspects and vocabulary improvement. Edit their work.	• Can edit and amend explanation texts. • Can share changes made and good examples of language use.
3	1	RWR: 1 RC: 1, 7, 16	Discuss character descriptions from *How to Train Your Dragon*, match characters to settings. Select outstanding vocabulary to share with a partner.	• Can discuss characters including inferred characteristics and understand importance of how they fit into settings.
	2	RC: 12	Predict parts of the plot in Chapter 3, discuss how Hiccup's character is developing, give reasons for suggestions and opinions.	• Can demonstrate, by giving examples and reasons, that they can draw inferences from text.
	3	RC: 11 WC: 3	Using Chapters 5, 6 and 7, draw inferences about Hiccup's relationships with his father and grandfather.	• Can complete 'Family values' sheets, following paired discussion. Then use as basis for further consideration as a class.
	4	RC: 16	Groups discuss favourite parts of the plot so far, noting good examples of vocabulary for later use.	• Can recap the story so far and words and phrases are noted for future use. A top favourite event may be chosen.
	5	WC: 3, 7	Orally compose and write the opening of the story in role as Hiccup.	• Can write and share diary entries relating the start of the story from Hiccup's point of view.
4	1	RC: 1, 11, 12	Discuss the developing characters of Toothless and Hiccup. List changes in Hiccup's character since the start of the story.	• Can discuss and identify character development and consider its effect on the reader.
	2	WT: 2	Select the correct homophones in a playscript. Share results, checking in dictionaries if necessary.	• Can select the correct homophones and share ideas for recalling the correct homophones.
	3	WC: 1	Read a playscript and identify and discuss the conventions of a playscript.	• Can identify playscript conventions and understand their purposes.
	4	WC: 3, 7	Select a scene to write as a script. Discuss ideas, write first draft and read-through to identify possible amendments.	• Can draft scenes using playscript conventions, read through and change as necessary.
	5	WC: 7, 10	Final versions of playscripts written, rehearsed and performed.	• Can write playscripts for two or more characters, including stage directions. Then rehearse perform and evaluate it.

Chapter at a glance

Week	Lesson	Curriculum objectives	Summary of activities	Outcomes
5	1	WC: 3	View images of Viking dragon ships, gathering descriptive vocabulary. Enact role plays of Britons seeing the ships approaching. Kennings introduced and devised.	• Can create group role plays, rehearse and present, with self- and peer-assessment.
	2	WT: 4, 6 WC: 16, 18	Recap possessive apostrophe, complete sheet, write dictated sentences using both singular and plural possessive apostrophes.	• Can complete activity sheets showing possessive apostrophes for both singular and plural nouns.
	3	WC: 2, 4	Consider, plan, discuss and write a descriptive text to accompany a Viking ship exhibit in a museum.	• Can complete planning sheets and share with a partner, and use to write finished descriptive text.
	4	WC: 1, 2	Read 'Boudicca our queen' and highlight non-fiction elements in the text. Learn about creative non-fiction and analyse fictional language aspects.	• Can identify elements of fiction in a non-fiction text to develop an understanding of how the two can be woven together.
	5	WC: 3, 5	Discuss as a class and in pairs, text about the Viking raid on Lindisfarne, and write in role as a monk recalling the events.	• Can write in role reports about the Viking invasion on the monastery at Lindisfarne, as creative non-fiction.
6	1	RC: 6, 8	Read and discuss the character of the dragon in the poem 'Not My Best Side'. Prepare and perform the first verse.	• Can show through discussion and performance an understanding of the poem and the free-verse form.
	2	RC: 8	Use books and the internet to source poems about dragons.	• Can work in pairs to source, select and note their choice of dragon poems.
	3	RC: 8 WT: 7, 8	Decide on criteria for copying selected poems, write them in best handwriting and illustrate appropriately.	• Can copy and illustrate selected poems for compiling into a class anthology.
	4	WC: 1	Read description of Tolkien's Smaug, look at illustration and discuss use of language. Make notes on own dragon including potential vocabulary.	• Can conceive ideas for dragons, gather vocabulary and share in preparation for writing free-verse poem.
	5	WC: 3	Use notes to discuss, plan and write a free-verse dragon poem in the third person. Select best lines to share with the class.	• Can plan and write free-verse dragon poems, using varied and rich vocabulary.

Background knowledge

Chinese dragons: Are seen as helpful, friendly creatures associated with good luck, long life, wisdom and life-giving rain. They can fly, swim and walk. They have the horns of a stag, the scales of a fish and the footpads of a tiger.

Compound sentence: A sentence with more than one clause, the clauses joined by connectives.

Conjunctions: Link two words or phrases together.

Connectives: Is an informal name for words that connect the ideas expressed in different clauses; connectives may be prepositions, conjunctions or adverbs.

Creative non-fiction: It is a story based on real historical events. It introduces place, scene and setting, adds characterisation to involve the reader, employs a literary voice, allows the reader to hear the author's perspective and ideally does not invent dialogue, facts or events.

Homophones: Words which sound the same but have different meanings and spellings.

Kenning: A metaphor of Viking origin, used to describe things, usually consisting of a two-word phrase which is sometimes hyphenated.

Week 1 lesson plans

As they will have met some dragons already, the unit begins with the children completing a 'Dragonfile sheet', recording their current dragon knowledge. Over the week, they will read a dragon myth from China and read and compare two dragon legends, reinforcing their understanding of how myths and legends differ. They will look for similarities and differences in the two legends. They will create together a dragon word wall, gathering vocabulary for use in their writing over the unit. The week concludes with them using their new knowledge to write a short guide for authors on how to create dragons for their stories.

1: What do we know about dragons?

Introduction
● Show the class a variety of images of dragons on the interactive whiteboard, as a stimulus to thinking and discussion. Select a wide range of types from different illustrative techniques and include a photograph of a real-life Komodo dragon.
● Explain to the children that they will be using dragons as the theme for this half-term's work. They will start by thinking about what they already know about them.

Independent work
● Hand out photocopiable page 104 'Dragonfile' for the children to complete individually before discussion begins.
● The photocopiable sheet asks them a number of questions about what they know about dragons. Reassure the children that you are not expecting them to have extensive knowledge – this is a starting point from which they will build, and it is good to know what information they already have, and to compare with each other.

Paired work
● After they complete their photocopiable sheet, invite the children to find a partner to share and compare their results with. Do they have similar knowledge and if not, what differences are there? Encourage the children to discuss their work, asking each other questions for extra information or further clarification.

Group work
● Now ask the pairs to form into small groups to further compare their answers about dragons. Do they notice any common features that all or most of them have recorded? Does anyone have a piece of knowledge that no-one else has recorded? Are they building up a picture of dragons that most people would recognise?

Review
● Bring the class together and ask a representative from each group to summarise their group's results. When all the groups have reported back, pick up on both common and unusual points as the basis for a class discussion. Are there any particular named dragons or dragon stories that come to the fore? Do most people agree on the characteristics of dragons, and if so, what are they? Does anyone mention friendly dragons? Where does their knowledge of dragons come from – is it books, TV, film or elsewhere? Tell the children to bear this introductory thinking in mind as they go through the week, to see how their knowledge and ideas match with what they will learn.

Curriculum objectives
● To increase their familiarity with a wide range of books, including fairy stories, myths and legends, and retell some of these orally.
● To discuss and record ideas.

Resources
Photocopiable page 'How the Dragon came to be' from the CD-ROM; photocopiable page 105 'Dragon words'

2: Mythical dragons

Introduction
● Read to the class the story on photocopiable page 'How the Dragon came to be' from the CD-ROM.

Whole-class work
● Ask what type of story it is – what other stories does it remind them of? (They should recall myths from Year 3.)
● Invite them to explain what types of character they would expect to find in myths. They may suggest heroes, gods, giants, monsters, centaurs and so on. This story is a myth about a dragon. Do they know any other mythical creatures? For example, *mermaids*, *unicorns*, *cyclops* or *the phoenix*.
● Remind them that myths are often used to try and explain how things are, such as creation myths. Does the story therefore suggest that dragons are real? What do they think?
● Read the story again, asking for comments on how this dragon fits into what they already know from their work in the previous lesson.

Independent work
● Hand out photocopiable page 105 'Dragon words'. Ask the children to begin to build their own dragon word wall by writing words and phrases on the scales. They can add to it as the half term progresses.

Review
● Select some of the children to share a few of their dragon words with the class. Encourage the rest of the class to comment on these.

Curriculum objectives
● To identify main ideas drawn from more than one paragraph and summarise these.
● To increase their familiarity with a wide range of books, including fairy stories, myths and legends, and retell some of these orally.

Resources
Photocopiable page 'The Dragon of Krakow' from the CD-ROM; photocopiable page 'St George and the Dragon' from the CD-ROM; photocopiable page 104 'Dragonfile'; photocopiable page 105 'Dragon words' (previously started)

3: Legendary dragons

Introduction
● Divide the class randomly into two halves. Give one half of the class photocopiable page 'The Dragon of Krakow' from the CD-ROM and the other half photocopiable page 'St George and the Dragon' from the CD-ROM. Don't tell them they have different texts.
● Ask the children to read their stories quietly to themselves, making no comments to anyone else.

Paired work
● Arrange each half of the class into pairs. Ask them to work together to identify what type of story they have read and to summarise the main points.

Group work
● Now invite pairs from the separate halves of the class to join into small groups and share their observations about the stories.

Whole-class work
● Draw the class together and ask for their comments. Did they recognise the stories as legends? What features led them to this? They should recall the key features from their Robin Hood work.
● What similarities did they notice between the two stories? (There are several.) Did this surprise them? What differences were there? What other observations did they make?

Review
● Refer the class to their work on photocopiable pages 104 'Dragonfile' and 105 'Dragon words'. Ask them what new knowledge they now have about dragons. Allow time for them to add to their 'Dragon words' sheet.

Curriculum objectives
● To discuss and record ideas.

Resources
Children's copies of photocopiable page 105 'Dragon words'; large dragon outline on sheets of paper on the wall; paper cut in the shape of scales (approx 12 x 8cms); felt-tipped pens

4: Build-a-dragon

Introduction
● Fix the large dragon outline on the classroom wall.
● Explain to the class that they will be using the ideas they have been gathering in the week to create a large dragon wall for everyone to share.

Group work
● Organise the class into mixed-ability groups and give each group a pile of paper dragon scales and felt-tipped pens.
● Ask the children to share the words and phrases they have written on their photocopiable page 105 'Dragon words', to agree on those they will write on the paper scales and which will be stuck on to the large dragon.
● Allow time for the groups to discuss their work and complete the paper scales.

> **Differentiation**
> ● You may wish to appoint group leaders to guide the discussions.

Review
● As the children are working, gather their paper scales, and begin to attach them to the large dragon outline on the wall. When the groups have finished, summarise their results briefly, noting where similar words, phrases or information occurs more than once, as these were obviously popular suggestions. Invite representatives from each group to tell the class something about their discussions and how they came to agreement about which words and phrases to include. Leave the dragon wall available for reference in future work.

Curriculum objectives
● To organise paragraphs around a theme.
● To compose and rehearse sentences orally (including dialogue), progressively building a varied and rich vocabulary and an increasing range of sentence structures (See Appendix 2).

Resources
Access to the dragon word wall created previously; children's completed photocopiable page 104 'Dragonfile'

5: How to create a dragon

Introduction
● Ask the children to reflect on what they have learned about dragons since they first completed their photocopiable page 104 'Dragonfile' at the beginning of the week. Ask for some examples, and require them to say where the new information came from.
● Explain that today they will be using what they know to write a short guide for other authors, giving them information about what they would need in order to create a convincing dragon for their stories. They should include a physical description, key features, common characteristics and any particular aspects they feel would be important. They can use the questions on their photocopiable sheet as a further guide, and should write in paragraphs.
● Encourage them to include questions to enliven their writing, such as: *So, you want to write about a dragon? Here's what you need* or *How will you make your dragon convincing? Here are some pointers.* They could also use subheadings for their paragraphs.

Independent work
● Provide time for the children to work quietly to create a guide for authors wishing to create dragon characters. Remind them to use their own work and the dragon word wall for reference.

Review
● Ask the children to swap their completed guides with a partner. When the work has been read quietly, invite several children to select the best paragraph from their partner's work to read out to the class, and invite positive comments from others.

Expected outcomes
● All children can research and write an explanation text about Chinese New Year, including compound sentences.
● Most children can include paragraphs, subheadings and a wider range of connectives to join clauses.
● Some children can extend sentences further to include more than two clauses.

Curriculum objectives
● To extend the range of sentences with more than one clause by using a wider range of conjunctions.

Resources
Photocopiable page 106 'Types of connective'; interactive whiteboard screen with prepared sentences (as suggested in lesson plan); individual whiteboards and pens

Week 2 lesson plans

This is primarily a non-fiction week, with the children learning about and researching Chinese New Year and the ways in which it is celebrated, which includes the famous Dragon dance. They will formulate questions as a guide to their research which will be done using a range of non-fiction texts, including, where possible, online sources. With the information they find, they will imagine themselves as party planners to create a list of activities suitable for Chinese New Year celebrations, together with required resources. They will also write an explanation of Chinese New Year, using subheadings. Work on clauses and connectives should also be reflected in this final piece of writing.

1: Clauses and connectives

Introduction
● Use starter activity 5 'Start with the connection' to refresh the children's knowledge about subordinate clauses and connectives.

Whole-class work
● Remind the children that clauses are special types of phrase, whose main word is a verb; that main clauses can stand as sentences on their own but subordinate clauses would not make sense without the main clause. When we join the clauses to make a compound sentence, we use connectives.
● On the interactive whiteboard, show the children the sentences:
  ● *The dragon roared when the knight approached*
  ● *Chi Yu walked to the meadow, cut the grass and took it to the farmer.*
  ● *Although she was afraid, the princess tried to be brave as she waited for the dragon.*
● Invite several children to come to the board and highlight the verbs. Ask how many verbs are in each sentence, thus defining the number of clauses.
● Next, invite other children to highlight the connectives, further defining the clauses which will be separated by the connectives. Can they spot a fronted adverbial?

Paired work
● Ask the children to spend some time working together to list as many connectives as they can. If possible, they should group them according to type. You can remind them about the work they have done on connectives of time and place as a starter. They should list their words on their individual whiteboards.

> **Differentiation**
> ● For the children who find it difficult to think of connectives beyond the basics, allow them to browse through books to spot others that they might not have thought of.

Review
● As a class, invite pairs of children to firstly suggest the ways in which they have categorised their connectives, writing useful headings on the board. Then ask for examples of each type. You may find that it is useful to hand out photocopiable page 106 'Types of connective'.
● When the lists are created, ask for oral examples of sentences containing any of them, allowing the children a little time to think and write them on their whiteboards. Encourage them to use three clauses and fronted adverbials as well as using more unusual connectives.

Curriculum objectives
● To retrieve and record information from non-fiction.
● To ask questions to improve their understanding of a text.

Resources
Media resource 'Chinese dragon' on the CD-ROM; books and online sources for finding out about the Chinese New Year

2: Chinese New Year dragon festival

Introduction
● Show the class the photograph 'Chinese dragon' on the CD-ROM.
● Explain that they will be finding out about the Chinese New Year which includes the part played by dragons in the celebrations. Today they will be working with a partner.

Paired work
● Allow the children access to books and the internet to see what they can find out about the Chinese New Year and how dragons are perceived in China, which is very different to the dragons they have read about so far.
● Explain that one piece of information may lead them to the next piece of their research and encourage them to think of questions to carry their research forward. For example: *When do the dragon dances happen? How big are the dragons? Why is red a lucky colour in China?*
● The children should keep notes of what they discover, including their sources, so they can find the information again, if necessary.

> ### Differentiation
> ● It may be useful to source appropriate books and internet sites beforehand, to save time and ensure the information is at an appropriate reading level for the children to access and understand.

Review
● Draw the class together and ask for examples of what the children have found out. Are they surprised to discover how different Chinese dragons are from those in Western culture?

Curriculum objectives
● To identify main ideas drawn from more than one paragraph and summarise these.

Resources
Children's notes from previous lesson

3: New Year celebrations

Introduction
● Invite the children to imagine themselves as party planners who have been asked to organise events to celebrate Chinese New Year. Explain that they will use the information from the previous lesson's research and will work with their partner to make a detailed list of suggestions for activities that guests at the party could have fun carrying out.

Whole-class work
● Ask the class for suggestions of ideas for activities that could be included. These might be: making paper cut-outs to decorate doors and windows, making red envelopes for people to put money in, making lanterns, learning a dragon dance and creating music to go with it, cleaning the party area beforehand, making dragon masks or puppets, preparing and eating certain foods.

Paired work
● Allow time for the children to discuss and list their suggestions in note form. They should include resources that might be needed for each activity they suggest.

Review
● Group pairs of children together to share their ideas, using their notes as prompts. Ask for some ideas to be shared with the whole class.
● If possible, time would be ideally found elsewhere in the day for some of the practical activities to be carried out. These would need additional planning and preparation but would reinforce the factual learning the children have completed.

Curriculum objectives
● In non-narrative writing, to use simple organisational devices.
● To organise paragraphs around a theme.
● To use fronted adverbials.
● To use commas after fronted adverbials.

Resources
Children's lists from previous lesson; media resource 'Chinese dragon dance' on the CD-ROM

4: Chinese New Year explained

Introduction
● Show the class the video 'Chinese dragon dance' on the CD-ROM.
● Explain that today they will use this week's work to write an explanation text about Chinese New Year celebrations.

Whole-class work
● Ask the children to recap on what an explanation text does, for instance that it explains how to do something – it is not the same as an information text which provides information without explaining how to do it. Explanation texts usually use imperative verbs.
● Ask the children for examples of explanation texts – they may suggest recipes or explanations for how to make something or how to play a game. Encourage them to offer suggestions for how one activity for Chinese New Year might be explained.
● Remind the children that their work should include paragraphs organised according to content with appropriate headings, use a range of connectives in compound sentences and use fronted adverbials.

Independent work
● Allow time for the children to use their notes to write their explanation texts. Explain to them that this is their first draft and they will have the opportunity to edit it tomorrow.

Review
● Encourage the children to work again with their partner from the previous lesson, swapping their work for reading and comments. Invite some of the children to share the best parts of their partner's writing with the class.

Curriculum objectives
● To assess the effectiveness of their own and others' writing and suggest improvements.
● To propose changes to grammar and vocabulary to improve consistency.
● To proofread for spelling and punctuation errors.
● To learn the grammar for Year 4 in Appendix 2.

Resources
Children's drafts of explanation texts (from lesson 4)

5: Editing explanation texts

Introduction
● Explain to the class that today the children have the opportunity to re-read their explanation texts from the previous lesson, to edit and improve them.

Whole-class work
● Encourage the children to provide suggestions of what technical aspects of their writing they will be checking first of all. They should suggest spelling and punctuation, and may also realise that there are aspects of grammar that may need to be changed in order to make the meaning of sentences clear (for example, are words missing, or is there verb agreement).
● Ask how they might then edit the language and sentence structure to improve their work. They may think of choosing more interesting vocabulary, looking for unnecessary repetition, changing clause order to use a fronted adverbial or increasing the range of connectives to make the piece more interesting for the reader.

Independent work
● Allow sufficient time for the children to read and edit their explanation text.

Review
● As a class, invite some of the children to share any changes they made to their work. Did anyone change a sentence to include a fronted adverbial? What examples of interesting connectives can they offer? Which imperative verbs have been used? Which activities would the children most enjoy doing, and why?

Week 3 lesson plans

This week the class will be introduced to the story *How to Train Your Dragon*. They will write character descriptions, identifying how the use of language enhances the individuality of key characters. They will consider how the setting and characters fit together and also study the plot so far. They will predict what might happen next, based on their understanding of the story and how the characters are developing. They will use inferential clues to talk about character relationships. The week concludes with them writing in role as Hiccup, relating events from his perspective, from the beginning of the story.

1: *How to Train Your Dragon*

Introduction

● Explain to the class that over a two-week period you will be reading *How to Train Your Dragon* by Cressida Cowell (or listening to the audio version). You may wish to share the book as a class serial separate from normal English lessons, using only those parts with particular relevance in individual lessons.
● Introduce the story by reading some of the character descriptions in the first two chapters. Provide the children with copies of these on photocopiable page 'Horrendous descriptions' from the CD-ROM to read for themselves. Also, show them the book illustrations which may remind them of those found in Roald Dahl stories they met in Year 3.

Whole-class work

● Ask the class what else can be inferred from the physical descriptions of the characters. For example, we are told that Gobber *didn't do noises quieter than screaming*, so what does this suggest about him? What do Snotlout's skeleton tattoos say about him? What other inferred characteristics can the children find?
● Can anyone spot similes in the descriptions? What do these add to our engagement and enjoyment? What adjectives can they find?

Independent work

● Allow the children to spend some time reading through the descriptions on the photocopiable sheet, highlighting or underlining parts of the text that they consider to be particularly good. This can be individual words, phrases or whole sentences.
● Encourage them to use word-building skills for unknown or unusual words.

Paired work

● Encourage the children to share their work with a partner, comparing selections and explaining the reasons for their choices.

Review

● Ask for some examples of the children's favourite pieces of writing from the character descriptions, with their reasons for choosing them. Did partners make similar decisions or were there differences?
● Read aloud to the class descriptions of settings from the first two chapters. For example: *Long ago, on the wild and windy isle of Berk a smallish Viking with a longish name stood up to his ankles in snow; They were standing on a bleak little beach at the bleakest spot on the whole bleak island. A heavy snow was falling*; (both from page 16). You can find other examples to share. Ask how the settings fit with the characters. Would it work if those characters were set in a 21st century town, or a sunny beach environment? Talk about the effects of matching setting and character and how this adds to the story and emphasises the main characteristics of both.

Expected outcomes

● All children can identify character differences and offer suggestions for relationships between some of them. They can outline the plot so far and predict what might happen next.
● Most children can write in role as Hiccup, showing events from his point of view.
● Some children can show a deeper understanding of inference and greater insight into the relationships between characters.

Curriculum objectives

● To discuss words and phrases that capture the reader's interest and imagination.
● To listen to and discuss a wide range of fiction, poetry, plays, non-fiction and reference books or textbooks.
● To participate in discussion about both books that are read to them and those they can read for themselves, taking turns and listening to what others say.
● To apply their growing knowledge of root words, prefixes and suffixes (etymology and morphology) as listed in Appendix 1, both to read aloud and to understand the meaning of new words they meet.

Resources

How to Train Your Dragon by Cressida Cowell; David Tennant's reading of *How to Train Your Dragon* (optional); photocopiable page 'Horrendous descriptions' from the CD-ROM; highlighter pens or ordinary pens

Curriculum objectives
● To predict what might happen from details stated and implied.

Resources
How to Train Your Dragon by Cressida Cowell

2: Predicting events

Introduction
● Talk about the first two chapters of the book, asking the children to predict what they think might happen next and giving reasons for their suggestions. If they were the writer, what would they put next to keep the reader's interest, whilst maintaining the integrity of the characters? Discuss the children's predictions.

Whole-class work
● Carry on reading the story to the class, pausing at the break on page 51 to ask the class what they think will happen next, now that it appears that Hiccup doesn't have a dragon. They may suggest Fishlegs gives Hiccup his dragon, or Hiccup returns to the cave to try again.
● Carry on reading to the end of Chapter 3 and ask the children to predict what might happen in the next part of the story, now that Hiccup has such a small and apparently useless dragon. What reasons can they give for their predictions? They may draw on previous reading experience to suggest that as Hiccup is obviously the hero of the story, Toothless may turn out not to be as useless as he appears, or there would not be a happy or heroic conclusion.

Review
● Talk about how Hiccup's character is developing. Is he developing to be stronger and more resourceful than we were first led to believe? What examples can they give for this?

Curriculum objectives
● To draw inferences such as inferring characters' feelings, thoughts and motives from their actions, and justify inferences with evidence.
● To compose and rehearse sentences orally (including dialogue), progressively building a varied and rich vocabulary and an increasing range of sentence structures (See Appendix 2).

Resources
How to Train Your Dragon by Cressida Cowell; photocopiable page 107 'Family values'

3: Family values

Introduction
● Read Chapters 5, 6 and 7 with the class. Ask them as they listen to focus particularly on Hiccup's relationships with his grandfather Old Wrinkly, and his father Stoick.

Paired work
● Ask the children to talk together about the conversations Hiccup has with his two relatives, and the differences between them. They should think about the sorts of thing each adult says to Hiccup and what his responses are.
● Encourage them to consider which of the two men Hiccup seems to be more like. Ask: *What do Old Wrinkly and Stoick feel about Hiccup and what does he feel about them?* They should give reasons for their opinions. If possible, they should have access to the texts for reference.

Independent work
● Allow time for the children to write a summary of their paired discussion, using photocopiable page 107 'Family values' to guide them.

Review
● Ask some of the children to share their thoughts on Hiccup's family relationships and discuss as a class similarities and differences in the children's opinions. Are they able to give reasons for their thinking? How would they feel about the two men's feelings towards them if they were Hiccup? How do they think these relationships might affect what Hiccup does in the rest of the story?

4: The story so far

Curriculum objectives
● To participate in discussion about both books that are read to them and those they can read for themselves, taking turns and listening to what others say.

Resources
How to Train Your Dragon by Cressida Cowell

Introduction

● Ask the children to share with the class some of their favourite parts of *How to train your dragon*, so far. Divide this up into characters, settings and plot.
● Explain that they will be working in groups to consider just the plot today, although obviously this will contain characters and have a setting. They will talk together, recapping the story so far, sharing ideas and opinions.

Group work

● Invite the children to work in mixed-ability groups of 4–6 (if possible with access to at least one copy of the text), to recall the story so far, identifying the main elements of the plot. (What is the story is about and what has happened?) Encourage them to enjoy sharing their favourite events in the story.
● Ideally the children will use the book to find and note any particular words or phrases that they thought worked especially well, as they may wish to use or adapt them for their own use later.

Review

● Ask each group to report back to the class on any parts of the plot that several of their group members chose as being a favourite. Note these briefly on the board. When all have fed back, invite the children to vote for just one of the events to see if a top favourite can be found.

5: Hiccup's diary

Curriculum objectives
● To compose and rehearse sentences orally (including dialogue), progressively building a varied and rich vocabulary and an increasing range of sentence structures (See Appendix 2).
● To assess the effectiveness of their own and others' writing and suggest improvements.

Resources
Children's notes (from lesson 4); *How to Train Your Dragon* by Cressida Cowell

Introduction

● Read to the class the extract 'Note from Hiccup' that precedes the story and ask them to think about it.

Whole-class work

● Explain to the children that today they will be planning, discussing and writing the start of the story as though they were Hiccup recording the events in his diary.
● Also, explain that this should include what some of the other characters said, and that as they speak in different ways the children should reflect this in their writing. Ask the class for some examples of how they might do this.

Paired work

● Allow the children to spend a little time working with a partner to compose and rehearse some of what they will include in their writing. They can refer to their work from the previous lesson, using some of the vocabulary they noted.

Independent work

● Invite the children to compose their diary entries, using paragraphs and punctuating direct speech correctly.

> **Differentiation**
> ● You may need to remind some of the children about writing in the first person and maintaining this throughout the piece. If they are using the word 'he' it is because they will be writing about one of the other characters, and not Hiccup.

Review

● Allow the children time to read their finished pieces to their partner, before asking the partners to tell the rest of the class what they thought worked well in their partner's writing.

Week 4 lesson plans

During this week, the children will talk and write about the development of Hiccup and his dragon, Toothless, citing evidence from the text to support their observations. They will contribute to a word wall of comparisons between Hiccup at the start of the story and how he changes as the story develops. They will use a playscript to identify and select correct homophones and as a reminder of playscript conventions. They will select a scene from the story to write as a playscript, having first discussed and drafted it. The scenes will then be acted out for the class.

1: Toothless to toothful

Introduction
● Ask the children for a reminder of the characteristics of Hiccup's dragon, Toothless, when he first found him. How would they sum up the young dragon at that stage in the story?

Whole-class work
● Ensure the children are familiar with Chapters 8, 9 and 10 before the lesson. Using the information in these three chapters, carry out a discussion about the developing character of Toothless. As he grows, what do we see about his emerging character? What are some of the things he does and says that show he is not the timid creature he first appeared to be?
● Now focus on the developing character of Hiccup and use the interactive activity 'Hiccup' on the CD-ROM. With the class read through the statements on the two screens, asking them to choose whether each statement is true or false.

Paired work
● Ask the children to work together to think of ways in which the character of Hiccup is developing alongside his dragon. If possible, they should have access to a copy of the book. They should consider:
    ● our first impressions of Hiccup, especially in comparison to the other Viking boys
    ● his actions as the story developed (such as the bravery he showed at the dragons' cave)
    ● the things we have learned about him from his conversations with different people (including Old Wrinkly and Fishlegs)
    ● his determination to master his dragon despite the odds
    ● what his character seems to be like now, in comparison with that at the start of the story. Do the children have a different opinion about him now? Can they predict how he might continue to develop and what might happen to him later in the story?
● Encourage the children to write their observations on sticky notes, which they will attach to the two large sheets of paper pinned to the classroom wall. Comments on Hiccup's character at the start of the story should go on the sheet labelled *Then* and those relating to him later in the story on the sheet labelled *Now*.

Review
● Use the two sheets of sticky notes to summarise the children's observations. Does everyone broadly agree? Engage the children in a discussion on points of agreement and on any differences of opinion. Ask how they might see the character of Toothless developing as the story continues. Will he turn out to be brave and courageous, or end up as the disappointment he first seemed to be? If they were the author, what would they do to satisfy their readers? Can they think of other stories where the characters have changed in a dramatic way? What does this do for the story, and how does it engage us as readers?

Expected outcomes
● All children can suggest ways in which characters are developing, write and act a short scene as a playscript and identify correct use of homophones.
● Most children can give textual evidence for their observations on character development and include appropriate stage directions in their playscripts.
● Some children can convey appropriate characteristics in the dialogue they give their characters in their playscripts.

Curriculum objectives
● To listen to and discuss a wide range of fiction, poetry, plays, non-fiction and reference books or textbooks.
● To draw inferences such as inferring characters' feelings, thoughts and motives from their actions, and justify inferences with evidence.
● To predict what might happen from details stated and implied.

Resources
How to Train Your Dragon by Cressida Cowell; sticky notes and pens; two large sheets of paper that are labelled *Then* and *Now*; interactive activity 'Hiccup' on the CD-ROM; computer access

Curriculum objectives
- To spell further homophones.

Resources
Photocopiable page 108 'Harald and Firestorm: a short scene'; dictionaries; the following rhyme to display: *Whether the weather be fine, or whether the weather be hot, we'll weather the weather, whatever the weather, whether we like it or not*

2: Whether the weather...

Introduction
- Show the class the rhyme (see Resources). Invite them to repeat the rhyme, and ask for its meaning. What do they notice about the spelling?
- Remind them about homophones which they have worked on previously and then use starter activity 10 'Homophones'.

Whole-class work
- Ask if any of the children have developed their own ways for remembering which homophones to choose. Discuss their ideas. Explain that they must try to remember the meanings and spellings of homophones, as usually there is no easy way to know which to choose, other than that they just look right.

Independent work
- Hand out photocopiable page 108 'Harald and Firestorm: a short scene' and first read through it with the class.
- Direct the children to choose and underline which they think are the correct homophones on the photocopiable sheet. Allow time for them to do this.

Paired work
- Encourage the children to check their work with a partner. If there is any disagreement, invite the pairs to use dictionaries to check the words' meanings.

Review
- Ask the class if any of them changed their choice of homophone after checking their work with a partner or using a dictionary. Were any words changed by several children? Ask for suggestions for how to remember specific words.

Curriculum objectives
- To discuss writing similar to that which they are planning to write in order to understand and learn from its structure, grammar and vocabulary.

Resources
Photocopiable page 108 'Harald and Firestorm: a short scene'; DVD of the film of *How to Train Your Dragon* (optional)

3: Playscripts

Introduction
- If possible, show the children a short scene from the film version of the novel, perhaps the first conversation between Hiccup and his father. If this is not possible, read the scene from the book.
- Explain that books are often made into films. Can the children offer any examples?
- Ask them what the scriptwriter would have to do to turn a book into a script. What is kept the same as the book and what has to be changed? They should suggest that dialogue remains, but everything else becomes visual. Encourage them to recall what they know of the conventions of a written playscript.

Paired work
- Invite the children to use photocopiable page 108 'Harald and Firestorm: a short scene' to practise reading a playscript scene. Each partner should take one character's lines. While reading through the scene, encourage them to consider what was effective about the script.

Whole-class work
- As a class, discuss how the script was written to help them to read it effectively. They should mention the character names, so they knew who should speak, and the stage directions telling them how to deliver the lines.
- Ask: *Why was the initial stage direction given, about the pair being alone?* (To provide information for the actors to get the right atmosphere.) *Would they suggest any further stage directions, such as movements or facial expressions?*

Review
- Select several pairs of children to act out the scene for the class.

Curriculum objectives
• To compose and rehearse sentences orally (including dialogue), progressively building a varied and rich vocabulary and an increasing range of sentence structures (See Appendix 2).
• To assess the effectiveness of their own and others' writing and suggest improvements.

Resources
How to Train Your Dragon by Cressida Cowell

4: Writing a playscript

Introduction
• Ask the children for some of their favourite scenes from the story which they think would make a good film.
• Explain that they will be choosing a scene to write as a playscript which they can rehearse and perform. They will spend some time discussing ideas and trying out a few bits of dialogue. They do not have to use the exact words in the book, but can adapt them, using the same basic plot and characters.

Paired work
• Arrange the children into partners and ask them to discuss possible scenes.
• Encourage them to try out some of their potential dialogue and make notes.

Independent work
• Invite the children to write a first draft of their scenes, using playscript conventions as discussed in lesson 3.

> **Differentiation**
> • Using just two characters is the easiest way to write the script. More experienced writers can be encouraged to use three characters, but more would be unwieldy in a short scene. The children should try to give the characters dialogue that reflects their personality, so more flamboyant ones are easier to portray. Encourage confident writers to extend speeches, injecting humour, tension or emotion into their dialogue.

Review
• In pairs, encourage the children to do a first read-through of their scripts, making notes for any changes they feel may be necessary.

Curriculum objectives
• To read aloud their own writing, to a group or the whole class, using appropriate intonation and controlling the tone and volume so that the meaning is clear.
• To assess the effectiveness of their own and others' writing and suggest improvements.

Resources
Children's drafted work (from lesson 4)

5: Lights, camera, action!

Introduction
• Invite several pairs of children to perform their run-throughs of the scripts they wrote in lesson 4.
• Ask each pair whether they will be making any changes to their first drafts when they write their final pieces.

Independent work
• Allow time for the children to write final versions of their playscripts, including any amendments they have decided to make.
• Encourage them to use their best handwriting, in order that other actors can easily read their work.

Group work
• Depending upon how many parts there are in the scenes, organise the children to work in pairs or small groups. Allow them time to rehearse their short scenes, remembering the criteria they have used in previous units of work, for giving an effective performance.
• Remind the children to take notice of any stage directions their characters have been given by the playwrights.

Review
• Invite the children to perform their scenes for the class. Afterwards, ask how useful the actors found the stage directions and ask the authors whether they would add any further directions now they have seen their scenes acted. Encourage the children to assess how near to the originals they have managed to get the characters. Have they been given the right sort of language to convey their character?

Week 5 lesson plans

This week, the children will link the Viking setting of How to Train Your Dragon with real Vikings and their dragon ships. Using images of the vessels, they will work in groups to act out a scene depicting the Britons' reactions to the approaching Viking invaders, also creating kennings for them. After working on the use of the possessive apostrophe, they will write explanatory notices that could accompany a Viking ship exhibit in a museum. Using a text about Boudicca (who they should remember from their work on the Romans in Year 3), they will see how fiction and non-fiction can be blended, culminating in writing in role as a monk on Lindisfarne, describing the Viking invasion.

1: Viking dragon ships

Introduction
● Show the class the media resource 'Viking dragon ship' on the CD-ROM. Explain that these large longships had the heads of dragons or other mythical creatures carved in their wooden prows. Such ships belonged to chieftains or kings and the dragon heads gave visual messages about their status. The Vikings believed the dragon heads would scare off their enemies, protect the ship and crew and ward off evil spirits.
● Ask the children to imagine how these vessels would seem to the British as they saw them arriving across the sea, crewed by ferocious-looking, armed Vikings. Invite suggestions for vocabulary to describe both the ships and the feelings of the British on the shore. Scribe responses on the board.

Independent work
● Invite the children to freeze-frame a stance and appropriate facial expression in role as a Briton, viewing the approaching dragon ship. Ask them to imagine how they would feel and what they would be thinking.
● Circulate around the class, lightly tapping individual children on the shoulder for them to speak aloud their thoughts in role.

Group work
● In informally organised small groups, ask the children to create a short scene, in role as Britons, talking about the sight they have witnessed and what this might mean. Some may feel brave, others afraid, others simply curious or excited.
● Ask the children for suggestions of what will make their short scenes good presentations. They should recall features, such as using a clear voice with appropriate intonation, having varied and interesting dialogue, using their faces to show emotions, using their bodies as actors (not just standing still in a row, for example they may point towards the approaching ships). They should also be listening to each other and not just concentrating on their own lines.
● Allow them some time to discuss, create and rehearse their scenes before presenting them to the class.
● After the presentations, invite the actors themselves and the rest of the class to offer comments on both the performance and the content of the role plays.

> ### Differentiation
> ● Mixed-ability groups would be appropriate, to allow children whose performance skills may be greater than their reading ability to have a more prominent role.

Review
● Share with the class the Viking kennings for their ships, including *wave-floater, sea-goer, wave-steed* or *sea-steed*, and for the sea, such as *whale's-way, fishes' realm, or sail-road*. Working as a whole class, ask for other suggestions. Can they also think of kennings for real dragons?

Curriculum objectives
● To indicate possession by using the possessive apostrophe with plural nouns.
● To write from memory simple sentences, dictated by the teacher, that include words and punctuation taught so far.
● To learn the grammar for Year 4 in Appendix 2.
● To place the possessive apostrophe accurately in words with regular plurals and in words with irregular plurals.

Resources
Photocopiable page 109 'Get the apostrophe right'; individual whiteboards

2: Vikings or Viking's?

Introduction
● Write: *The Vikings ships sailed across the sea.* Ask the class whether the sentence is correctly punctuated. Invite a child to come and punctuate it to indicate one Viking, then another to show more than one Viking, by placing the possessive apostrophe correctly. Ask why the word 'ships' does not need an apostrophe (because it is just a plural noun with no possession attached).

Independent work
● Hand out photocopiable page 109 'Get the apostrophe right'. Explain that there are plural nouns in the sentences as well as words requiring possessive apostrophes, so the children should not assume that all plurals need apostrophes. Allow time for the children to complete the photocopiable sheet.

Whole-class work
● Ask the children to write short dictated sentences requiring either singular or plural apostrophes, on their whiteboards. For example, singular: *The king's ship was huge*; plural: *The dragons' wings were like leather.*

> **Differentiation**
> ● For some of the children you may need to reinforce the difference between plural nouns where no possession is suggested and therefore no apostrophe required, and those where possession is indicated.

Review
● Show the children the correct punctuation for the sentences on their photocopiable sheet, for them to mark themselves.

Curriculum objectives
● To organise paragraphs around a theme.
● To discuss and record ideas.

Resources
Media resource 'Viking dragon ship' on the CD-ROM; photocopiable page 110 'Viking ship plan'

3: Viking ship on show

Introduction
● Show the children this caption: *This is a Viking ship. It is very old. It is made of wood.* Tell them this is a caption for a museum exhibit and ask for comments. They should identify that it is very basic and conveys little information.

Whole-class work
● Challenge the children to write a better explanatory text for the Viking ship and ask for ideas on the kind of information that could be included in the description, drawing on the work they have done earlier in the week. Explain they will have the opportunity to think and plan their text before writing.
● Hand out photocopiable page 110 'Viking Ship plan', briefly talking the children through it before allowing them time to complete it with their ideas and potential vocabulary.

Paired work
● After completing the photocopiable sheet, invite the children to briefly outline their ideas to a partner, each offering comments and suggestions, enabling amendments to the plans if the children wish.

Independent work
● Allow time for the children to use their plans to write a lively, informative text.
● Remind them to use paragraphs with headings as appropriate. They should aim to engage the museum visitors who would be the readers.

Review
● Bring the class together and show them again the initial description on the interactive whiteboard, asking for suggestions for how to improve it.

Curriculum objectives
● To discuss writing similar to that which they are planning to write in order to understand and learn from its structure, grammar and vocabulary.
● To discuss and record ideas.

Resources
Photocopiable page 111 'Boudicca our queen'; highlighter pens or coloured pencils

4: Creative non-fiction

Introduction

● Read aloud to the class photocopiable page 111 'Boudicca our queen'.
● Ask them whether it is fiction or non-fiction, asking for reasons for their opinions. It is likely that they will find evidence of both.

Paired work

● Hand out the photocopiable sheet and ask the children to work in pairs to discuss and highlight those parts of the story they consider to be non-fiction.

Whole-class work

● As a class, have a discussion about the decisions the children made in their pairs. Did everyone select the same parts of the text? Why did they choose the parts that they did?
● Ask them to look now at the parts left unhighlighted. How would they classify these? Could they be called fiction? For example, do we know who the writer was? Can we prove any of the pieces of personal information about him?
● Explain that there is a genre of writing called 'creative non-fiction' which uses real historical events woven into a story with added characterisation to involve the reader, and give a fictional author's perspective. It doesn't invent dialogue, facts or events, apart from those of the fictional author.

Review

● Look again at the text with the class, discussing the types of language used for the fictional elements of the writing, analysing and categorising them and discussing what they add to the story.

Curriculum objectives
● In narratives, to create settings, characters and plot.
● To compose and rehearse sentences orally (including dialogue), progressively building a varied and rich vocabulary and an increasing range of sentence structures (See Appendix 2).

Resources
Prepared text on interactive whiteboard (outlined in lesson plan)

5: Vikings invade Lindisfarne

Introduction

● Display on the following information:
  ● *There were whirlwinds and lightning storms and fiery dragons were seen flying in the sky. These signs were followed by great famine and on 8th January the ravaging heathen men destroyed God's church at Lindisfarne.*
  ● *Never before has such terror appeared in Britain as we have now suffered from a pagan race... The heathens poured out the blood of saints around the altar, and trampled on the bodies of the saints in the temple of God.*
● Explain to the class that these were reports written near the time, in 793, when Vikings invaded the island of Lindisfarne, committed terrible violence against the monks and stole church treasure.

Whole-class work

● Remind the children about creative non-fiction and invite them to imagine they are one of the surviving monks who fled Lindisfarne. They will write in role a report describing the events. Recap on the key elements and explain that they should use a range of sentence structures to enhance their writing.

Paired work

● Ask pairs to discuss their ideas and make brief planning notes.

Independent work

● In role as a monk, ask the children to use the information on the interactive whiteboard to write a report on the events.

Review

● Select children to read out parts of their reports to the class. Encourage the rest of the class to offer their opinion.

Expected outcomes
● All children can talk about free-verse poetry, find and copy examples of dragon poems and write their own free-verse dragon poem.
● Most children can explain the key features of free verse, including the importance of punctuation, and include these in their own poem.
● Some children can take ideas from their reading of poetry and prose to enhance their vocabulary and sentence structure in their poems.

Curriculum objectives
● To prepare poems to read aloud and to perform, showing understanding through intonation, tone, volume and action.
● To recognise some different forms of poetry.

Resources
First verse of the poem 'Not My Best Side' by UA Fanthorpe to hand out (available online); image of the painting 'St George and the Dragon' by Paolo Uccello (available online)

Week 6 lesson plans

Poetry about dragons is this week's focus, looking at the story of St George from the dragon's point of view, through the poem 'Not My Best Side'. The children will identify the poem as free verse and discuss the importance of punctuation in this poetic form. They will use the context of the writing to deduce the meanings of unfamiliar words and rehearse and perform the poem. They will use books and the internet to find dragon poems, selecting some to write in their best handwriting for inclusion in a class anthology. Studying Tolkien's description of Smaug provides the stimulus for the children creating their own dragon, which they will write about in a free-verse poem.

1: Not my best side

Introduction
● Show the class the painting 'St George and the Dragon', and ask if they recognise the subject.
● Ask who the characters are, and for a brief reminder of the legend.

Whole-class work
● Hand out copies of the first verse of the poem 'Not my best side'. Read it aloud to the class before they read it to themselves. Tell the children the poem is written from the perspective of one of the characters in the painting, and that while they are reading they should try to decide which one it is.
● When they have finished, ask for suggestions of which character's voice the poem is written in, giving reasons for their choices. They should identify it as the voice of the dragon.
● Enquire if there are any words the children are unfamiliar with, *ostentatiously* perhaps. Can they define the meaning from the context? If not, provide the definition.
● Ask how the dragon is feeling about his situation, and what his opinions are of the princess and St George, again asking for reasons so that the children have to refer to and quote from the text, showing their understanding. Why is the poem called 'Not My Best Side'? Does this portrayal of the dragon fit with what they know of the original legend? What similarities or differences do they notice?

Group work
● In groups of 4–6, encourage the children to practise reading the verse aloud for performance. They must decide how they are going to divide the poem up for individuals or pairs to read a section at a time. The punctuation should guide them. Remind them to use clear voices and good intonation.
● Allow time for them to practise several times, before each group performs their version to the whole class.

Differentiation
● If some children find difficulty in understanding aspects of the poem, it could be because they are not taking enough notice of the punctuation. Familiarity with rhyming verse may lead them to pause at line ends and read in a rhythm. Explain that in free verse, we read the poem differently, almost like a story; it is the punctuation that guides us, telling us when to pause. They should not try to fit a regular rhythm to their reading.

Review
● After the presentations, talk with the class about what makes this a free-verse poem. Why might the poet have chosen to write in this way, rather than use rhyme and rhythm? What do they think this form adds to the content? Do they find this easier to read and understand than rhyming verse, and why?

Curriculum objectives
● To recognise some different forms of poetry.

Resources
A selection of poetry books; internet access to source poetry

2: Finding dragon poems

Introduction

● Show the children several of the books you have selected and ask what they have in common and what connection they have with the previous lesson. The children should identify them as poetry books.

Whole-class work

● Explain that they will be searching through books and online for poems about dragons.

● Spend some time discussing how they will go about that. They should know about searching contents and indexes of books for themes or titles, and using the phrase *dragon poems* for an internet search. If you are providing sites yourself, they will need to know how to navigate each one, perhaps using the site's own search facility.

● Explain that they will be choosing one or two poems to write out for inclusion in a class anthology of dragon poems. Ask how the collection can be made as interesting as possible. Encourage the children to select a range of poetic forms and different types of dragon, some may have humour, others tension or adventure, and to choose poems that differ in length.

Paired work

● Allow the children to spend time enjoying finding, reading and selecting their poems, noting the titles, authors and where they were found, so they can be accessed easily in the next lesson.

Review

● Invite the children to share their poem choices with the class.

Curriculum objectives
● To recognise some different forms of poetry.
● To use the diagonal and horizontal strokes that are needed to join letters and understand which letters, when adjacent to one another, are best left unjoined.
● To increase the legibility, consistency and quality of their handwriting.

Resources
Children's notes for their sources (from lesson 2); poetry books; internet access

3: Compiling a dragon anthology

Introduction

● Remind the class that they will be using the poems they found in lesson 2 to create a class anthology. Can they see any problems that might be encountered? Discuss and ask for solutions to any points they raise, which may include duplication of selected poems. It will be yours and the class's decision on whether duplications should be allowed.

Whole-class work

● As a class, decide on how the poems will be presented – size of paper, lined or unlined, how they will be illustrated, how to attribute the work to both the poet and the child who chose the poem, and so on.

● Ensure the children know you expect this to be their best handwriting, particularly as the work is intended for a wide audience.

● As the poems will be of different lengths, you should decide whether children should write one or more.

Independent work

● Encourage the children to find and write their chosen poems, illustrating them appropriately.

> **Differentiation**
> ● Bear in mind that some children, can find copying work difficult. Reading a text, lifting the eyes while remembering the words, refocusing on the paper and then writing may take considerable effort and must be taken into account.

Review

● Enjoy listening to some of the poems before compiling the anthology.

Curriculum objectives
● To discuss writing similar to that which they are planning to write in order to learn from its structure, grammar and vocabulary.

Resources
Photocopiable page 'Smaug' from the CD-ROM; media resource 'Smaug by Carol Emery Phenix' on the CD-ROM; highlighter pens

4: Famous dragons

Introduction

● Show the children the illustration 'Smaug by Carol Emery Phenix' on the CD-ROM, inviting comments. Inform the class that this is one artist's vision of Tolkien's famous dragon, Smaug, from *The Hobbit*, which they may be familiar with from the film version. Read them Tolkien's description of Smaug from photocopiable page 'Smaug' from the CD-ROM.

Paired work

● Hand out the photocopiable sheet. Ask the children to work together to highlight parts of the text that they consider to be good use of vocabulary and descriptive writing.

Whole-class work

● Discuss the highlighted text with the class, talking about why the writing is so effective and why the children have chosen particular parts of the language. What has Tolkien done to engage us as readers and enable the artist to produce such an arresting image of the dragon?
● Explain to the children that tomorrow they will be writing a free-verse poem about an awesome dragon of their own creation. They will now have time to think about their dragon and begin to gather vocabulary that they may use.

Independent work

● Allow the children to spend some time making notes about the nature of their dragon based on all their previous work, and gathering first ideas for vocabulary they may use to describe it.

Review

● Invite the children to share some of their potential vocabulary with the class, discussing its effectiveness in portraying the dragon's nature.

Curriculum objectives
● To compose and rehearse sentences orally (including dialogue), progressively building a varied and rich vocabulary and an increasing range of sentence structures (See Appendix 2).

Resources
Children's notes (from lesson 4)

5: Dragon verse

Introduction

● Ask the children to use their notes to describe their dragon to a partner, trying out some phrases and sentences that they may use in their free-verse poems and discussing these to make any amendments they feel would improve their work.

Whole-class work

● Invite the class to share some of their thoughts following their paired discussions. What changes have been made?
● Talk about the importance of a good opening line. Will we see, hear or smell their dragon first? Or will we learn about its nature before we meet it in the poem?
● Suggest that although UA Fanthorpe chose to use the first-person voice for her dragon, they should write in the third person (the same as Tolkien), in order to have the opportunity to provide an outsider's view of their dragon. Remind them about the importance of punctuation in writing their poems.

Independent work

● Allow time for the children to write their free-verse poems, using a rich and varied vocabulary to describe both the physical appearance and the nature of the dragons they have created.

Review

● Ask the children to select what they think is the best sentence in their poems and invite them to read these out to the rest of the class.

Curriculum objectives
● To extend their range of sentences with more than one clause by using a wider range of conjunctions.

Resources
Photocopiable page 106 'Types of connective'; interactive activity 'Start with the connective' on the CD-ROM; computer access

Grammar and punctuation: Clauses and connectives

Revise
● Carry out starter activity 5 'Start with the connection' with the class.
● Hand out photocopiable page 106 'Types of connective'. Talk about each category, asking what jobs they are doing, for example, qualifying connectives are giving some sort of alternative or suggesting a problem, while emphasising connectives draw attention to something, making more of it. Ask for examples of sentences containing some of the connectives, including those where the connective starts the sentence. Which of the words on the lists would not be used to begin a sentence?
● Use interactive activity 'Start with the connective' on the CD-ROM, asking the children to select the correct words from the drop-down lists to begin each sentence.

Assess
● Encourage the children to write one or more sentences containing a connective from each of the lists, thereby composing sentences with more than one clause. They must also underline the main clause in each sentence. You may wish to differentiate the assessment by asking some of the children to write two sentences for each list and/or write some sentences with three clauses. Encourage them to write at least one sentence where the connective begins the sentence.

Further practice
● Continue to use starter activity 5 'Start with the connection' to consolidate the children's understanding.
● When reading with the children, encourage them to notice where connectives have been used, particularly where they are more unusual.

Curriculum objectives
● To spell further homophones.

Resources
Class list of homophones gathered over time; photocopiable page 108 'Harald and Firestorm: a short scene'

Spelling: Homophones

Revise
● Use starter activity 10 'Homophones', making use of the wide variety of these words that the children have managed to collect.
● Challenge the class to find three-word homophones, such as *to, too, two*; *there, their, they're*; or *he'll, heel, heal* and dictate sentences for them to write, choosing the correct spelling.
● Look again at the homophones on photocopiable page 108 'Harald and Firestorm: a short scene' and talk about those which the children found difficult to choose between. Many adults are still unsure of when to use *affect/effect* and *accept/except*. Explain that *affect* links to the word *affection* so that something which affects us has to do with our feelings, whereas *effect* is when something makes a difference to something else. Can they suggest how the etymology of *accept/except* can help them remember which to choose?

Assess
● Dictate sentences for the children to write, including a range of the homophones they have been working on. Ensure the sentences give a clear indication of the meaning of the homophones to make the choice obvious.

Further practice
● Challenge the children to compose short pieces that include pairs or triplets of homophones. For example: *Two of us went to the café and we ate too much.* or *He'll hurt his heel in those boots and it may take a long time to heal.*

Curriculum objectives
● To increase familiarity with a wide range of books including myths and legends.
● To identify themes and conventions.
● To identify main ideas drawn from more than one paragraph and summarise these.

Resources
Children's completed photocopiable page 104 'Dragonfile' (from week 1, lesson 3); photocopiable page 'St George and the Dragon' on CD-ROM; first verse of the poem 'Not My Best Side' (available online)

Reading: Dragons

Revise

● Ask the class to recall all the dragon stories they have been reading throughout this unit of work and list them on the board. Ask them to classify the stories, for example which were myths, which legends and which fiction. What factual information do they remember (perhaps the Chinese Dragon dances and Viking dragon boats). Which texts did they most enjoy and why? Did any of the stories or information surprise them in any way?

● Talk about the different writing styles they have encountered, such as the more formal style of the traditional legend, the direct style of information texts, the humorous writing in *How to Train Your Dragon*, the chatty and informal style of UA Fanthorpe's poem. What marks the differences between them? They may suggest the choice of vocabulary, the sentence structure or the inclusion of direct speech.

● Ask the children to look at their work on photocopiable page 104 'Dragonfile', which they completed at the very start of this half-term, listing what they knew at that time about dragons. Allow them some time to read through the sheets quietly.

Assess

● This assessment is in two parts and should take place on separate days. For the first part of the assessment, ask the children to use the questions from photocopiable page 104 'Dragonfile' to write about the new knowledge they have gained from their reading over the half-term. They are likely to need more space than is available on the sheet, so encourage them to write their answers to the questions on a separate piece of paper, leaving a spare line between each answer. If you wish, you can require the children to answer in complete sentences, allowing you to assess their punctuation and sentence structure.

● For the second part of the assessment, ask the children to consider the writing styles of three of the text types they have been reading: the legend of St George, *How to Train Your Dragon* and the poem 'Not My Best Side'.

● Explain to the class that they will be comparing the writing styles of the three texts, looking for what identifies them as a particular text type and how the writers have used language to engage and interest their readers. Give the children the photocopiable page 'St George and the Dragon' from the CD-ROM and also display the first verse of the poem 'Not My Best Side' on the board. You could read the opening chapter of *How to Train Your Dragon* as a reminder if you wish.

● For each text, invite them to think about: *How you would describe the writing – the choice of vocabulary, the sentence structure, is it funny, serious, informative or something else?; What it is about the writing that makes it different from the others?; What kind of reader would enjoy the text?; What has each writer done to engage and interest the reader?*

● Then compare the texts by asking: *How do they differ from each other? Is there anything that is the same about them? Which writing style did you most enjoy, and why?*

Further practice

● Using the questions on photocopiable page 104 'Dragonfile', have a class discussion about how much the children have learned from their reading. In what ways has their knowledge about dragons extended and which were their favourite texts?

Curriculum objectives

● To compose and rehearse sentences orally (including dialogue), progressively building a varied and rich vocabulary and an increasing range of sentence structures (See Appendix 2).
● To choose nouns or pronouns appropriately for clarity and cohesion and to avoid repetition.
● To use fronted adverbials.
● To use commas after fronted adverbials.
● To use and punctuate direct speech.
● To indicate possession by using the possessive apostrophe with plural nouns.

Resources

Photocopiable page 'St George and the Dragon' from the CD-ROM; first verse of the poem 'Not My Best Side' (available online)

Writing: Dragons

Revise

● Talk with the class about the kind of writing usually found in diary entries, identifying key features. For example, being written in the first person, giving one person's point of view about events, including direct speech to record what people said, usually but not exclusively being written for the writer alone.
● Explain that sometimes the writers of diaries intend that their writing will be read by others, such as the fictional monk they used who recorded the events on Lindisfarne. Politicians and others in the public eye often write diaries or journals in this way, many of which are published for people to buy. Ask the children why this could be, such as the writers wanting their opinion on people and events to be shared and understood.

Assess

● Explain to the children that they will write a diary entry in role as either Princess Sadra or St George, from the story on photocopiable page 'St George and the Dragon' from the CD-ROM.
● Give the children copies of the story to read to themselves in order to refresh their memories of the events. Also, read them the first verse of the poem 'Not My Best Side' as an example of how things were seen from the dragon's perspective.
● Allow them some time to talk with a partner about their choice of character, how they might view the situation and what their feelings might be at different points in the series of events.
● Explain that they will choose their own writing style for their diary entry. Will they write in a humorous way or be very serious about the events? Will they imagine that they are writing only for themselves or ultimately for a wider audience? Talk about how, because the story is a legend, they should include those elements that are historical fact, such as names and places, but that beyond that they can use their imagination. They should enjoy creating short snatches of dialogue, and may give the dragon a voice if they wish. They can extend the story beyond the main events, to include things that happened before or after, remembering that everything is to be seen from their character's point of view. This will include writing about their thoughts and feelings as well as chronicling events.
● Inform the class that you will be looking for a well-told story that uses interesting and engaging vocabulary, making their character's perspective and personality clear. They must include some direct speech, take care to use pronouns to avoid repetition and add clarity to their writing, and ensure their punctuation is correct. You will also expect them to include some sentences with fronted adverbials. Remind them to maintain the first person as they write.
● Allow the children some thinking and planning time before they write their diary entries.

Further practice

● Pair the children up so that those who wrote as the Princess share their writing with those who wrote as St George, to compare their versions of events.
● Invite the children to read out a section of their diary for others to guess who they are from what they say. What clues gave it away?
● Find examples of a variety of diaries to share with the children, discussing the writers' styles and opinions on the events and people they write about.

Dragonfile

■ What do you know about dragons? Answer the questions to get you thinking.

1. What stories do you know containing dragons? _____

_____

2. Write the names of any dragons you know _____

_____

3. What do dragons look like? _____

_____

4. What do dragons eat? _____

_____

5. How do dragons move? _____

_____

6. What sounds do dragons make? _____

_____

7. Where do dragons live? _____

_____

8. What makes dragons different from other creatures? _____

_____

9. What words might describe a dragon's personality? _____

_____

10. Do you think dragons are real? Why, or why not? _____

_____

I can answer questions about what I know about dragons.

How did you do?

Name: _____

Dragon words

■ On the dragon's scales, build a collection of words, phrases and pieces of information about dragons.
Add to it as you discover more.

I can select and record vocabulary and information from my reading and discussion to use in my own writing.

How did you do?

Types of connective

■ Here are lists of categorised connectives.

Qualifying connectives	Emphasising connectives
although	above all
unless	in particular
except	especially
if	indeed
yet	clearly
as long as	obviously

Contrasting connectives	Illustrating connectives
whereas	for example
alternatively	including
instead of	such as
unlike	for instance

Comparing connectives	Additional connectives
equally	and
similarly	also
like	as well as
in the same way	furthermore

Family values

■ Complete these phrases to summarise Hiccup's relationships with
Old Wrinkly and Stoick, giving reasons for your opinions.

Hiccup is most like _____ because _____

_____

Hiccup is least like _____ because _____

_____

Old Wrinkly thinks that Hiccup _____

_____

_____

_____

Stoick thinks that Hiccup _____

_____

_____

_____

Hiccup thinks that _____

_____

_____

_____

I can summarise character relationships and give reasons
for my opinions.

How did you do?

Harald and Firestorm: a short scene

- Underline the correct homophones in this short playscript.

Harald is talking to his dragon, Firestorm. No-one else can hear.

Harald *(despondently)*	I don't know **weather/whether** you'll ever do as I say, Firestorm.
Firestorm *(complaining)*	If you **ball/bawl** at me, I'll pretend **not/knot** to **here/hear** you.
Harald	OK, but let's make it **plain/plane**. You have to **accept/except** that I am your master.
Firestorm	That doesn't sound very **fare/fair** to me.
Harald *(defiantly)*	Well, I'm sorry about that. But if you don't obey me, it will **affect/effect** my **whole/hole** future. Not to mention yours, too.
Firestorm *(complaining again)*	You **grown/groan** too much.
Harald *(losing his you patience)*	Give me some **piece/peace**, you disobedient creature! When we **meet/meat** the others and you do what want, I'll be **scene/seen** as a failure!
Firestorm	It's **not/knot** my fault you **mist/missed** your chance to choose a different dragon.
Harald	Stop sulking, Firestorm. The **mane/main** thing is that for both our sakes, we make a **grate/great** impression at the competition.
Firestorm *(confidently)*	Don't worry young Viking. I'll show them **who's/whose** best.

I can identify correct homophones.

How did you do?

Get the apostrophe right

■ Put possessive apostrophes in these sentences to show they are written in the singular.

The ships prow was decorated with a dragons head.

The dragons claws were as sharp as knives.

The chiefs helmet had imposing horns.

The sailors oars gave him blisters on his hands.

The boy was afraid when he saw the Vikings ship.

The Vikings name for his ship was 'wave-breaker'.

■ Place the possessive apostrophe in these sentences to show they are written in the plural.

The Vikings beards were long and straggly.

The ships oars looked like a hundred spiders legs.

The Vikings ships cut through the waves like huge wooden monsters.

The people fled from the dragons fiery breath.

The marauding Vikings ignored the Britons cries for mercy.

■ Now write two sentences of your own about Vikings, one with a possessive apostrophe in the singular and one in the plural.

I. _____

_____

_____

2. _____

_____

_____

I can use the possessive apostrophe to show both singular and plural.

How did you do?

Viking ship plan

■ Use this sheet to write down your ideas for a description of a Viking ship on display in a museum.

How old is the ship? _____

What is it made of? _____

What size is it? _____

How was it powered? _____

How many people would it carry? _____

What special features does it have? _____

_____

Where was it found? _____

When was it found? _____

Who was the original owner? _____

Where did it sail from and to? _____

■ Now write some words, phrases and ideas you might use when you describe the ship.

_____

_____

_____

_____

_____

_____

_____

I can use my knowledge to plan a descriptive text.

How did you do?

PHOTOCOPIABLE   ■SCHOLASTIC
www.scholastic.co.uk

Boudicca our queen

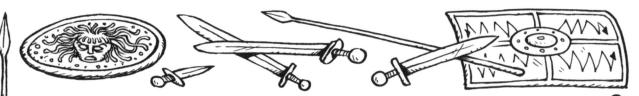

News has arrived in our village that our courageous leader, Queen Boudicca, has died. No longer will we see her tall figure and flaming red hair. No longer do we have this brave woman as our protector and guide.

In the days when her husband, Prasutagus was king, there were amongst us Iceni, those who did not agree with the arrangement he made with the invading Romans. In return for being left in peace, we were obliged to follow Roman ways, which were strange to us. But when Prasutagus died and Boudicca became queen, she rebelled against the Roman rulers, and many Iceni tribesfolk supported her. I was one of those loyal followers, for I was most unhappy obeying our conquerors.

Brave Boudicca trained us in warfare, armed us and hatched a plan to attack the Roman garrison at Camulodunum. We marched for two days until we reached the town, which looked very different to our villages. No simple thatched huts for the Romans – they lived in stone houses and had built huge public buildings in their own style. But defeating them was easy. The Romans had become comfortable in our country and Camulodunum was home to old soldiers long past fighting.

Boudicca's plan was to set fire to the town and this we did. The people fled to hide in the great temple of their emperor Claudius, and there many hundreds of them died. I confess I was sorry for the women and children, but they were our enemies after all. I myself was injured in the battle and was forced to return to my home village while Boudicca led our remaining brave warriors to lay siege to the cities of Londinium and Verulamium. It was at this last battle that our leader lost her life. There is no news of how she met her fate; perhaps it will never be known. But her memory will live long in the Iceni tribe she led so fiercely. For us, her bravery will long be remembered and her name will never die.

Normans

The Bayeux Tapestry and the Domesday Book, the two key texts used for this half-term's work, are very different from those texts the children have encountered so far. Both primary historical documents, particular skills are needed to interpret them, and the children will learn that the bias of the writer has to be taken into consideration when reading factual texts. They will also work on monologues, including Marriott Edgar's 'The Battle of Hastings' which presents the challenge of using colloquial English. The children will write narrative versions of part of the tapestry and create their own pictorial story to which they will add a narrative and later use this to write a monologue. They will use the Domesday Book as a stimulus to create a personal contemporary version of their own.

Expected prior learning
- Can use a dictionary.
- Can discuss a text and poems.
- Can infer characters' thoughts and feelings.
- Can understand the features of narrative text.
- Can understand and use punctuation for direct speech.
- Can plan their own stories.
- Can comment appropriately on other people's work.
- Can use joined handwriting.
- Can identify rhyme.

Overview of progression
- The children will learn how to interpret wordless pictorial text and develop an understanding of the work that words have to do to provide the same information. They will realise that opinions can be inferred from the position of the writer of factual texts.
- They will use dictionaries to look for meanings, revise possessive apostrophes and the perfect form of verbs. They will learn to spell some words that are often misspelled. By self- and peer-assessment they will use their growing knowledge and understanding of grammar, punctuation and composition to suggest and make changes when editing work.

Creative context
- There are obvious links to a study of the Normans in history.
- The Bayeux Tapestry can link to the study of art history and the children can be asked to try some basic embroidery.
- Scenes from the tapestry or scenarios relating to the Domesday Book could be interpreted at greater length in dramatic form.
- Timelines of events can be linked to work in mathematics.

Preparation
Before starting this unit you should familiarise yourself with the basic story of the Bayeux Tapestry, the Norman invasion and the Battle of Hastings. It would be beneficial for you to select and view relevant websites, such as the Museum of Reading and the National Archives.

You will also need:
Online images of the Bayeux Tapestry and the Domesday Book; plain paper; dictionaries; individual whiteboards and pens; visualiser (if possible); wordless picture book; felt-tipped pens, coloured pens, highlighter pens; scissors; image of your choice for oral storytelling; internet access; a free-verse poem of your choice; mixing bowl and spoon.

On the CD-ROM you will find:
Media resource 'Pictorial storytelling'; interactive activities 'We done that', 'That is perfect'; photocopiable pages 'Domesday Book', 'The Battle of Hastings', 'Norman and Saxon', 'William of Malmesbury's account of the Battle of Hastings'

■SCHOLASTIC

Chapter at a glance

An overview of the chapter. For curriculum objective codes, please see pages 8–10.

Week	Lesson	Curriculum objectives	Summary of activities	Outcomes
1	1	RC: 1, 2, 9, 14	Children introduced to and discuss and interpret images of the Bayeux Tapestry. Complete KWL grid to guide further learning.	• Can complete KWL grids, recording current knowledge and what they want to learn about the subject.
	2	RC: 11 WC: 1, 2	Study a scene from the Bayeux Tapestry, deciding on characters' thoughts and speeches, rehearsing orally and writing as a playscript.	• Can discuss, rehearse and write playscripts which are practised, performed and discussed.
	3	WC: 16	Suggest speeches for tapestry characters. Consider differences between correct and incorrect use of grammar in sentence construction.	• Can understand and demonstrate orally appropriate use of formal and informal grammar in sentence structure.
	4	RC: 2 WC: 1	Establish link between tapestry and comics. Make comic strip of event with speech bubbles, call-outs and text boxes. Watch animated tapestry.	• Can establish link between tapestry and comics, create comic strip of tapestry event, understand value of written language.
	5	WC: 3	Consider, discuss and devise questions for the tapestry makers. Write up list of questions and use to role play answers.	• Can consider needlewomen's perspectives, write list of questions and use in role play.
2	1	RC: 3, 14 WT: 5	Identify and discuss value of words when added to visual texts. Gather vocabulary to describe Tapestry scenes, checking spellings in dictionaries.	• Can discuss and write potential vocabulary for settings, character and plot for use in narrative retelling part of Tapestry story.
	2	WC: 3, 19	Mime, then add dialogue to a character's actions. Write it as a short piece, including correct punctuation.	• Can demonstrate understanding of punctuating direct speech by writing piece about tapestry character, including dialogue.
	3	WC: 5	Discuss ways to begin a section of the tapestry story as a class and in groups. Make initial notes.	• Can form ideas for how to structure narrative version of scenes from Bayeux Tapestry, with notes to guide planning.
	4	WC: 7, 8	Use starter activity 14 'Edit it'. Use plans to draft Bayeux Tapestry narrative, editing as the writing develops.	• Can use plans to aid writing first drafts, which are edited and completed.
	5	WT: 7, 8 WC: 7	Write final versions of their narratives in clear joined handwriting. Share with a partner.	• Can write final narratives in legible, consistent handwriting.
3	1	WC: 1, 2	Look at ways of pictorial storytelling. Read a wordless picture book. Discuss ideas for writing stories in pictures and words.	• Can discuss and decide on stories to be told. • Can note initial ideas about characters and scenes.
	2	WC: 5	Look at storyboard examples. Use notes to make storyboard of own story.	• Can plan key scenes in the form of a storyboard.
	3	WT: 4 WC: 16, 18, 20	Revise possessive apostrophe. Use starter activity 6 'One or more?'. Learn about exceptions including its.	• Can demonstrate understanding of the use of possessive apostrophes by correct completion of sheet and showing given examples on whiteboards.
	4	WC: 12	Revise perfect form of verbs. Use starter activity 12 'The perfect verb'. Complete sheet 'The perfect verb'. Give examples of sentences using perfect tense.	• Can show, by completing sheet and giving oral responses, their understanding of the perfect form of verbs.
	5	WC: 5	Read storyboards, decide on size and form for final versions of stories. Draw illustrations to include speech bubbles and discuss difficulties.	• Can complete pictorial elements of stories.
4	1	WC: 3	Using teacher modelling for guidance, children use their picture stories for oral storytelling to a partner. Feedback given, discussed and noted.	• Can complete all picture stories and use for oral storytelling; make notes for reference when writing accompanying narrative text.
	2	WC: 5	Teacher models drafting written narrative for picture. Reminder of what to include. Children write narratives for each illustration.	• Can complete drafts of narrative text for each scene and discuss helpfulness of partner response.
	3	WT: 3, 6	Identify the patterns 'ce', 'ff', 'ss', 'ei' in the spellings of tricky words. Practise spelling the words.	• Can highlight, group and test words with common spelling patterns.
	4	WT: 5 WC: 7, 8, 9	Review elements to consider when editing. Edit own work and compare with partner, offering positive feedback and constructive suggestions.	• Can review and edit first drafts of narratives.
	5	WT: 7, 8	Write final text. Discuss reading, planning and writing process. Complete KWL grids started in first week.	• Can complete stories combining pictures and text, and decide how to share them.

Chapter at a glance

Week	Lesson	Curriculum objectives	Summary of activities	Outcomes
5	1	RWR: 1 RC: 2, 13, 16 WC: 1	Look at images of Domesday Book. Read 'Domesday Book' sheet, summarise paragraphs orally and in writing. View book online, investigating place names.	• Can summarise paragraphs orally and in writing about the Domesday Book.
	2	RC: 3	Look at medieval words no longer in use. Guess then check word meanings to complete 'Word investigations' sheet.	• Can use dictionaries to find meanings of words taken from the Domesday Book. • Can write and discuss definitions.
	3	RC: 11, 16	Watch National Archive videos depicting Norman and Saxon viewpoints on Domesday. Groups discuss and class debates in role. Discuss value as historical document.	• Can make inferences from videos, and develop deeper understanding of effects of Domesday on those involved.
	4	WC: 2	Compare Domesday with modern Census; look up census information for your area. Complete 'My Domesday information' sheet and discuss.	• Can complete 'My Domesday information' sheets and discuss feelings about it as a class.
	5	WT: 7, 8 WC: 6	Consider handwriting in the Domesday Book. Write up information from lesson 4 as own modern version of the book, using best handwriting.	• Can write individual personal Domesday Books, using paragraphs with appropriate subheadings.
6	1	RC: 7, 8 WC: 1	Read and discuss Marriott Edgar's poem 'The Battle of Hastings', noting language effects and finding the facts.	• Can identify and articulate the effectiveness of the poet's deliberate language choices, and read the poem aloud.
	2	RC: 6	Read and discuss Rudyard Kipling's 'Norman and Saxon'. Groups rehearse a verse each then perform as whole class and evaluate.	• Can make comparisons with previous day's poem.
	3	WC: 1	Identify key features of monologues. Discuss and list as a checklist. Recall known forms of poetry.	• Can write and discuss a list of key features for a monologue for use in next lesson.
	4	WC: 3, 7	Use checklists and pictorial stories from Week 4 to draft, rehearse orally, and share monologues. Partners comment on each other's work.	• Can edit and redraft monologues, ready for final draft.
	5	WT: 7, 8	Write final drafts of monologues. Share and discuss with partner who selects their favourite part to read to class. Discuss writing process.	• Can produce final drafts in best handwriting and discuss writing process.

Background knowledge

Bayeux Tapestry: 11th century embroidery created by the Normans chronicling the events leading up to the invasion of England, including the Battle of Hastings in 1066.

Domesday Book: Survey carried out in 1086 under the orders of William the Conqueror, listing land, buildings, people and domesticated animals and used for gathering taxes. Originally spelled 'Doomsday'. Not all of the country was included, for example Northumberland.

Freeze frame: Drama technique where children freeze an action, showing a character frozen in time, with appropriate facial expression and body position.

KWL grid: A simple grid for recording what is Known about something, what the learner Wants to know about it, and afterwards, what they have Learned.

Participles: Verbs in English have two participles, called 'present participle' (such as, *walking, taking*) and 'past participle' (such as, *walked, taken*).

Perfect form of verbs: The perfect form of a verb generally calls attention to the consequences of a prior situation. It is formed by taking the past participle of the verb (such as, *thrown, taken, helped*); adding the verb *have* before it (for example, *she has helped*). It can also be combined with the continuous (for example, *he has been reading*).

■ SCHOLASTIC

Week 1 lesson plans

Set in the time of the Norman invasion, the children start this half-term's unit by looking at the pictorial text of the Bayeux Tapestry. They will consider what they already know about it and begin to interpret the scenes. They will put words into the mouths of characters, and use these to write short playscripts. They will compare the use of colloquial language for speech and formal written language. Also, they will use the comic-strip style of the tapestry to add speech bubbles and text boxes to chosen scenes. Finally, they look at the creation of the tapestry from the needlewomen's point of view, formulating questions they would ask them.

1: Introducing the Bayeux Tapestry

Introduction

- Ask the children if they have heard or know anything of the Bayeux Tapestry.
- Explain that it is a large piece of needlework, 70 metres long by 50 centimetres wide. Although it is called a *tapestry* (which is a picture woven as a piece of fabric is made), it is actually an *embroidery*, which is a picture stitched on to a piece of ready-made cloth. Made over a thousand years ago, it can still be seen in Bayeux, France. It is important because it records the events leading up to the Norman invasion of England, and the Battle of Hastings in 1066, when William of Normandy defeated Harold of England and became king.

Whole-class work

- Show the class images of the tapestry on the whiteboard. (These can be sourced from an image search or dedicated tapestry websites, such as that at: www.bayeuxtapestry.org.uk.)
- Select one image to focus on and ask if the children can work out what is happening. Ask what makes it difficult for us to understand. They may suggest the lack of words, or that the writing in some images is in a different language. They may feel that the artistic style is not one we are used to, making it difficult to interpret. Explain that when the tapestry was made, few people could read so visual depictions of significant events were an important way to convey information.
- Ask what the children know about the Battle of Hastings. Explain that it is perhaps the best-known date in English history, when William's invading Normans fought Harold's Saxon soldiers, defeating them and killing Harold. After this, England was ruled by a French king.

Independent work

- Explain that they will be finding out more about the tapestry, the battle and the Normans. To guide their learning, they will complete a KWL grid, where they will record what they already Know about these things, what they Want to know and later they will record what they have Learned.
- Hand out photocopiable page 136 'KWL grid' for the children to complete. It may help if the middle section is explained as those things that puzzle you, or that you are curious about.

> **Differentiation**
> - Reassure children who have little knowledge of English history that this is not important, but they may have more questions to consider which will guide their learning.

Review

- Encourage the children to share some of their questions with the class, noting common threads.

SPRING 2

WEEK 1

Expected outcomes
- All children can infer characters' thoughts from a visual image and use this to write appropriate dialogue. They can recognise grammatically incorrect speech patterns.
- Most children can form questions about what they have read and write correct versions of grammatically incorrect sentence structures.
- Some children can inject a sense of character into the dialogue they write, showing a greater insight into characters' thoughts, feelings and motives.

Curriculum objectives
- To read books that are structured in different ways and read for a range of purposes.
- To listen to and discuss a wide range of fiction, poetry, plays, non-fiction and reference books or textbooks.
- To check that the text makes sense to them, discussing their understanding and explaining the meaning of words in context.
- To identify how language, structure, and presentation contribute to meaning.

Resources
Images of the Bayeux Tapestry (available online); photocopiable page 136 'KWL grid'

SCHOLASTIC

100 ENGLISH LESSONS · YEAR 4 ■ 115

Curriculum objectives
● To draw inferences such as inferring characters' feelings, thoughts and motives from their actions, and justify inferences with evidence.
● To discuss writing similar to that which they are planning to write in order to understand and learn from its structure, grammar and vocabulary.
● To discuss and record ideas.

Resources
Selected scene from the Bayeux Tapestry (available online)

2: Hidden clues

Introduction
● Show the class your chosen scene from the Bayeux Tapestry. Select one with several different characters, perhaps one including Harold and William. Explain that because the story is told visually, we must decide for ourselves what the characters might be thinking or saying to each other.

Paired work
● Encourage the children to talk with a partner about what the characters in the scene could be thinking, and what they might be saying to each other. Suggest that these may not be the same – a character may be thinking one thing, but saying something entirely different.
● After their discussion, the children should improvise and rehearse a short scene, speaking the characters' words.

Independent work
● Allow time for the children to write down their ideas of what each character is both thinking and saying, in the form of a short playscript, with the thoughts forming the basis for stage directions. Remind them of the playscripts they wrote when working on dragons (in the last half term) to refresh their memories about playscript conventions.

Review
● Invite the children to swap their scripts with a different partner, and to read each others' work aloud, as in a read-through. After practising a few times, they should perform these for the class. How much similarity and difference was there in the children's interpretations?

Curriculum objectives
● To learn the grammar for Year 4 in Appendix 2.

Resources
Another scene from the Bayeux Tapestry (including several different characters); photocopiable page 137 'We done good'; interactive activity 'We done that' on the CD-ROM; computer access

3: The boys done well!

Introduction
● Show the class your chosen scene from the Bayeux Tapestry – perhaps one with the cooks or soldiers. Invite the children to identify what is happening in it.

Whole-class work
● Ask the children to imagine the conversations that might have gone on in the scene. What sorts of thing might the characters have been saying to each other?
● After taking suggestions, write on the board: *I think William done a good job* as one example of what might have been said. Ask the children if they can see anything wrong with the sentence. They should identify the grammatical error: that *done* should be *did*.
● Explain that sometimes we do not speak grammatically correctly, often making the wrong verb choice. This can be useful to use to convey character when writing direct speech, but in normal written English it is incorrect.

Independent work
● Hand out to the children photocopiable page 137 'We done good!' and invite them to complete the sheet individually to assess their grammar.

> **Differentiation**
> ● Be sensitive to those children whose dialect includes this form. Reinforce the difference between formal and informal and the times when each are appropriate and acceptable.

Review
● With the class use the interactive activity 'We done that' on the CD-ROM, asking them to identify the verbs used incorrectly for you to click and highlight. Invite them to say or write down what the correct sentences should be.

Curriculum objectives
● To read books that are structured in different ways and read for a range of purposes.
● To discuss writing similar to that which they are planning to write in order to understand and learn from its structure, grammar and vocabulary.

Resources
Bayeux Tapestry scene (used in lesson 3); plain paper folded to make six squares; animation of Bayeux Tapestry (available online)

4: Comic-strip history

Introduction
● Show the children several more scenes from the Bayeux Tapestry.
● Ask them if they know of a modern text type that uses strips of pictures in a similar way to tell a story, and establish a link to comics. What comics do the children know?

Whole-class work
● Ask the class what is missing from the tapestry that they would expect to find in a modern comic strip, identifying speech bubbles, call-out shapes and text boxes. Discuss what sort of writing goes in each of these, such as speech in the bubbles, sound-effect words in the call-outs and information in the boxes.
● Using the same scene from the tapestry as lesson 3, ask the children to freeze-frame the characters, choosing several to speak their thoughts aloud.

Independent work
● Using a sheet of paper folded to form six squares, invite the children to draw simple outline sketches of an event from the tapestry, adding their own speech bubbles, call-outs and text boxes. Explain that they will need to spread the event over several boxes, as in a comic, although the tapestry fits all the aspects of an event into one scene.

Review
● Show the class the animated version of the tapestry (available online), which travels through the story, replacing the Latin wording with English translations. Ask: *Does the captioning make it easier to understand?*

Curriculum objectives
● To write by composing and rehearsing sentences orally, including dialogue, building a varied and rich vocabulary and a range of sentence structures (See Appendix 2).

Resources
Bayeux Tapestry scene (used in lesson 3)

5: Tell me about the tapestry

Introduction
● Encourage the children to imagine they were one of the people who made the tapestry and to think of the work involved in creating such an intricate and large work of art. The needlewomen would have had to follow a designer's plan of the entire story and made sure their work matched that of the other women in every way. Ask for suggestions about their working days, and how they might have felt about helping to create the tapestry.

Paired work
● Invite the children to discuss with a partner the questions they might ask one of the needlewomen about her work, the events she is helping to depict and her feelings about the task. Explain that no one knows for sure if the tapestry was made by French or English embroiderers, so they must choose, as the woman's views would differ depending upon her nationality (she was either on the winning or losing side).

Independent work
● Allow time for the children to compile a set of questions they would ask one of the tapestry makers.

Review
● Arrange the children into different pairings and invite them to ask each other questions from their list, with each partner taking their turn to answer in role. Reassure them that there is no right answer, so they can use their imaginations. Encourage the children to ask you some of their questions and answer in role yourself.

Week 2 lesson plans

The children will be looking in greater detail at scenes from the Bayeux Tapestry this week, not simply to retell the story, but to interpret events from the various points of view of depicted characters. They will select characters to whom they will give appropriate dialogue. They will write their character's words in correctly punctuated direct speech. They will plan, discuss, draft and write a narrative version of the scene, after choosing a good starting point. In order to develop their editing skills, the children will begin to work on editing as they write, a paragraph at a time. Final drafts will be written in their best handwriting.

I: A picture speaks a thousand words...

Introduction
● Present the class with the following puzzle: *Why are radio and chapter books the same, but different from TV, comics and films?* Take their suggestions, agreeing on the answer that the former don't have pictures, while the latter do. Ask what difference this makes to us as readers/viewers. What do the visual images add to our understanding of what we read and watch?
● Refer to the Bayeux Tapestry, which is a story told in pictures. Ask: *What difference would it make to our understanding if there were words?*

Whole-class work
● Explain to the children that they will be using scenes from the tapestry to write a narrative, telling the story in their own words. As it is a long story, they will be concentrating on just one series of linked events. This means they will be able to include details and focus on characters, interpreting their thoughts as well as giving them some dialogue to enliven their story.
● Show the class the series of scenes you have selected. Can they identify which part of the story this is, and explain what is happening? What characters can they see and what are they doing?
● Under the headings *Setting, Characters* and *Plot* begin to gather suggestions from the class for vocabulary the children might use in writing their narratives. Encourage them to think of adjectives and adverbs, phrases with fronted adverbials, similes and samples of dialogue for particular characters. Suggest the words *hawk, estate, lance, oath, embark, invade, nobles,* for them to include to add authenticity. They can use dictionaries to check meanings.

Paired work
● Invite the children to work with a partner, in order to study the selected scenes and write down their own ideas for words and phrases they might use in their writing, as well as those already suggested. Explain that they should write these in note form under the three headings and check spellings they are unsure of in a dictionary.

Differentiation
● In selecting the scenes for the narrative, take your group's interests and sensibilities into consideration. For example, some children may find the gory battle scenes distressing, while others may have little interest in the cooks preparing food. If you are able to print and copy scenes, you may be able to offer children a choice.

Review
● Show the children the series of scenes again, this time adding your own narration to the events, as in a voice-over. Ask the children if your version bore any resemblance to their own interpretations. What were the similarities and differences? Ask for examples of both.

Curriculum objectives
● To use and punctuating direct speech.
● To compose and rehearse sentences orally (including dialogue), progressively building a varied and rich vocabulary and an increasing range of sentence structures (See Appendix 2).

Resources
Interactive whiteboard screen containing short unpunctuated text, including dialogue

2: Hello, Normans speaking

Introduction
● Select one of the characters from the scenes worked on in lesson 1 and mime their actions for the class, using varied facial expressions to indicate thoughts. Ask the children to suggest some speech for your character at different points, and then act it out again using the suggested speeches.

Paired work
● Invite the children to mime their own choice of characters from the scenes, adding speech to their actions. Select several to share with the class.

Whole-class work
● Revise punctuation for direct speech, using your character's lines as an example and adding description. For example: 'This armour is about as comfortable as wearing bedsprings,' Edwin complained. 'I really hope it doesn't rain, or it'll go rusty.' Once on his horse, however, his spirits rose. 'Ah, my trusty sword. Sharp enough to do damage to those miserable Saxons!'

Independent work
● Encourage the children to write a short piece of dialogue for their own character, using accurate punctuation.

Differentiation
● Children commonly struggle with the concept of inverted commas and tend to include words such as 'he said' inside the marks. Remind them that the only words to go inside the quotation marks are the words actually spoken – just like those in speech bubbles.

Review
● Display the prepared passage and work together to punctuate it correctly.

Curriculum objectives
● In narratives, to create settings, characters and plot.

Resources
Images of selected scenes from the Bayeux Tapestry (from lesson 1); children's vocabulary notes (from lesson 1); children's written dialogue (from lesson 2); individual whiteboards

3: Planning the narrative

Introduction
● Explain that as they plan their narrative versions of the story, they will be like the original tapestry-makers, stitching together the settings, characters and plot. How will they start? Show them the scenes again, with no comment.

Whole-class work
● Talk about different ways the story could begin, for example with a description of the setting, opening event, or with the thoughts or words of one of the characters. Work on the opening scene together, gathering suggestions.

Group work
● Organise the class into groups of 3–4, to look together at the story, discussing ways they could narrate it and making notes on whiteboards.
● To guide their discussion, pose the following questions: Which characters will you focus on? What is their role? What are their names? Where is this part of the story set? Is there more than one setting? How can paragraphs help you divide the story and link the scenes together? How might you begin your narrative?

Independent work
● Invite the children to spend time selecting from their notes those ideas they will use in their plans, writing these on paper to use in the lesson tomorrow.

Review
● As a class, share some of the points raised in the discussions. Remind the children that they have some thinking time overnight to consider their plans.

Curriculum objectives
● To assess the effectiveness of their own and others' writing and suggest improvements.
● To propose changes to grammar and vocabulary to improve consistency.

Resources
Children's notes (from lesson 3); photocopiable page 77 'Editing checklist'

4: Drafting the narrative

Introduction
● With the class, use starter activity 14 'Edit it'.

Whole-class work
● Inform the children that they will be using their planning from the previous lesson to write and edit a first draft of their narrative version of the scenes from the Bayeux Tapestry.
● Explain that as they will also be editing their draft today, they should re-read as they are writing, perhaps at the end of each paragraph or two, checking for ways to improve their work, as with the starter activity.
● Recap how to include fronted adverbials and how to correctly punctuate dialogue, reminding them to be consistent in their use of pronouns.

Independent work
● Allow time for the children to individually write their drafts, using their plans.

> **Differentiation**
> ● If children are experiencing difficulty with the editing process they may find it helpful to use photocopiable page 77 'Editing checklist', which they used in the Science fiction unit. Encouraging the children to re-read and edit as they write will help them to see ongoing redrafting as an essential part of the writing process, and not something which is simply bolted on at the end.

Review
● Discuss with the class how useful their planning was and how they coped with the ongoing editing.

Curriculum objectives
● To use the diagonal and horizontal strokes that are needed to join letters and understand which letters, when adjacent to one another, are best left unjoined.
● To increase the legibility, consistency and quality of their handwriting.
● To assess the effectiveness of their own and others' writing and suggest improvements.

Resources
Children's edited drafts of their Bayeux Tapestry narratives (from lesson 4)

5: The final narrative

Introduction
● Ask the class what differences there will be between the edited drafts and final versions of their writing. Agree that the presentation of the final versions will be neater and therefore easier for others to read. However, this does not preclude them from making any extra changes that they decide would improve their work, as they write.
● Remind them about using the right sitting position, holding the pen correctly and angling the paper in order to produce their best handwriting.

Independent work
● Encourage the children to work quietly, writing the final drafts.

Paired work
● As they finish, invite pairs of children to share their narratives, comparing how they have each retold the story.

> **Differentiation**
> ● Bear in mind that left-handed writers can be prone to use an incorrect pencil grip, often hooking their hand around their work in order to see what they have written. This can be largely corrected by using the correct sitting position, which tends to be directly facing the desk, not sitting at an angle, instead angling the paper at 45 degrees.

Review
● Invite the children to comment positively on their partner's work, perhaps selecting particularly effective passages to read aloud to the class. Finally, vote on whether they prefer a pictorial or written version of the story, asking for reasons for their preference.

Week 3 lesson plans

Following on from studying the Bayeux Tapestry, this week the children will be creating their own pictorial story. They may use a known story or invent their own. Through discussion they will develop their characters and the sequence of events they will include. They will plan their scenes in the form of a storyboard, having first looked at examples. As they will be including writing to go with their pictures, they will revise the use of the possessive apostrophe and look at the perfect form of verbs. They will finish the week by drawing the final drafts of their pictorial stories, including speech bubbles for some of the characters.

1: Create your own tapestry

Introduction
- Show the class the photographs of the mosaic and stained glass window from 'Pictorial storytelling' on the CD-ROM, which show different forms of pictorial storytelling. You may also wish to source images of a cave painting of a hunt, narrative paintings, Inuit story sticks or the willow pattern story.
- Discuss the different ways these artistic forms convey stories.

Whole-class work
- Use a visualiser (if possible) to share with the class a wordless picture book, such as Philippe Dupasquier's *Dear Daddy* or a Jeannie Baker title. As you go through the book, invite the children to tell each part of the story to the class.
- Discuss how and why they were able to interpret the picture books more easily than the earlier examples. They may realise it is to do with familiarity – that we do not possess the necessary knowledge and experience to fully understand pictorial images of the past.
- Explain that using what they have learned from their work on the Bayeux Tapestry, the children will be creating a story, as though designing their own tapestry. In their stories they will incorporate pictures and words, and they will devise, plan, draw, write and evaluate them over the next two weeks. Inform them that today they will choose the story they wish to tell and start to think about the characters and events they will be depicting.
- Advise them that their stories can be real or imaginary. They could use a myth, legend, historical event or religious story they are familiar with or invent a new story of their own.

Group work
- In groups of 4–6 ask the children to discuss possible ideas for their stories, sharing suggestions, beginning to get ideas for the story they will tell. If they are considering stories they already know, they can help by reminding each other of the characters and events.
- Invite the groups to summarise and share the ideas they have with the rest of the class.

Independent work
- Encourage the children to decide on their story and begin to note the main characters and sequence of events. As this will begin as a pictorial story, they will need to think about how many scenes they will need to show the events of the story, in chronological order. Stress that this is early planning which can be changed as the planning process develops.

Review
- Bring the class together to find out what sort of stories the children have chosen. How many are devising their own story? What other stimuli has been selected from those discussed earlier?

Expected outcomes
- All children can plan and create a sequential story using a storyboard, use the possessive apostrophe for singular and plural nouns and the perfect form of verbs.
- Most children can include speech bubbles in their pictorial stories that mostly use possessive apostrophes and the perfect form of verbs accurately.
- Some children can consistently use possessive apostrophes accurately, including knowing when not to use them and have a clear understanding of when and how to use the perfect form of verbs.

Curriculum objectives
- To discuss writing similar to that which they are planning to write in order to understand and learn from its structure, grammar and vocabulary.
- To discuss and record ideas.

Resources
Media resource 'Pictorial storytelling' on the CD-ROM; visualiser (if possible); wordless picture book of your choice; other pictures that tell a story, see Introduction (optional)

Curriculum objectives
● In narratives, to create settings, characters and plot.

Resources
Children's notes (from lesson 1); plain paper folded into quarters or sixths and pencils; examples of storyboards

2: Storyboarding

Introduction

● Show the class several storyboard examples, such as those made for producing films. Introduce the term 'storyboard', and ask what they think their purposes are as part of the planning process. Agree that they are a quick way of organising and outlining the plot and settings, without worrying about the words. Do they notice a similarity to the Bayeux Tapestry?
● Explain that today they will create a storyboard for the stories they devised in lesson 1. They need only do rough sketches in pencil – their detailed pictures and the writing will come later. The main purpose is to plan their scenes, telling the story in order. They may need to use several sheets of paper and should number their scenes. No colour is needed.

Independent work

● Using their notes from the previous lesson, invite the children to sketch out the scenes for their story, forming a linear narrative.

> **Differentiation**
> ● Some of the children may find it difficult to identify their key scenes, ending up with more than they need. Tell them to choose the events that their stories could not do without. Background detail can be included later in the written text.

Review

● Ask the children how many scenes they have made. If they have too many their story will be too long, but too few scenes and they will have more writing to do.

Curriculum objectives
● To indicate possession by using the possessive apostrophe with plural nouns.
● To learn the grammar for Year 4 in Appendix 2.
● To use and understand the grammatical terminology in Appendix 2 accurately and appropriately when discussing their writing and reading.
● To place the possessive apostrophe accurately in words with regular plurals and in words with irregular plurals.

Resources
Individual whiteboards and pens; photocopiable page 138 'Today's offers'; felt-tipped pens or coloured pencils; scissors (optional)

3: Revising the possessive apostrophe

Introduction

● Write *possessive apostrophe* on the board and ask the class what this means. They should be able to explain its meaning, referring to previous work.
● Then write: *girls, girl's, girls'*, and ask for an explanation of the difference between the three. Can anyone suggest a sentence for each form of the word?
● Choose one of the activities from starter activity 6 'One or more?'.

Whole-class work

● Explain that there are some instances where using the possessive apostrophe is more tricky.
● Write on the board: *men, women, children, sheep, cattle, mice* and ask the class how they are similar (they are plural nouns). Explain that because they are already plural, the possessive apostrophe goes after the word, and before the letter 's', for example *the men's hats*.
● Write: *its, hers*. Ask what type of words they are (pronouns). Explain that pronouns don't need apostrophes, for example *The dog wagged its tail; It was hers without a doubt.*

Independent work

● Invite the children to complete photocopiable page 138 'Today's offers'.
● Afterwards, have fun writing correct versions as large signs which can be cut out for display

Review

● Assign the children words of all types requiring possessive apostrophes to write and show you on their whiteboards. Ensure you include examples where no apostrophe is required.

Curriculum objectives
● To use the present perfect form of verbs in contrast to the past tense.

Resources
Photocopiable page 139 'Perfect verbs (1)'; interactive activity 'That is perfect' on the CD-ROM; computer access

4: Perfect verbs

Introduction
● Write on the board: *has, have, had, has been*. Ask the class for anything they notice or know about the words. Some may remember using them to form the perfect forms of verbs in Year 3.
● Recap on the perfect form of verbs, noting that they are linked to another verb and mark relationships of time and cause. Provide reinforcement with the following examples: *He has been working on the farm for years; They had noticed a change in the weather.*

Whole-class work
● With the class, use starter activity 12 'The perfect verb'.
● Use interactive activity 'That is perfect' on the CD-ROM, inviting the children to select the correct option from the drop-down list in order to complete each sentence.

Independent work
● Hand out photocopiable page 139 'Perfect verbs (1)' and encourage the children to complete it individually.

Review
● Invite the children to suggest in what forms of writing they would use the perfect tense of verbs. For each that they suggest, ask for an example of a sentence that might fit that particular form. For example, a report could have *The Saxons had fought bravely.* A first-person diary entry might use *My brother has been driving me mad...* or a piece of dialogue in a story could be *'You have helped me enormously'.*

Curriculum objectives
● In narratives, to create settings, characters and plot.

Resources
Children's storyboards (from earlier in the week); coloured pencils and pens

5: Drawing stories

Introduction
● Allow the children time to look over their storyboards to refresh their memories of their story outline. Explain that today they will be drawing the final versions of their 'tapestries'.

Whole-class work
● Discuss with the class suggestions for the ideal size for their work. Bear in mind that each picture will need to be big enough to show sufficient detail and include some speech bubbles, and that there needs to be space either beside or underneath each picture for one or two paragraphs of writing to be added later. Allow each individual to choose their own size and page arrangement, although you may recommend that two pictures per A4 sheet would probably work best.

Independent work
● Encourage the children to spend the majority of the lesson drawing their illustrations, including some speech bubbles. Ensure they take care to use possessive apostrophes and perfect verb forms correctly.

Review
● At the end of the lesson, find out how far the children have got with their illustrations. They may have not had sufficient time to complete them all. Reassure them that if this is the case they will be able to have extra time next week. Ask them what difficulties they have encountered with the task. How easy is it to tell a story in pictures?

Expected outcomes
● All children can orally rehearse, plan and write narrative text to accompany their pictorial texts. They can identify common spelling patterns.
● Most children can include correctly punctuated dialogue and fronted adverbials. They can usefully review and edit their own and others' work.
● Some children can plan and write their written narrative to significantly enhance their pictorial text. They can consistently spell identified words that are commonly misspelled.

Curriculum objectives
● To compose and rehearse sentences orally (including dialogue), progressively using a varied and rich vocabulary and a range of sentence structures.

Resources
Children's pictorial story scenes (from previous week); an image of your choice to use as a basis for oral storytelling; individual whiteboards and pens

Week 4 lesson plans

Continuing from their work last week, the children will use their pictorial stories as the basis for telling their story orally to a partner, each evaluating the other's work. They will then draft, review, edit and write up a final version of a narrative to accompany each scene of their stories. To finish their work on the tapestry they will revisit the 'KWL grid' completed at the start of the unit to complete the L for Learning section. During the week, they will also work on spelling tricky words in the context of the Norman invasion, with the letter patterns 'ce', 'ff', 'ss' and 'ei'.

1: Tell me a story

Introduction
● Show the class the image you have selected. This could be a *Bayeux Tapestry* scene not previously used or any other image you feel you can effectively use as the basis for a short piece of oral storytelling. Model how to use the image in order to tell the story, including dialogue for one or more of the characters.

Whole-class work
● Invite the children to comment on how you told the story. What was included? Did they notice the dialogue? Can they recall descriptions of the setting or the characters? Were characters' thoughts or feelings mentioned? Were there any particular words they noticed that they thought were good vocabulary choices? Was there a mixture of short and longer sentences and a range of connectives?
● Explain that they are going to use their pictures to tell their story in the same way as you, but to a partner.

Independent work
● Allow the children a few minutes to look over their pictures, considering how they will tell their stories. If there are any children who didn't complete the picture sequence the previous week, then time will need to be allocated for them to do this later in the lesson. However, at this stage they can just use those pictures they have completed.

Paired work
● Invite the children to show their partner their pictures while telling their stories. Partners should comment helpfully. As they work, encourage the children to make notes on their whiteboards that they may find useful for the next stage, which requires them to write the narrative that will accompany the pictures. One way to do this is to ask partners to quickly jot down words, phrases or ideas they thought worked well, while they are listening.

> **Differentiation**
> ● If it has not been possible to find extra time for those children who need to complete their pictures, they should be paired with others in the same situation. This should provide them with extra time to finish their illustrations before rejoining the class for the review.

Review
● Draw the class together and talk about their storytelling experience. How well did they think they told their stories? How much guidance did they take from their pictures? Did other things occur to them while they were speaking? Then ask partners for examples of the things they noted that worked particularly well. Allow the children time to transfer their notes and any other thoughts they have had, onto paper for use later.

Curriculum objectives
● In narratives, to create settings, characters and plot.

Resources
Children's pictorial stories and notes (from lesson 1); your chosen image (from lesson 1)

2: Adding the narrative

Introduction
● With the image you used in lesson 1 for modelling oral storytelling, ask the children to help you compose a first draft of written narrative to accompany it. Remind them of the discussions they had about choosing where to start their retelling of the Bayeux Tapestry scenes and use this to help decide how to begin. Ensure you include some dialogue, well-chosen vocabulary and a range of sentence structures.
● Explain to the children that they will write first drafts of one or two short paragraphs to accompany each of the pictures in their story, using their experiences and notes from the previous lesson to guide them.
● Remind them to include elements of setting, character and plot. Some of their dialogue can be taken from the speech bubbles, but must be correctly punctuated. They should aim to include some fronted adverbials and take care to use pronouns for clarity and cohesion.

Independent work
● Provide time for the children to work individually on drafting the narratives to accompany their pictorial text. They should not work directly onto the finished illustrations, as these are drafts that will be edited before final versions are written at the end of the week.

Review
● Discuss with the class their writing. When writing their narratives, how helpful was the partner work they did yesterday? Ask for examples.

Curriculum objectives
● To spell words which are often misspelled. (See Appendix 1).
● To write from memory simple sentences, dictated by the teacher, that include words and punctuation taught so far.

Resources
Photocopiable page 140 'Some tricky words'

3: Some tricky words

Introduction
● Show the class the following sentences on the interactive whiteboard: *Extreme exercise can make it extremely hard to get your breath. But if you get up early, take regular runs and learn how to breathe properly you could soon become healthier.*
● Ask for suggestions for which words may be the hardest to learn to spell, and underline them.
● Can they see any spelling patterns that could help to make learning these words easier, such as those words starting with 'ex' and those containing 'ea'?

Individual work
● Hand out photocopiable page 140 'Some tricky words' for the children to complete individually. If they are unsure about the tasks, briefly recap the previous activity on the board.

Paired work
● Arrange the children into pairs and ask the partners to compare and discuss their results, before testing each other on the selected words.

Differentiation
● Challenge the more confident spellers to find other words to add to each group of spellings.

Review
● Invite the children to share their word selections with the class, explaining how they grouped them. They should have words with 'ce', 'ff', 'ss' and 'ei'. What tricky words did they find? Draw attention to the word *island*, then tell them one way to remember the spelling is to learn the mnemonic *An island is land surrounded by water.* Conclude by dictating the words individually and in short sentences for the children to write and show you on their whiteboards.

Curriculum objectives
● To assess the effectiveness of their own and others' writing and suggest improvements.
● To propose changes to grammar and vocabulary to improve consistency.
● To proofread for spelling and punctuation errors.
● To use the first two or three letters of a word to check its spelling in a dictionary.

Resources
Children's drafts of their narratives (from earlier in the week); dictionaries

4: Reviewing and editing

Introduction
● Review the work the children have done to arrive at their drafted narratives. Remind them that the purpose is to consider all aspects of their writing and look for ways to improve, so that they produce the best version they can.

Whole-class work
● Ask the children what things they will look for when reviewing their work, listing them on the board. Ensure they do not focus solely on technical aspects, as they also need to consider the quality of writing in their sentence construction and choice of words. They must also consider the amount of space available next to their illustrations.

Independent work
● Invite the children to spend some time reading through their drafts, making any changes they feel are necessary, including using dictionaries to check spellings.

Paired work
● After they have proofread and edited their own work, ask the children to exchange their writing with a partner and encourage each of them to read through the other's work, offering further suggestions as well as making positive comments. Encourage them to ask their partner's opinions on any aspects they are unsure about. For example, they might want advice on which words to choose in particular instances or whether a piece of dialogue works.

Review
● Some of the children may feel reluctant sharing their writing in this way. Reassure them that this process is as much about receiving positive feedback as it is looking for errors, and ask for examples of encouraging responses to share with the class.

Curriculum objectives
● To use the diagonal and horizontal strokes that are needed to join letters and understand which letters, when adjacent to one another, are best left unjoined.
● To increase the legibility, consistency and quality of their handwriting.

Resources
Children's edited drafts (from lesson 4); children's final drafts of their illustrations; children's copies of photocopiable page 136 'KWL grids' (from week 1)

5: Completing the story

Introduction
● Inform the class that today they will be finalising their tapestry stories, by adding their edited narratives to the pictures they created earlier. Ask if they are confident that they have enough space next to their pictures for their writing. They will need to consider the size of their handwriting in relation to this. Remind the children to use their best handwriting for these final drafts.

Independent work
● Allow the children to spend most of the lesson writing their edited text to accompany the pictorial versions of the stories they completed earlier.

Review
● Discuss as a class the processes the children have gone through in order to achieve their final products, from studying the Bayeux Tapestry and thinking about telling stories in pictures and what text can add to that, to devising, planning and creating their own stories combining words and pictures. Decide together how the work will be shared – perhaps as a linear wall display, echoing the original tapestry. Finally, ask the children to return to photocopiable page 136 'KWL grid' they began at the start of their work on the Bayeux Tapestry. Give them the opportunity to record their learning by completing the 'L' for Learning section and use this as the basis for further discussion.

Week 5 lesson plans

Work on the Normans now changes focus to the Domesday Book – a very different form of information text. From a given explanation of the document, the children will summarise the paragraphs. Word study involves investigating place-name changes since Norman times as well as suggesting and looking up the meanings of unusual words from the period. They will watch short videos giving Norman and Saxon opinions of the gathering of information for the Domesday Book before debating the opposing viewpoints. After looking at online Census summary information the children will gather their own personal contemporary information to write up using headings and subheadings.

1: Introducing the Domesday Book

Introduction

● Show the children some images of the Domesday Book. Ask if they can read any of it. It is written in medieval Latin, which was the clerical and administrative written language of the period. Ask if anyone has heard of the Domesday Book. Explain that it was a hand-written document which listed information about England 20 years after the Battle of Hastings. The information about who owned what land and how much it was worth, was collected on the orders of King William I (the Conqueror), so he knew how much tax he could collect.
● Hand out photocopiable page 'Domesday Book' from the CD-ROM, and read it twice. Ask the class how they can tell that this is a piece of non-fiction writing. What makes it different from fiction? Can they explain how the paragraphs have been organised? What sort of information is included them?

Paired work

● Invite the children to work together to summarise the paragraphs on the photocopiable sheet, writing a sentence about each one on their whiteboards. They should answer the basic question: *What is each paragraph about?*

Whole-class work

● Work through the photocopiable sheet, a paragraph at a time, and ask some children to read their summaries to the class and compare them. Is there agreement about the main content of each paragraph?

Independent work

● Using the heading *Domesday Book*, invite the children to write their paragraph summaries on paper, making any changes they feel would improve their originals.

> **Differentiation**
> ● To simplify the summarising process for those finding it difficult, suggest they underline key words. These tend to be nouns and some verbs. Where these occur more than once, only one mention is usually needed. This method helps to isolate and therefore draw attention to, the main points of the paragraph.

Review

● Show the class the Domesday Book pages from the National Archives at www.nationalarchives.gov.uk (search for 'Domesday')
● Here they can see the original entry for part of Essex, which is automatically translated into modern English when the cursor is held over the image. This will allow them to see details of the type of information collected.
● Then use the Domesday Book online www.domesdaybook.co.uk and find places familiar to the children. Compare the original spellings of place names. What parts of the names still exist? Can they see any patterns, and discern their meanings? (Note that Northumbria was not included in the Book.)

Expected outcomes
● All children can both summarise and write non-fiction texts in paragraphs with appropriate subheadings. They can use a dictionary to find definitions.
● Most children can explain the reasons for their summaries and paragraphing. They can interpret inferences in non-fiction, judging how events might affect different people.
● Some children can derive the meanings of place names from etymological sources. They can express the views of characters from the past, based on their reading.

Curriculum objectives
● To read books that are structured in different ways and read for a range of purposes.
● To participate in discussion about both books that are read to them and those they can read for themselves, taking turns and listening to what others say.
● To discuss writing similar to that which they are planning to write in order to understand and learn from its structure, grammar and vocabulary.
● To apply their growing knowledge of root words, prefixes and suffixes (etymology and morphology) as listed in Appendix 1, both to read aloud and to understand the meaning of new words they meet.
● To identify main ideas drawn from more than one paragraph and summarise these.

Resources
Images of the Domesday Book; photocopiable page 'Domesday Book' from the CD-ROM; individual whiteboards; internet access

Curriculum objectives
● To use dictionaries to check the meanings of words that they have read.

Resources
Photocopiable page 141 'Word investigations'; a range of dictionaries

2: Investigating ancient words

Introduction

● Write on the board the words *demesne, cottar, muid*.
● Explain that they are words used in the Domesday Book, but which are no longer in use. Can anyone suggest what any of them might have meant? How could they find out?
● Give the meanings as follows: land used by the lord of the manor; an unfree peasant who lived in a cottage; a French term for a measure of liquid.

Independent work

● Hand out photocopiable page 141 'Word investigations'. Explain to the children that they should first write down what they think the words might mean in the context of the Domesday Book.
● Next, they should select a dictionary and check the meanings, using the first two or three letters of each word to make finding them quicker. The dictionary definitions they find should be added to the photocopiable sheet. Where more than one definition is given, they should choose the one most likely to be correct in context and leave blank any words they cannot find.

> **Differentiation**
> ● Words such as *hide* and *villein*, in the context of the Domesday Book, may not appear in school dictionaries. Have an adult dictionary for more confident users, who can share their definitions with the others. (Definitions of all the words can be found at: www.nationalarchives.gov.uk search for 'Domesday').

Review

● Ask the children to share some of the definitions they have found. Did any surprise them?

Curriculum objectives
● To participate in discussion about both books that are read to them and those they can read for themselves, taking turns and listening to what others say.
● To draw inferences such as inferring characters' feelings, thoughts and motives from their actions, and justify inferences with evidence.

Resources
Online access to Domesday video clip at: www. nationalarchives.gov.uk (search for 'Domesday collecting the information'); printed transcripts of the above videos (available as a link)

3: What did the Normans do for us?

Introduction

● Share with the class the four videos on the National Archive site, which talk about collecting the information for the Domesday Book from the viewpoint of a Norman commissioner and a Saxon land-holder. (Each lasts just over a minute.)

Group work

● Organise the class into mixed-ability groups of 4–6. Give them copies of the video transcripts for reference.
● Ask them to discuss the opposing viewpoints of the Norman and Saxon. What does each of them think about William's survey? How do they feel about it? How would this make the Norman and Saxon feel about each other? What are their views about King William?

Whole-class work

● Hold a whole-class debate, with one half in role as Norman commissioners and the other half as Saxons. Conduct the debate yourself, calling on representatives from each half to state their views, and answer questions from the opposing side. You may need to ask leading questions, such as: *Tell us why you are gathering this information. How will it help the Saxons? What worries you about the king having this information?*

Review

● Out of role, ask the children for their own views on the survey. What difference do they think it made to the country? As a historical resource, how valuable is it to us today?

Curriculum objectives
● To discuss and record ideas.

Resources
Photocopiable page 142 'My Domesday information'

4: My own Domesday

Introduction
● Ask the class if they know of any information-gathering survey, similar to the Domesday Book. Some may know about the national Census that is held every 10 years. Go to the website for the Office for National Statistics at www.neighbourhood.statistics.gov.uk and select information for the school's postcode area.
● Ask the children how this compares with the Domesday Book survey. Explain that its purposes are different. Can they think why the government might want to have such information?
● Explain that today they will be compiling information for their own mini-version of a modern Domesday Book survey.

Independent work
● Hand out photocopiable page 142 'My Domesday information'. Read through it with the children so that they understand the questions, answering any queries they may have. Reassure them that the information is only for them – this is not like a national equivalent where information is read by others.
● Encourage them to complete the sheet as far as they can. They may need to get some information from home, or find out for example, distances from shops and so on. Be sensitive to individual circumstances, so it is fine if some children prefer not to answer some of the questions.

Differentiation
● Distances between locations can be checked using an online mapping search. More experienced computer users could be given this job to do for several of the other children.

Review
● Talk together with the class about how the children felt, when writing this kind of information. How might they feel if, like the Saxons, it was for a conquering army?

Curriculum objectives
● In non-narrative material, to use simple organisational devices.
● To use the diagonal and horizontal strokes that are needed to join letters and understand which letters, when adjacent to one another, are best left unjoined.
● To increase the legibility, consistency and quality of their handwriting.

Resources
Children's completed sheets (from lesson 4); image of page from the Domesday Book (available online)

5: Writing up the survey

Introduction
● Show the children an original Domesday Book page (source online). Ask about the handwriting. Can they imagine writing the whole book like that with a quill and ink? It isn't surprising that the writer did make some mistakes, but we can still read his work over 1,000 years later.
● Explain to the children that they will be using the information they gathered in the previous lesson to write their own 'mini Domesday Book'. They will write in paragraphs, using appropriate subheadings.
● Discuss how they could group the information on their sheet, which may not be in the same order as the questions. Ask how they could turn the information into grammatically correct sentences. For instance, *In my house, 4 people live. Their names are…*
● Remind the children about the importance of legible handwriting. Imagine their work will also be read a thousand years from now.

Independent work
● Encourage the children to write up their survey information, under the heading *My Domesday Book*. They should organise the work under their own choice of subheadings, using neat, legible joined handwriting.

Review
● Ask the children to reflect on their final product. Is it as neatly written as they would wish? How would it be useful to a historian in the future?

Week 6 lesson plans

An unusual poetic way of describing the Battle of Hastings starts this week's work. Marriott Edgar's colloquial monologue offers the opportunity to discuss informal language. A second, more serious approach by Rudyard Kipling is studied and prepared for performance. The form and key features of monologues are discussed and listed, to be used by the children when they draft and write their own monologues, based on the pictorial stories they created last week. The monologues are shared and evaluated.

1: I'll tell of the battle of 'astings...

Introduction
● Ask the children what they remember about the Battle of Hastings. Was it a serious or funny event? Read 'The Battle of Hastings' by Marriott Edgar from the photocopiable sheet from the CD-ROM.

Whole-class work
● Ask the children for their first reactions to the poem. They may be struck by the humour, the colloquial language, the rhyme or rhythm, or even simply the length. Discuss their comments. It is intended to be a funny poem, but do they find it so? What makes it effective? How does the poet's choice of language add to its overall effect?
● Introduce the term *monologue*, inviting the children to work out its meaning. Explain that *mono* means *one*, so it is written as the voice of one person.
● Remind the children of the work they have done on writing direct speech, where it can be effective to use grammatically incorrect sentences in dialogue to add character.
● Examine together the written version of the poem using photocopiable page 'The Battle of Hastings' from the CD-ROM. Find examples of grammatical errors such as *were* being used instead of *was*, missing the 'h' from many words, the truncated use of the word *the* to *t*, the double negative in *hadn't no*.
● Also, look for unusual words, such as *toff, by gum, swank, regatta, 'aughty, knaves, cads*. Can the children work out their meaning from the context?
● Invite the children to read a few verses together, taking note of the punctuation.

Paired work
● Hand out photocopiable page 'The Battle of Hastings' from the CD-ROM and ask the children to identify three things, using different coloured pens or pencils to highlight them.
   ● Firstly, can they find words written in dialect, primarily those with apostrophes of omission?
   ● Secondly, encourage them to spot unusual words or phrases they are not familiar with.
   ● Finally, can they identify elements of the poem that they recognise from the real story of the battle?

> ### Differentiation
> ● Children for whom English is not their first language may experience particular difficulty in understanding the poem. Discuss with them colloquialisms and differences between the spoken and written word in their own language. Can they give you examples?

Review
● Invite the children to share their findings. Focus particularly on the unfamiliar words. How much does this interfere with their enjoyment and understanding of the poem? For example, does it matter if they don't know what a *buckler* is? Could they work out what was meant by *put breeze up the Saxons*? Finish the lesson by enjoying another reading of the poem together, in dialect.

Curriculum objectives
● To prepare poems to read aloud and to perform, showing understanding through intonation, tone, volume and action.

Resources
Photocopiable page 'Norman and Saxon' from the CD-ROM

2: Another monologue

Introduction
● Display photocopiable page 'Norman and Saxon' from the CD-ROM, and read Rudyard Kipling's poem aloud to the children.
● Ask if the children notice any similarities to 'The Battle of Hastings' poem. They may notice that it also rhymes, the rhythm is very similar and both are about Norman and Saxon. Ask in what ways this poem is different to the other, for example it is more serious and it doesn't include colloquialisms.
● Invite the children to say if they have noticed any unfamiliar vocabulary. Use the same method as yesterday to see if they can they ascertain meaning from the context.

Group work
● Arrange the class into six groups, allocating one verse of the poem to each, appointing group leaders if you feel this would help. Invite the children to practise reading their verses in their groups, before coming together as a class to perform the whole poem. Remind them to take notice of the punctuation – particularly in the first verse.
● Encourage the groups to do more than just read it chorally – they will need to consider pace, intonation, volume and adding appropriate actions to enliven their performance. Remind them to rehearse several times.

Review
● Draw the class together and perform the entire poem, a group at a time. Invite the children to offer feedback on the performances. Do they prefer the 'Norman and Saxon' poem or 'The Battle of Hastings' poem? Why?

Curriculum objectives
● To discuss writing similar to that which they are planning to write in order to understand and learn from its structure, grammar and vocabulary.

Resources
Photocopiable page 'Norman and Saxon' from the CD-ROM; photocopiable page 'The Battle of Hastings' from the CD-ROM; a free-verse poem of your choice; individual whiteboards

3: What makes a monologue?

Introduction
● Select any free-verse poem and read it aloud to the class.
● Ask the children what differences they notice between this poem and the two monologues they have been reading.

Group work
● Arrange the class into groups of 3–4. Using the two monologues (photocopiable pages 'Norman and Saxon' and 'The Battle of Hastings'), ask the children to work together to discuss them, listing key features.
● Explain that they should focus on the form of the poems, answering the question: *What do I need to include in a monologue?* Invite them to note their ideas on whiteboards.

Whole-class work
● Bring the class together to discuss their lists. What key features are common to most groups? The lists should include rhyme and rhythm, the poems tell a story chronologically and that direct speech has been used.
● Explain to the children that tomorrow they will be planning their own monologues, based on the tapestry stories they wrote earlier.

Independent work
● Invite the children to use both the group and class discussions to compile a list of key features for writing a monologue to help them write their own.

Review
● Talk together about different forms of poetry the children are familiar with. They should remember writing ballads and free verse from earlier this year and may also recall rhyming couplets and haiku. What others do they know?

Curriculum objectives
● To compose and rehearse sentences orally (including dialogue), progressively building a varied and rich vocabulary and an increasing range of sentence structures (See Appendix 2).
● To assess the effectiveness of their own and others' writing and suggest improvements.

Resources
Children's checklists (from lesson 3); children's pictorial stories (from week 4); mixing bowl, spoon, pieces of cut-up paper of different sizes; two or three verses of one of the monologues ('Norman and Saxon' or 'The Battle of Hastings')

4: Drafting a monologue

Introduction

● Use the mixing bowl to act out mixing a cake, adding pieces of paper and stirring with the spoon. Explain that when the children draft their monologues today it will be like bringing together several ingredients from their previous work to create something new, like making a cake.
● As it is crucial to get the rhythm of the poem right, read out and clap the rhythm of part of one of the monologues, demonstrating how the rhythm works. They may choose to use the same rhythm for their own work.

Independent work

● Using their story and checklist, invite the children to begin to draft the first two or three verses of their monologues. Remind them to check the rhythm of their lines, and decide on their rhyme scheme.
● Encourage them to rehearse their lines orally to check on the rhythm.

Paired work

● With the monologues part-written, ask the children to swap their work with a partner, each reading through the other's poem, using their checklists as a guide.
● Encourage them to offer feedback to each other, focusing particularly on how effective the rhyme and rhythm of the pieces are, and suggesting improvements where appropriate.

Review

● Provide time for the children to continue writing their monologues independently, consulting with their partner again when they have finished the draft. Then they may make subsequent changes if they wish.

Curriculum objectives
● To use the diagonal and horizontal strokes that are needed to join letters and understand which letters, when adjacent to one another, are best left unjoined.
● To increase the legibility, consistency and quality of their handwriting.

Resources
Children's drafts of monologues (from lesson 4)

5: The final monologue

Introduction

● Ask the children if they have any questions about their monologues, following the drafting and editing process yesterday. Discuss how the poems should be set out, for example centred on the page or written against the margin. Remind the class to use their best handwriting, aiming for consistency in joining strokes as well as evenly-sized letters.

Independent work

● Allow time for the children to write final drafts of their poems, first reading through to see if any final changes are needed.

Paired work

● When the poems are completed, encourage the children to work again with their partner from yesterday, to share and discuss their finished monologues.
● Ask the children to select their favourite parts of each other's poems to share with the class.

Review

● Invite the children to read out to the class their chosen sections of their partner's monologues, saying why they chose it. Do the partners agree that this is the best part? Would they have selected a different part? Ask how successful the children think they have been in maintaining rhyme and rhythm throughout the poems. Have they successfully translated their stories into poems? What advice would they give to others undertaking the same task?

■ SCHOLASTIC

Curriculum objectives
● To use fronted adverbials.
● To choose nouns or pronouns appropriately for clarity and cohesion and to avoid repetition.
● To use conjunctions, adverbs and prepositions to express time and cause.
● To use and understand the grammatical terminology in Appendix 2 accurately and appropriately when discussing their writing and reading.

Resources
Photocopiable page 143 'How good is your grammar?'; coloured pencils (red, blue, green and yellow)

Grammar and punctuation: Fronted adverbials, pronouns, connectives, prepositions

Revise
● There are four starter activities which you can use to remind the children of the elements of this assessment: 3 'Improvise it', 5 'Start with the connection', 7 'Fronted adverbials' and 8 'Spot the pronoun'. Depending upon how well the children understand the concepts, you may wish to use any or all of these for revision purposes.

Assess
● Hand out photocopiable page 143 'How good is your grammar?' and ask the children to identify and underline all four of the elements of grammar.
● Advise them to first read through the text about the Bayeux Tapestry, and to identify and underline one element at a time. Advise them to start with the element with which they feel most comfortable and to work independently.

Further practice
● Using books, challenge the children to do a timed print hunt, requiring them to find and list examples of any of the elements of grammar previously assessed. Vary the types of text used, such as poetry, non-fiction and fiction, to compare the usage of the grammatical elements in each type of writing. This knowledge can be used by the children to enable them to select appropriate language for use in their own writing of different text types.

Curriculum objectives
● To spell words which are often misspelled (see Appendix 1).

Resources
Individual whiteboards

Spelling: Words starting with 'ce' and words containing 'ff', 'ss' or 'ei'

Revise
● Use starter activity 9 'Spellchecker'.
● Remind the children of the spellings they worked on in week 4, noting that those containing 'ei' may have different sounds.
● Ask them to try and spell the following words on their whiteboards, which contain the same four letter-patterns: *cease, celery, cement, offer, scaffold, coffee, eight, freight, vein, lesson, gossip, massive.*

Assess
● Use the following words to more formally assess the children's knowledge of the spelling patterns, by encouraging them to write sentences which include the words: *celebration, census, centimetre, difference, difficulty, office, foreign, eighteen, neighbour, casserole, passenger, essential.*
● As an extra challenge, ask them to spell these words, which contain two of the patterns combined: *ceiling, caffeine, conceited, deceitful, receive.*

Further practice
● There are many words containing these letter patterns. Challenge the children to make a class collection, which they can add to whenever they find appropriate words. This can be done using dictionaries, online searches or simply noticing them in their everyday reading.

Curriculum objectives
● To understand what they read, in books they can read independently, by checking that the text makes sense to them, and explaining the meaning of words in context.
● To use dictionaries to check the meanings of words they have read.
● To draw inferences such as inferring characters' feelings, thoughts and motives from their actions, and justify inferences with evidence.
● To identify main ideas drawn from more than one paragraph and summarise these.

Resources
Photocopiable page 'William of Malmesbury's account of the Battle of Hastings' from the CD-ROM; a range of dictionaries

Reading: Normans

Revise

● Remind the class about the two primary sources of evidence they have looked at, which gave them information about the Norman invasion – namely the Bayeux Tapestry and the Domesday Book. Talk about the fact that these two historical documents were created near the time the events took place, and both were written from a Norman point of view, so are possibly biased. When we read ancient texts today, we have to interpret them for ourselves, but this can be difficult as we are very far removed from events and may not be experienced in reading that type of writing. Ask the children what they have learned from studying the two texts.

Assess

● Hand out photocopiable page 'William of Malmesbury's account of the Battle of Hastings' from the CD-ROM, which provides abbreviated extracts from a modern translation of this historical document. Explain that William was a 12th century monk who wrote a history of England. His father was Norman and his mother English, so he could view events from both sides.
● Use the text for two assessments. Firstly, ask the children to use dictionaries to check the meanings of words. Sixteen words have been highlighted on the text, as these are the words the children are most likely to find unfamiliar. Instruct them to read the text through twice, to get the sense of the piece. Then invite them to copy each of the highlighted words in list form, writing next to each what they think the words' meanings might be, from the context of the writing, and similarity to known words. For example, they may work out *juncture* from its similarity to *junction*. Next ask them to use dictionaries to check the words' meanings which they will copy next to their own suggestions. Remind them that where words have more than one meaning (for example *standard*) they must select the most appropriate.
● The second assessment focuses on comprehension and inference. Encourage the children to re-read the piece, a paragraph at a time, and write a sentence or two to summarise each paragraph, in their own words. Finally, they will consider the writer's point of view. What can they infer from the way in which he tells the story of the battle and its preparations? Does he favour one side or not? Can we tell if he thinks it was a good thing? The children must give evidence from their reading to support their views.

Further practice

● After the assessments, read through and discuss the text together. How does this compare with the story told in the tapestry? Look for scenes that match the written text. The whole of William's account can be found at www.fordham.edu (search for 'Malmesbury').
● You could look at this to see what else he has to say about the battle and its aftermath. Discuss with the class the values and problems of reading and interpreting primary historical documents.

Curriculum objectives

● To compose and rehearse sentences orally (including dialogue), progressively building a varied and rich vocabulary and an increasing range of sentence structures (See Appendix 2).
● To choose nouns or pronouns appropriately for clarity and cohesion and to avoid repetition.
● To use conjunctions, adverbs and prepositions to express time and cause.
● To use fronted adverbials.
● To use commas after fronted adverbials.
● To proofread for spelling and punctuation errors.
● To use and punctuate direct speech.
● In narratives, to create settings, characters and plot.

Resources
Internet access

Writing: Normans

Revise

● Remind the class of the two monologues they worked on recently, and the key features they identified which they then used to write their own monologue. Talk particularly about the rhyme and rhythm and how a story was told from a particular viewpoint.

● Discuss the difficulty for the writer in composing rhyming verse, for instance that it limits the choice of words to those which rhyme and how that then has an impact upon the lines themselves. Ask the children how they managed this while also maintaining the rhythm when they wrote their own monologues. Did anyone have any method they devised that they found useful? For example, what did they do if they had chosen a word that worked in a line, but they couldn't find a rhyme for it?

● Select some words that the children might use in the monologues they will be writing, such as *fight, battle, horse(s), swords, king*. Invite them to suggest rhyming words for each that could be used in the context of a poem about the Battle of Hastings.

● Remind the class that the Bayeux Tapestry and the Domesday Book were both created for the conquering Normans, and that William of Malmesbury was half Norman, so none of those documents were entirely Saxon in their viewpoint. Remind them also about the short videos they watched about collecting the information for the Domesday Book, where we were given a fictional account of what a typical Saxon's opinions might have been.

Assess

● Using the knowledge and insight they have gained from their work, encourage the children to write a monologue about the gathering of information for the Domesday Book from the Saxons' point of view.

● Ask them to imagine themselves as a chronicler of the events, writing in the past tense. They may choose an amusing style, like Marriott Edgar, or follow a more serious approach. They should make the Saxon perspective obvious from the way they tell the story, which will include correctly punctuated quotes from fictional characters, as in the monologues they read. Remind them to take care to use pronouns carefully, so as not to confuse the reader.

● Allow them time to plan their monologues, deciding on a starting point. They may choose to write in the first person, for example *I'll tell you about the Normans...* or take a more distant perspective, such as *It was twenty years after the battle, that the king's men they did come to call*. If you wish, you could provide opening lines such as these to give the children a start.

● Inform them that the monologues must have at least four verses of four lines each, and that they can choose their own rhyme scheme. You should expect more experienced writers to produce more verses.

● After planning and drafting, allow the children to work independently to write their poems.

Further practice

● Provide the children with access to a range of poetry books, asking them to find rhyming poems. Remind them to look carefully at how the poets have constructed their lines, noting how sentence structure might have been affected by the necessity to maintain rhyme and rhythm. They can also look for particularly clever rhymes, including those where a two-word phrase has been chosen to rhyme with a polysyllabic word. What different rhyme schemes can they find? Can anyone find an example that they think is unsuccessful, perhaps where the poet has lost the rhythm or chosen a word that they think doesn't work? (You may like to read short selections from the work of William McGonagall at: www.mcgonagall-online.org.uk a Victorian poet famous for his bad poetry!)

Name: _____

Date: _____

KWL grid

■ Use this grid to write down what you know, what you want to know and what you have learned.

| K
This is what I already know | W
These are the things I want to know | L
This is what I have learned |
|---|---|---|
| | | |
| | | |
| | | |
| | | |

I can record my knowledge, questions and learning about a subject.

How did you do?

PHOTOCOPIABLE

We done good!

■ Rewrite these sentences using the correct grammar.

1. We done good! _____

_____

2. She seen the biggest spider ever. _____

_____

3. For her birthday, Sam give Sunita a bunch of flowers. _____

_____

4. When we went to the fair, we was very excited. _____

_____

5. I were the fastest runner in the race. _____

_____

6. The puppy done a bad thing. _____

_____

7. Alfie said he seen the Loch Ness monster. _____

_____

8. Mum said we was the best children in the world. _____

_____

9. I give my sister a big hug when she fell over. _____

_____

10. I were pretty scared on the big roller coaster. _____

_____

I can identify and correct grammatically incorrect sentences.

How did you do?

Today's offers

- Circle the mistakes in these signs and write the correct version of the words underneath.

Todays special offer

_____

Quality childrens' clothes

_____

Fresh tomatoe's

_____

Town gets it's bypass

_____

Womens team victorious

_____

Lovely local carrot's

_____

Genuine sheeps wool

_____

Local team wins' again

_____

Everything for your pet's

_____

I can identify and correct errors in the use of possessive apostrophes.

How did you do?

Perfect verbs (1)

■ Write any of the parts of the verb 'to have' that can be used to form the perfect tense of these verbs. Choose from:

have	has	had	has been

_____ walked

_____ spoken

_____ taking

_____ forgotten

_____ enjoyed

_____ sung

_____ singing

_____ collecting

_____ ridden

_____ danced

_____ eaten

_____ cooking

_____ borrowing

_____ played

I can choose the correct forms of the verb 'to have' to create perfect verbs.

How did you do?

Some tricky words

- In the passage below, underline the words you think are the most difficult to spell.

In the 11th century, this island felt the full weight of the Norman army. Hastings was the centre of the invasion when Duke William's men took possession of the land. The reign of King William had begun. This was certain to be a difficult time for the English, for whom life would be very different. It would be possible that the pressure could prove too much.

- Look at your underlined words and write them in groups according to similarities in their spelling. Any words that do not fit a pattern can be grouped together as 'others'.

_____
_____
_____
_____
_____
_____
_____
_____
_____
_____
_____
_____

I can identify tricky words and group them according to similarities in spelling.

How did you do?

Word investigations

■ Write down what you think each word from the Domesday Book means, then find and write its dictionary definition.
(Beware! Some words didn't have the meaning you might expect!)

	My idea	**Dictionary definition**
vill		
hide		
villein		
manor		
plough		
shilling		
meadow		
pasture		
livestock		
abbot		

I can use the first three letters in a dictionary to check the meanings of words.

How did you do?

My Domesday information

- Complete the sections below.

Family name _____

Address _____

Postcode _____

Telephone number _____

Type of property _____

Is there a garden? _____

How far from a shop? _____

How far from a bus stop? _____

How far from a railway station? _____

Who lives there? _____

_____

What jobs do they do? _____

_____

Which people go to school? _____

What animals live there? _____

Number of cars _____

Number of TVs _____

Is there a computer? _____

I can gather, research and record information.

How did you do?

PHOTOCOPIABLE

■ SCHOLASTIC
www.scholastic.co.uk

How good is your grammar?

■ In the passage below, underline fronted adverbials in red, pronouns in blue, connectives in green and prepositions in yellow.

Over 1,000 years ago, England was invaded by Duke William of Normandy. Because we have the Bayeux Tapestry, we know the story of the Norman invasion of England and the Battle of Hastings. But does it tell the true story? Did everything happen just as the tapestry suggests? For example, the death of Harold seems to be shown twice. In one scene we see him with an arrow shot through his eye, while later he is seen being attacked by a Norman knight.

We need to bear in mind that history is written by the victors and in this case it was the Normans who won the battle. Their king became the new King of England, so the tapestry tells the story from their point of view.

No one knows who designed the tapestry, or whether it was the work of one or many people. Historians disagree about where it was made. Some suggest Canterbury while others say it was Winchester, which was the old capital of the country. Both ideas are interesting, as neither are in France, where Norman needlewomen would no doubt relish telling the story of their victory. One wonders how English embroiderers felt, telling the world the story of their defeat.

Whatever the truth, the tapestry gives us lots of information about this period of history. We know what people wore and ate, what their hairstyles were and what armour and weapons they used. It is up to us to work out the thoughts of our long-ago ancestors.

I can identify fronted adverbials, pronouns, connectives and prepositions.

How did you do?

Jacqueline Wilson

Stories with issues is the focus for this half-term's work, with Jacqueline Wilson's *The Suitcase Kid* and *Cliffhanger* and Charles Causley's poem 'Timothy Winters' being read as the basis for study. The children will consider how the writers have conveyed information about their character through the use of inference. They will use this in their own work, writing a story and several haiku based on a range of issues they have identified. The children will find out about Jacqueline Wilson, including using her website. They will write a blurb, tell a story in postcards and formulate questions. Also, they will do further work on grammatical features. Spelling work will cover further prefixes and suffixes.

Expected prior learning
● Can talk about the work of a single author.
● Can understand that themes and ideas can be compared across an author's work.
● Can understand how a theme can be explored through a novel.
● Can understand the perfect tense.
● Can discuss inference and say why writers use it.
● Can discuss the planning, writing and editing processes.
● Can understand that poems have a variety of forms following different conventions.

Overview of progression
● Close reading offers the opportunity for further insight into the interpretation of inference about characters' feelings. The children will transfer this developing knowledge to their writing. They will broaden their experiences by writing in different forms.
● They will reinforce their knowledge of conjunctions, prepositions and adverbs of time and cause, fronted adverbials and the use of pronouns for clarity and cohesion. Spelling will focus on prefixes and suffixes.

Creative context
● There are clear links with PSHE where the issues covered can be investigated in greater depth and from different perspectives.

Preparation
Before you start this half term read the two Jacqueline Wilson books it features – *The Suitcase Kid* and *Cliffhanger*. Familiarise yourself with the author's website. Collect as many of her novels as possible, reading several other titles to become familiar with the themes in her work.

It would be a good idea to start reading *The Suitcase Kid* to the class as a serial during the first week of the term, in order for them to quickly become familiar with it.

You will also need:
Internet access; picture of Jacqueline Wilson; individual whiteboards and pens; images of mascots and lucky charms; scissors; glue sticks; postcards with messages; dictionaries; A3 paper; leaf-shaped paper, twigs in a solid base to form a small tree

On the CD-ROM you will find:
Interactive activities 'Character comparisons', 'Absolutely lovely!'; photocopiable pages 'Timothy Winters', 'Some haiku', 'Perfect verbs', 'Choose the spelling'

Chapter at a glance

An overview of the chapter. For curriculum objective codes, please see pages 8–10.

Week	Lesson	Curriculum objectives	Summary of activities	Outcomes
1	1	RC: 1, 4, 5 WC: 2	Establish knowledge of Jacqueline Wilson. Look at website and blurbs of books. Identify key themes. Hear beginning of *The Suitcase Kid*.	• Can identify and discuss genre and themes of Jacqueline Wilson's works.
	2	RC: 5	Recall characteristics in Roald Dahl and mythology characters. Complete 'Comparing characters' sheet. Hear next part of *The Suitcase Kid* and discuss characters.	• Can identify and compare three character types, recognising Wilson's as being realistic.
	3	RC: 15	Answer questions about Jacqueline Wilson from website biography. Use answers to tell partner facts orally in sentences. Look at Children's Laureate site.	• Can retrieve and record information successfully from online information and understand Laureateship.
	4	RC: 10 WC: 2	Watch question and answer video from Wilson's website. Formulate own questions, watch FAQ video and discuss.	• Can write questions to ask Jacqueline Wilson and compare with those on video. • Can consider effects as readers and writers.
	5	WT: 1	Recap on known prefixes and suffixes. Play challenge game in groups and make timed lists of examples of both types of words.	• Can demonstrate knowledge and understanding of known prefixes and suffixes by matching words to given criteria.
2	1	RC: 1, 4, 11, 12 WC: 2	Read 'B for Bathroom' in *The Suitcase Kid*. Identify main characters, discuss and list characteristics. Write paragraphs for three characters, including Andy.	• Can suggest and discuss reasons for characters' behaviour and consider alternative viewpoint, bearing first-person biased narrative in mind.
	2	RC: 11, 16	Re-read opening chapter of *The Suitcase Kid*. Discuss role of counsellor and effects on Andy. Make mini role-on-the wall noting her feelings and actions.	• Can demonstrate understanding of inferential details.
	3	RC: 11 WC: 5	Look at and talk about mascots and why Radish is important to Andy. Design a mascot, labelling its key features.	• Can identify reasons for Radish's importance, design and label mascot with appropriate features.
	4	RC: 5	Recall themes in previous work. Suggest themes for *The Suitcase Kid*. Complete cut-and-paste activity, grouping statements under themes.	• Can discuss and group statements under headings, giving reasons for choices.
	5	WC: 13, 20	Recap on use of pronouns, identifying where they are needed and suggesting which pronouns to use.	• Can demonstrate understanding of pronoun use by completing the sheet and replacing pronouns with original nouns orally.
3	1	RC: 10, 11 WC: 2	Answer quick-fire and inferential questions about *The Suitcase Kid*. Discuss in pairs then write own questions about the text.	• Can formulate, write, share and discuss factual and inferential questions.
	2	RC: 1, 16	Look at book reviews and discuss purpose. Groups share remembered books, asking and answering questions about them.	• Can select books for discussion with a group, explaining reasons for their choice.
	3	WC: 1	Recap *The Suitcase Kid*, giving opinions. Read online top tips for writing book reviews. Plan review, discuss and refine with partner.	• Can plan book reviews of *The Suitcase Kid* in paragraphs under appropriate subheadings.
	4	WC: 4, 6, 12, 13	Discuss review plans, what are the most important things? Use notes to write first drafts of reviews. Check against top tips list.	• Can complete and check first drafts of book reviews.
	5	WT: 7, 8 WC: 7, 8, 9	View children's online reviews of *The Suitcase Kid*. Swap drafts with partner for editorial comments. Write final draft.	• Can write final drafts, incorporating editorial changes, in best handwriting; evaluate and discuss final version.
4	1	RC: 1, 11, 12	Read introduction and first chapter of *Cliffhanger*. Discuss characters. Predict outcomes. Complete 'All about Tim' sheet and share opinions with partner.	• Can infer characters' feelings about each other.
	2	WC: 12, 14	Identify time and cause words and perfect form of verbs. Write sentences using them.	• Can write sentences including all required elements.
	3	RC: 1, 2, 14	Read and discuss Tim's postcards. What do they tell us about his feelings? Note use of punctuation and sentence structure.	• Can discuss postcards and demonstrate awareness of what they add to the story.
	4	WC: 2, 5	Discuss language and tone of postcards and compare with novel. Discuss ideas, plan story outline and use to tell to partner.	• Can discuss, plan and orally tell stories in the form of postcards.
	5	WC: 5, 7	Remind about key elements for postcard stories. Children write final versions and share with partner for feedback.	• Can write final versions of postcard stories, which are then evaluated by partners.

Chapter at a glance

Week	Lesson	Curriculum objectives	Summary of activities	Outcomes
5	1	RC: 5, 16 WC: 1, 2	Define 'issue' in terms of stories. Pairs list titles of issues-based stories; share in groups and with whole class.	• Can create, share and discuss superlists of wide range of issues-based stories.
	2	WC: 2	Groups list ideas for stories to match issues. Lists shared and children choose possible ideas for stories.	• Can formulate two or three ideas about which to plan and write their stories.
	3	WC: 1, 7, 8	Discuss plot structure of issues-based stories. Plan own story, including character and plot. Tell orally to partner and discuss planning process.	• Can complete plan outlines for issues-based stories, including paragraphing.
	4	RC: 14 WC: 1	Explain difference between showing and telling in text. Children complete 'Show, don't tell' sheets.	• Can complete sheets that demonstrate understanding of inference in text.
	5	WC: 5, 9, 20	Plans used to write issues-based stories, taking grammatical conventions and 'showing, not telling' technique into account. Work checked and shared with partner.	• Can complete and edit stories, self-assessing and sharing with partner for comment.
6	1	RC: 5, 11	Listen to and read 'Timothy Winters'. Discuss theme and note unfamiliar words, using context to define. Draw picture of Timothy using evidence in the poem.	• Can demonstrate understanding of character by using the poem to draw a picture of Timothy.
	2	RC: 11 WC: 2	Re-read poem. Link to 'showing, not telling'. Pairs look for inferential clues in poem. Class discuss Timothy's life and feelings.	• Can demonstrate understanding through solving inferential clues.
	3	WT: 1, 3, 6	Identify adverbs as root words plus the '-ly' suffix. Practise spelling given words and write them in dictated sentences.	• Can learn to spell root words + '-ly' ending, and write dictated sentences using them in the context of 'Timothy Winters'.
	4	RC: 1, 8, 10	Summarise work on inference. Read and discuss issues-based haiku before writing own. Attach as leaves to 'poet tree' and share.	• Can produce a haiku that demonstrates their understanding of inference and the haiku form.
	5	RC: 6	Listen to a reading 'Timothy Winters'. Identify criteria for a performance. Groups rehearse, perform and evaluate the poem.	• Can effectively perform the poem in a group and evaluate against original identified criteria.

Background knowledge

Children's Laureate: The role of Children's Laureate is awarded once every two years to an eminent writer or illustrator of children's books to celebrate outstanding achievement in their field. It was first awarded in 1999.

Haiku: Japanese poetic form of three lines with the syllable count of 5, 7, 5.

Issues-based stories: A genre of stories based around problems. Contemporary books for young readers in this genre have grown in popularity in recent years.

Past participle: Verbs in English have two participles, called 'present participle' (such as *walking, taking*) and 'past participle' (such as *walked, taken*).

Showing not telling: A device used in writing where a character's feelings and emotions are inferred by describing their actions, what they say and how they react to others.

Week 1 lesson plans

This half-term the children will enjoy hearing two books by the popular author Jacqueline Wilson, *The Suitcase Kid* and *Cliffhanger*. They begin by finding out about her and the issue-based books she is most well-known for. They will compare her typical characters with those created by Roald Dahl and in legends, both of which they have met before. They will formulate questions they would like to ask Jacqueline Wilson and revise prefixes and suffixes. It is advisable to familiarise the class with the two books, starting with *The Suitcase Kid*, by reading it to them as a class serial, beginning this week. They will need to know most of the story by week 3.

1: Meet Jacqueline Wilson

Introduction

● Show the class a photograph of Jacqueline Wilson and ask if anyone knows who she is. Identify her and ask if the children have read any of her books or know any of her characters – they may be familiar with Tracy Beaker from the television series.
● Ask what sort of stories she writes from those they already know. They may suggest modern stories about separated families but, as her books for younger children are about dinosaurs, animals and adventures they may be more familiar with those. They may mention that the books contain humour, while some may pick up on themes like divorce, problems or growing up.

Whole-class work

● Show the class Jacqueline Wilson's official website (www.jacquelinewilson. co.uk), going to the 'Books' section, and looking at the book covers, arranged in age-appropriate order. Do they recognise any they didn't think of earlier? Notice that she has written more books for 9–11 year-olds than other age-groups. Ask the children why they think this might be.
● Go to the 'Cinema' section, and watch the four short videos where Jacqueline Wilson talks about Tracy Beaker – the character that the children are most likely to know. Can they suggest why Tracy is such a popular character?
● Select titles from the 7–9 and 9–11 sections, and invite individual children to read aloud the blurbs which appear on screen when each title is clicked on. Encourage the children to classify the books according to their themes. List them on the board and discuss the results.

Paired work

● Invite the children to talk together and make notes about the content and themes of the books they have been discussing, and compare them with other genres with which they are familiar (such as legends, myths and science fiction). What differences can they find? Are there any similarities?

> **Differentiation**
> ● Be sensitive to the individual circumstances of children for whom the issues covered may be personal. Some of the children may not wish to discuss certain things, and their situations must be treated with care. This may affect their pairings in the above activity.

Review

● Bring the class together and ask for feedback from the paired discussions. What differences did the children find between Jacqueline Wilson's books and other genres? Did anyone find any similarities? Introduce the class to *The Suitcase Kid*, explaining they will be studying it and reading the introductory chapter. How does this fit with their observations of the author's work? End the lesson by using starter activity 13 'Blurb matching', to familiarise the children with summarising texts and choosing appropriate titles.

Expected outcomes
● All children can identify and discuss generic themes and typical characters, formulate questions and give examples of words with known prefixes and suffixes.
● Most children can identify differences and similarities between genres.
● Some children can research extra facts from a website.

Curriculum objectives
● To listen to and discuss a wide range of fiction, poetry, plays, non-fiction and reference books or textbooks.
● To increase their familiarity with a wide range of books, including fairy stories, myths and legends, and retell some of these orally.
● To identify themes and conventions in a wide range of books.
● To discuss and record ideas.

Resources
Photograph of Jacqueline Wilson; online access to Jacqueline Wilson's website www.jacquelinewilson.co.uk; individual whiteboards

Curriculum objectives
● To identify themes and conventions in a wide range of books.

Resources
Photocopiable page 168 'Comparing characters'; interactive activity 'Character comparisons' on the CD-ROM; computer access

2: Comparing characters

Introduction
● Ask the children to recall characters any Roald Dahl characters they know. List them on the board. (They should be able to recall some from Year 3.)
● Use interactive activity 'Character comparisons' on the CD-ROM, asking the children to match characters they are likely to know with their character types.

Group work
● In groups of 3–4 invite the children to discuss similarities and differences between the characters in the lists.
● After a short time, ask them to add what they know of Jacqueline Wilson's characters and character types. In what ways are they similar to or different from those already discussed?

Independent work
● Hand out photocopiable page 168 'Comparing characters' for the children to complete. Reassure them not to worry if they don't yet know many Jacqueline Wilson characters – they will discover more as the half term progresses.

Review
● With the lists complete, ask the children if they can spot one main thing that separates Jacqueline Wilson's characters from the others – they are more realistic. Dahl's characters are pantomimic, unbelievable inventions, and those in myths have unworldly powers or talents. Read to the class the 'A' chapter from *The Suitcase Kid*, and identify characteristics of the main protagonists.

Curriculum objectives
● To retrieve and record information from non-fiction.

Resources
Access to Jacqueline Wilson's website www.jacquelinewilson.co.uk; photocopiable page 169 'Facts about Jacqueline Wilson'

3: Jacqueline Wilson facts

Introduction
● Show the children the biographical notes on Jacqueline Wilson's website www.jacquelinewilson.co.uk Read it aloud to them or invite children to read sections of it to the class.
● Ask the children what they find most interesting, surprising or impressive about the writer from this information. Do they have any questions about the information? Do they know what an OBE or Children's Laureate is?

Independent work
● Hand out photocopiable page 169 'Facts about Jacqueline Wilson' for the children to complete. Refer them to the displayed website information.

Paired work
● Remove the biography from view. With only their completed photocopiable sheets, challenge the children to turn their Q & A information into sentences, taking turns to tell their partner orally, the facts about Jacqueline Wilson. For example, for the first question they would say *Jacqueline Wilson was born in Bath in 1945*.

> **Differentiation**
> ● More confident readers could be given access to a 2012 Guardian interview with Jacqueline Wilson 'Jacqueline Wilson, my family values' at www.guardian.co.uk, (also linked from her website). Using this, they could be challenged to summarise the different information found in the interview.

Review
● Explain to the class more about the Children's Laureate, (you may find this a useful website: www.childrenslaureate.org.uk). You could also look at Jacqueline Wilson's page on the same site.

4: Questions for the author

Curriculum objectives
● To ask questions to improve their understanding of a text.
● To discuss and record ideas.

Resources
Interviews in the 'Cinema' section of Jacqueline Wilson's website www.jacquelinewilson.co.uk

Introduction
● Show the children the first three short video clips of Jacqueline Wilson answering questions sent to her by children on her website, and the first three from the Frequently Asked Questions video. Ask the children why the first three questions were answered individually, and not in the FAQ section (they are more unusual).
● Explain that they need to think about questions they would ask Jacqueline Wilson. The questions may be about herself, or how she writes, or her books. They should try to think of some more unusual questions as well as those that may be asked frequently, but are nevertheless interesting.

Independent work
● Provide time for the children to write their questions on paper. Remind them to use question marks. It may help their thinking if they group their questions according to the categories mentioned in the Introduction.

Review
● Return to the website, and show the children the rest of the Frequently Asked Questions video (just over eight minutes long). Encourage them to look out for any of the questions they thought of themselves. About halfway through, pause the video and ask for the children's comments. Do any of Jacqueline's answers surprise them? Watch the rest of the video and ask if knowing more about the author has any effect on their reading of her books, or their attitude to her writing.

5: Prefix and suffix challenge

Curriculum objectives
● To use further prefixes and suffixes and understand how to add them (Appendix 1).

Resources
Set of cards with the prefixes 'in-', 'il-', 'ir-', 're-', 'im-', 'super-', 'auto-', 'anti-' (to create); set of cards with the suffixes '-ing', '-ed', '-er', '-ation', '-ous' (to create); individual whiteboards

Introduction
● On the board write the words: *running, impossible, jubilation, jealous, illegal*.
● Invite the children to underline the suffix or prefix in each of the words ('-ing', 'im-', '-ation', '-ous', 'il-').

Whole-class work
● Explain to the class that they will be playing the 'Prefix and suffix' challenge. Invite a child to select a card at random from the two sets and show it to the class, who must write a word on their whiteboards to match the selected prefix or suffix and then show their results.
● Explain that the words must be spelled correctly and must use the prefix or suffix correctly, for example *incorrect* would be right because the prefix *in* means *not*, but *inside* would be wrong as *in* is not being used as a prefix.

Group work
● Divide the class into mixed-ability groups. Select a card to show them and ask them to write down possible words on their whiteboards. Then discuss as a group which they want to use, agreeing that the word is spelled correctly and fits the prefix/suffix criteria.
● Invite the groups to show their words at the same time. If they fit the criteria, they get one point and they gain a second if it is spelled correctly.
● Play several rounds of the game, keeping score as you go.

Review
● Challenge the children to list as many words as they can for each prefix and suffix in a given time.
● Use starter activities 4 'Suffix challenge' or 15 'Prefix game'.

Week 2 lesson plans

Continue to read *The Suitcase Kid* with the class, completing it by the end of the week. The main focus this week is developing the children's understanding of inference by thinking about what characters say and do, bearing in mind that we are seeing everything from the narrator's point of view. They will think about and summarise what Andy's responses to the family counsellor tell us about Andy herself and the role the counsellor plays in setting up the premise for the story. They will consider the importance of Radish, Andy's mascot, designing and labelling a mascot of their own. Also, they will identify themes in the story and recap on the value and use of pronouns.

1: Meet the cast

Introduction

● Remind the class about the first two chapters of the book *The Suitcase Kid* and read to them the 'B for Bathroom' chapter. (If you have been using the book as a serial, you may have read further than this.)
● On the board, ask the children to list the main characters so far in the story – Andrea/Andy, her Mum and Dad, the family counsellor, Katie, Paula, Graham, Uncle Bill. Give the children a short time to write the characters on their whiteboards, but in the order in which they know most about them.
● Ask the children which characters they think will be most important as the story unfolds, giving their reasons.

Paired work

● Encourage the children to work with a partner to discuss each character in turn, noting characteristics about each one, taken from what we learn about them via Andy's first-person voice. Explain to the children that they should consider what the characters are described as both doing and saying.

Whole-class work

● Bring the class together and ask for feedback from the paired discussions. Do the children have similar or differing opinions of the characters and their importance in the story?
● Ask for words or phrases to sum up each of the characters, writing the children's suggestions next to the names on the board. For example, they may suggest *angry* or *jealous* for Andy, *selfish* or *babyish* for Katie. They should give reasons for their opinions, referring to incidents in the story.

Independent work

● Invite the children to select at least three of the characters to focus on, one of whom must be Andy. She is a complex character, and the children should think about her actions, for example, why she chooses to lock herself in the bathroom. They must consider what her actions tell us about her, as well as what her opinions are of the other characters in the story.
● Provide time for the children to write a paragraph about each character, describing what they are like, citing evidence from the story. As they are writing their own opinions and perceptions, they can use the first person, such as *I think x is.... because...* or *When x said...it made me think they are....*

Review

● Remind the class that we are hearing the story from Andy's point of view. Ask them to consider what other characters in the story might say about Andy – Katie, for instance. Can they think why Katie is apparently so horrible towards Andy? Have they realised that Katie is having to share her room with her new stepsister, and that she might dislike the situation as much as Andy?

Curriculum objectives
● To participate in discussion about both books that are read to them and those they can read for themselves, taking turns and listening to what others say.
● To draw inferences such as inferring characters' feelings, thoughts and motives from their actions, and justify inferences with evidence.

Resources
The Suitcase Kid by Jacqueline Wilson

2: The counsellor

Introduction

● Re-read the opening chapter of *The Suitcase Kid*, where Andy first meets the family counsellor.
● Discuss with the class the conversation between Andy and the counsellor. The counsellor does most of the talking while Andy says very little. Can they suggest what she might be thinking? Do they think the session helped Andy, and in what way? (Bear in mind that some children may have gone through a similar situation.)
● Ask the children how this scene helps the story. What sort of information is it giving about the events and the characters, including Mum and Dad? Why do they think Jacqueline Wilson chose to start her story with this scene?

Paired work

● Ask the children to talk with their partner about what impression the family counsellor might have got of Andy. As she said very little, this would have to be gained mostly from her actions. What might Andy's silence have told the counsellor about how she was feeling?

Independent work

● Using plain paper, invite the children to draw a simple outline of Andy in the centre of the page, and create their own role-on-the-wall.
● Explain that they need to write her feelings and thoughts during the conversation with the counsellor inside the shape, and the things she says and does outside the shape.

Review

● Ask the children why the book is called *The Suitcase Kid*. How does this sum up Andy's feelings?

Curriculum objectives
● To draw inferences such as inferring characters' feelings, thoughts and motives from their actions, and justify inferences with evidence.
● In narratives, to create settings, characters and plot.

Resources
The Suitcase Kid by Jacqueline Wilson; images of mascots and lucky charms

3: Lucky mascots

Introduction

● Show the children images of mascots, including those representing football teams and lucky charms, for example a horseshoe. Ask what these objects have in common with *The Suitcase Kid* (Andy's mascot Radish).
● Do any of the children have special mascots? Perhaps they have a teddy from their early life. Can any of them explain how this makes them feel, and what it would be like if it were lost?
● Read paragraphs 2 and 3 from the 'G is for Garden' chapter of the book. Ask why Radish is so important to Andy, particularly in her current situation. Why would she talk to the toy when she knows it can't hear her?

Independent work

● Invite the children to design their own mascot. Explain that they can give it unique features, so that it can fulfil the owner's requirements. They should consider its size, what it is made from, what it looks like and how it might be able to respond to the owner's problems or wishes.
● Allow time for them to draw the mascot and label it, pointing out its key features. They should also give it an appealing and appropriate name.

Review

● Invite some of the children to share their ideas with the class, in role as a salesperson persuading someone to buy their newly designed mascot.

Curriculum objectives
• To identify themes and conventions in a wide range of books.

Resources
Photocopiable page 170 'Theme matching'; scissors; glue sticks

4: Finding themes

Introduction

• Ask the class to recall the themes they identified earlier in the year, in the stories of Robin Hood. What would they say are the themes in *The Suitcase Kid*? Ask for reasons for their suggestions, referring to incidents in the story.

Paired work

• Hand out photocopiable page 170 'Theme matching' and provide time for the children to work together to discuss how they will group the statements under the suggested headings. There may be different viewpoints about some of the statements. For example, while one child might consider Andy telling Radish how she feels fits with the theme of sadness, another might judge it to be friendship. As long as the children can justify their choices, either would be acceptable.

• Once they have made their decisions, ask them to stick the cut-out boxes on a sheet under the appropriate headings.

Review

• Use the children's completed sheets as the basis for a class discussion about their choices. Which statements are the class generally in agreement about? Where do they differ? Invite the children to give the reasons for their groupings.

Curriculum objectives
• To choose nouns or pronouns appropriately for clarity and cohesion and to avoid repetition.
• To use and understand the grammatical terminology in Appendix 2 accurately and appropriately when discussing their writing and reading.

Resources
The Suitcase Kid by Jacqueline Wilson; photocopiable page 171 'Pronouns please!'

5: Revising pronouns

Introduction

• Select a short section of the book where use is made of several different pronouns. Read it aloud to the class twice – once for them to get the sense of the extract and a second time with the instruction to listen out for the pronouns.

• Ask the children which pronouns they noticed. Why do we use pronouns? What do they do to make the text clearer?

Independent work

• Hand out photocopiable page 171 'Pronouns please!' for the children to read and correct.

• Explain to them that they must identify where pronouns are needed and write their suggestions for which pronouns to use. Warn the children that this doesn't mean that all names need to be replaced with pronouns – names are needed to signal who we are reading about. Remind them that we use pronouns for clarity and cohesion of the text, as well as to avoid ambiguity and repetition.

Differentiation
• Using pronouns correctly can be particularly difficult for children who do not have English as their first language. If this task is confusing for some children, let them spend time identifying pronouns in short sections of the book, to see how they are used.

Review

• Allow time for the children to select any book and have fun working with a partner, reading sections of the text aloud and replacing pronouns with the nouns they are being used instead of.

Week 3 lesson plans

In order to do this week's work, the children will need to have heard or read the whole of *The Suitcase Kid*. They will deepen their understanding of the text by formulating questions. They will read online reviews and read, discuss and use top tips for writing a good review. Working with a partner, they will discuss their approach to the review, making notes which they will use for a first draft which partners will comment on, suggesting improvements before final versions are written in good handwriting. Also, they will recap on the use of the perfect form of verbs. They will read children's reviews of the book on Jacqueline Wilson's website.

Expected outcomes
● All children can formulate questions about the text and write a review of the book.
● Most children can formulate inferential questions, with supporting evidence for the answers. Reviews are organised in paragraphs under appropriate subheadings.
● Some children can provide written explanatory answers to their questions. Their reviews clearly express their opinions.

Curriculum objectives
● To ask questions to improve their understanding of a text.
● To draw inferences such as inferring characters' feelings, thoughts and motives from their actions, and justify inferences with evidence.
● To discuss and record ideas.

Resources
The Suitcase Kid by Jacqueline Wilson; individual whiteboards and pens

I: Questioning the text

Introduction
● Challenge the children to answer a series of quick-fire questions about *The Suitcase Kid*. For example, ask: *Who wrote it? What is the name of the main character? Name three other characters in the story. What is Radish? Where did Andy live before her parents divorced? What did Graham make for Radish? Where was Radish lost?*
● Explain that these are simple, factual questions, the answers to which can be easily found in the book.
● Point out that other questions require more thinking about, where we have to work the answers out from clues in the text. For example: *Why is the book called* The Suitcase Kid? *Why is Radish so important to Andy? Why is Andy losing concentration at school?*
● Ask the class for answers to these and similar questions, that require the children to cite textual evidence for their answers – encourage use of 'because' to facilitate this.

Paired work
● Explain to the children that they will be formulating questions about the story. Some may be straightforward like the first examples, but most should be of the second kind – where we have to work a little harder to arrive at the answers.
● Suggest that they could work chronologically through the book and link their questions to particular incidents, use the relationships between characters for other inferential questions, or consider questions relating to the themes of the book.
● Ask the children to begin by discussing their ideas with a partner, making notes on whiteboards from which to formulate their questions.

Independent work
● Allow time for the children to work quietly, writing their inferential questions on paper. Remind them to use question marks.

Differentiation
● For children finding difficulty with formulating inferential questions, suggest looking back to the previous week's work on the relationships between Andy and Katie or the family counsellor. They could ask questions relating to those and this may then lead them on to think of similar relationship-based questions between other characters in the book. More experienced readers could also provide the answers to their own questions.

Review
● Pair the children with a different partner and invite them to take turns to ask each other questions from their lists, giving feedback on the answers. As a class, summarise the questions. Ask for examples and see how many other children formulated similar questions. What evidence can they cite from the story to support their answers – how many different examples can be given to answer individual questions? Did anyone have an unusual question that no-one else thought of?

Curriculum objectives
● To listen to and discuss a wide range of fiction, poetry, plays, non-fiction and reference books or textbooks.
● To participate in discussion about both books that are read to them and those they can read for themselves, taking turns and listening to what others say.

Resources
Online access to children's book review sites, such as: booksforkeeps.co.uk or www.justimaginestorycentre.co.uk; individual whiteboards and pens (one per group)

2: Reviewing books

Introduction

● Show the children a book review of your choice, for a book they may know or that they would find interesting. Talk about why people write and read book reviews, such as wishing to share books they have read, wanting to find a new book to read or to discover what others thought of a book they've read. Do any of the children or their parents read reviews?

Group work

● In groups of 4–6, invite the children to take turns to tell each other about books they have read, or that have been read to them. Encourage them to talk about books that particularly stick in their minds, either because they enjoyed them or disliked them. These could be non-fiction as well as fiction, and may be favourite picture books or books from their early childhood.
● Ensure each group member is prepared to say why they chose that book to talk about, and to ask and answer questions about the books discussed.
● Ask them to make a list of the books they talked about so they can share them with the class, including authors' names if they know them.

Review

● Encourage each group to read out the list of books they discussed. Are there any duplicates, or more than one title by the same author? Invite comments on known books, noting similarities and differences in the children's opinions.

Curriculum objectives
● To discuss writing similar to that which they are planning to write in order to understand and learn from its structure, grammar and vocabulary.

Resources
Online access to Rodman Philbrick's tips on writing book reviews at: teacher.scholastic.com; children's previous work on *The Suitcase Kid*; *The Suitcase Kid* by Jacqueline Wilson

3: Reviewing *The Suitcase Kid*

Introduction

● Show the class a copy of *The Suitcase Kid* and ask what they thought about the book. What would they say in recommending it to other readers? Who would they suggest would be the most likely readers for the book?
● Explain to the children that they will be writing a review of the book and show them the web page, see Resources where author Rodman Philbrick gives his top tips for writing book reviews. He offers a lot of useful information, which is worth spending some time discussing. Leave the page on display for the children to refer to during the lesson.

Independent work

● Invite the children to use Rodman Philbrick's tips, and start making notes for their review of *The Suitcase Kid*. They may find it helpful to number their notes to match the suggestions in the list. They can refer to the work they have already done on the book and the author.

Review

● Encourage the children to work in pairs and to compare their notes, using them to tell each other what they will be saying under each point. Reassure them that their opinions do not have to agree. Partners should help each other to group their ideas into possible paragraphs, and suggest appropriate subheadings.

Curriculum objectives

- To organise paragraphs around a theme.
- In non-narrative material, using simple organisational devices.
- To use the present perfect form of verbs in contrast to the past tense.
- To choose nouns or pronouns appropriately for clarity and cohesion and to avoid repetition.

Resources

Children's notes (from lesson 3), Rodman Philbrick's online tips (as in lesson 3)

4: Drafting the review

Introduction

- Remind the class about the work they did in lesson 3. Ask what they think will be the most important things for them to have in mind while they write the first drafts of their book reviews today, discussing their responses. Again show them Rodman Philbrick's list of top tips – have they taken all of these into account in their planning?
- Remind the children about the perfect tense of verbs, which they may find useful when writing their reviews. Provide some examples such as: *Andy had been upset since her parents' divorce; She had chosen to live with both of them.* Ask the children for other examples, in the context of the book.

Independent work

- Allow the children to spend the majority of the lesson using their notes to write a first draft of their review. Remind them to re-read and edit their writing as they go along, perhaps a paragraph at a time. Remind them to use nouns and pronouns effectively.
- Reassure them that they may make changes to their original plan as they are working, if they spot a possible improvement, or wish to change their mind about something.

Review

- Provide time at the end of the lesson for the children to quietly read through their completed reviews, making a final check against the top tips list.

Curriculum objectives

- To increase the legibility, consistency and quality of their handwriting.
- To use the diagonal and horizontal strokes that are needed to join letters and understand which letters, when adjacent to one another, are best left unjoined.
- To assess the effectiveness of their own and others' writing and suggest improvements.
- To propose changes to grammar and vocabulary to improve consistency.
- To proofread for spelling and punctuation errors.

Resources

Children's drafts (from lesson 4); online access to Jacqueline Wilson's website

5: Final reviews

Introduction

- Go to the book review section of Jacqueline Wilson's website at www.jacquelinewilson.co.uk where you will find 200+ reviews of *The Suitcase Kid* by children. Share some of the reviews with the class and ask their opinions, comparing them with their own drafted reviews. They may suggest that those on the site are more like comments than reviews.

Paired work

- Working with their planning partners from earlier in the week, invite the children to swap their drafts and offer comments to their partner on possible improvements. These could be about organisation, grammar, spelling, punctuation, vocabulary or content. It is up to the children whether to accept their partner's suggested changes or not.

Independent work

- Provide time for the children to use their best joined handwriting and write final drafts of their book reviews.

Review

- Invite the children to comment on their own reviews. How easy or difficult was it to write them? How satisfied are they with their final reviews? Do they think they have given potential readers a good overview of the story?

Week 4 lesson plans

Jacqueline Wilson's *Cliffhanger* is the basis for this week's work. Its six chapters take 8–10 minutes each to read aloud, so it will be easy to share it with the class over the course of the week. Chapter 1 is part of the first lesson, but the class can enjoy hearing the rest of the book at any time, perhaps as a class serial. They should have heard at least the first three chapters before lesson 3. They will investigate characters through inference, and discuss the use of postcards as a storytelling device, going on to plan and write their own. They will revise using the perfect form of verbs when writing sentences, including conjunctions, adverbs and prepositions of time and cause.

1: Introducing *Cliffhanger*

Introduction
● Introduce the class to Jacqueline Wilson's adventure story, *Cliffhanger*. Read the introduction from the author at the beginning of the book and ask how, based on what she says, this story might differ from *The Suitcase Kid*.

Whole-class work
● Read Chapter 1 to the class. (If multiple copies are available, children can take turns to read parts of it aloud while the others follow.) This will take 7–9 minutes.
● Ask the children for their first reactions to the story. What do they think of Tim? What are their feelings towards him? Are they sympathetic, like Mum? Do they agree with Dad or Giles that he needs to toughen up, or that he's pretty useless? How would they describe the other characters? Invite them to make predictions about what might happen in the story.
● Draw attention to the first-person narrative. Ask what this means about the views we get of characters and events (we are seeing things from Tim's perspective, as we did with Andy in *The Suitcase Kid*). Remind the children that this means that, to get a fuller picture of everyone involved in the story we have to do some detective work, using clues such as what people say and do, and what their reactions are to each other and to events.

Independent work
● Hand out photocopiable page 172 'All about Tim'. Ask the children to consider, based on what they say and do, how each of the characters, including Tim, might describe Tim.
● Encourage them to complete the sheet individually, remembering to write in the first person. If sufficient copies of the text are available, they may refer to these as they work.

Paired work
● Allow time for the children to share their opinions with a partner, discussing similarities and differences in their observations.

> **Differentiation**
> ● Some of the children may benefit from hearing the chapter read again.

Review
● Write each of the characters' names on the board and invite suggestions from the children for words or phrases to describe each of them, based on what the characters say and how they behave towards Tim. How do they think Tim feels about each of the other characters?

Curriculum objectives
● To use conjunctions, adverbs and prepositions to express time and cause.
● To use the present perfect form of verbs in contrast to the past tense.

Resources
Photocopiable page 173 'Because it happened yesterday...'; prepared sentences (listed in Whole-class work)

2: Revising the grammar of time and cause

Introduction
● Write the word *because* on the board and ask the children for examples of sentences containing the word. Point out that they all relate to cause and effect.
● Repeat this for the word *before*, pointing out that the sentences relate in some way to a time element.
● Ask the class for examples of other words which indicate cause or time.

Whole-class work
● Show the children the following sentences on the interactive whiteboard:
  ● *He 'had finished' **before** we arrived.*
  ● *She was off school **because** she 'had been' ill.*
  ● *He 'had eaten' sweets **after** his meal.*
  ● *She 'had fallen' asleep **during** the film.*
  ● *He 'has achieved' his goal **through** hard work.*
● Ask what they notice about the sentences. Draw attention to the perfect form of the verbs (here inside quotation marks) and the prepositions, conjunctions and adverbs of time and cause (here in bold).

Independent work
● Hand out photocopiable page 173 'Because it happened yesterday...' which lists common conjunctions, adverbs and prepositions of time and cause.
● Invite the children to write their own sentences using the perfect form of the verb, including at least one word from each category on the sheet. Leave the example sentences on display as guidance.

Review
● To reinforce the learning with the class use one or all of the starter activities 3 'Improvise it', 5 'Start with the connection' or 12 'The perfect verb'.

Curriculum objectives
● To read books structured in different ways and read for a range of purposes.
● To listen to and discuss a wide range of fiction, poetry, plays, non-fiction and reference books or textbooks.
● To identify how language, structure, and presentation contribute to meaning.

Resources
Cliffhanger by Jacqueline Wilson; photocopiable page 174 'Postcards from Tim'; individual whiteboards

3: Postcards home

Introduction
● Read to the class the first two postcards from Tim in *Cliffhanger*. Ask what we can tell about how he is feeling, and how this has been achieved.

Whole-class work
● Discuss the technique of using postcards to tell the story. What do they add? If we were to read just the postcards, what would we miss? How can we work out how Tim is feeling by the ways he writes the messages? How would Mum and Dad feel, receiving each day's card?

Paired work
● Hand out photocopiable page 174 'Postcards from Tim' for partners to read together. (Or, use copies of the book to read all of the postcards.)
● Invite them to note key elements of each postcard and how the tone changes. Ask them to consider Tim's use of punctuation, underlining, block capitals and sentence length as well as the content.

Review
● As a class, discuss the points the children have noted about the postcards. Conclude by reading the final two postcards in *Cliffhanger*, written as a post-script after the holiday, to Tim's new friends. Ask the children to think back to the beginning of the story. Was Dad right to insist on Tim going on the holiday after all? Has their opinion of Mum and Dad changed?

Curriculum objectives
- In narratives, to create settings, characters and plot.
- To discuss and record ideas.

Resources
Postcards with messages

4: Postcard story: planning

Introduction

- Read one or two real postcards to the class. Ask how the language and tone of them differs from the writing in a novel. For example, they are directed to a specific audience, they summarise events rather than give detail, they use informal language more like speech, they give information and usually don't include direct speech.
- Point out the opportunity for humour and the fun of leaving clues so that the reader becomes a detective working out missing details – and it's also shorter to write.

Whole-class work

- Explain to the class that they will be planning and writing a story of their own in the form of postcards. Discuss the challenge of choosing which events to relate and what to omit. Explain that, just as in the *Cliffhanger* postcards, a lot will be going on that won't find its way on to the postcards – they will need to know this detail, even though they don't write it.

Paired work

- Invite pairs of children to discuss ideas for their stories. Suggest the stories are based on events around a holiday, as that is when postcards are usually written. They must decide who the postcards are written from and to.

Independent work

- Allow time for the children to plan the outline for their story, noting what key events will be written on each postcard. About six postcards would be the best number.

Review

- Using their plans, ask the children to tell the story behind the postcards to their partner.

Curriculum objectives
- In narratives, to create setting, characters and plot.
- To assess the effectiveness of their own and others' writing and suggest improvements.

Resources
Children's plans (from lesson 4)

5: Postcard story: final draft

Introduction

- Invite some of the children to share their story outlines with the class.
- Explain the format for their postcard stories. You may wish them to be written one under the other on paper, or on postcard-sized-pieces of paper or card for more authenticity.

Independent work

- Provide time for the children to write their postcard stories and remind them to use an appropriate tone and informal language. The way they write their postcards should give us a clear idea of the writer's frame of mind, like Jacqueline Wilson did for Tim's postcards in *Cliffhanger*.
- Remind them how something as simple as the way he signed off, his use of punctuation and the length of his sentences gave us clues about how he was feeling.

> **Differentiation**
> - If you use postcard-sized-paper, bear in mind that some of the children may find difficulty in writing small enough for the size of the paper, so a larger size may be needed.

Review

- Working with their original partner, invite the children to read each other's postcard stories, offering feedback on the final products.

Week 5 lesson plans

Having read two books which deal with issues, this week the children will list other issues-based stories they know, in the widest sense. They will collect many issues on which stories can be based and select one to use for writing their own story. They will plan, discuss and write their story which they will edit as they write, before sharing it with a partner for feedback. They will learn about the technique of 'showing, not telling' in narrative to convey characters' feelings by inference, going on to use this in their writing, alongside incorporating the grammatical conventions they have worked on during the year so far.

I: Discussing ideas

Introduction

● Read out dictionary definitions of the word *issue*, for example: *outflow, one publication of a magazine, important topic, supply for use, to take out.* Consider the meanings of these and ask which of them fits the type of stories that they have been reading, which are generally known as stories that deal with issues. Agree on 'important topic' (or a similar definition). Further define this in terms of the stories as including a problem the characters have to deal with.

● Ask the children what the issues were in *The Suitcase Kid and Cliffhanger.* Talk about the differences between them, for instance that Andy's problems were not caused by her, while Tim was dealing with his own personal issues linked to the type of person he was. Note that in both cases the situations were fairly well resolved as there was a happy ending.

Paired work

● Invite pairs of children to make a list of all the stories they know that deal with as wide a range of issues as possible. As well as the Jacqueline Wilson stories, encourage them to recall stories such as Robin Hood or King Midas, which deal with different issues.

● Remind them about picture books that may have friendship issues as their focus, or feelings of inadequacy in various situations. They may know religious stories where issues of a different kind are encountered.

● Explain that issues in stories are not necessarily linked to just one person. In fact the whole theme of a story could be a wider issue such as war, famine or poverty, although it will be seen through the eyes of certain characters.

Group work

● Ask pairs to now join together to form groups of four, in order to share and compare their lists. They should combine their lists to create a 'superlist' of as many titles as they can.

> **Differentiation**
> ● Once again, be sensitive to individual circumstances in this exploration. Use your judgement about pairings and groupings, and be prepared to deal with children for whom particular issues are live.

Review

● Allow groups to share their 'superlists' with the class. Find titles common to all the lists as well as more unusual ones. Which stories did they think of first, and which came later? They can continue thinking and add to the lists tomorrow.

Expected outcomes
● All children can identify stories with issues, and select and write an issues-based story. They understand the difference between telling and showing.
● Most children can list a range of issues on which stories can be based and demonstrate how to show rather than tell about a character's feelings in a narrative.
● Some children can include all taught grammatical conventions in a written narrative. They can indicate a character's feelings by showing rather than telling.

Curriculum objectives
● To participate in discussion about both books that are read to them and those they can read for themselves, taking turns and listening to what others say.
● To identify themes and conventions in a wide range of books.
● To discuss writing similar to that which they are planning to write in order to understand and learn from its structure, grammar and vocabulary.
● To discuss and record ideas.

Resources
Dictionary

Curriculum objectives
● To discuss and record ideas.

Resources
Prepared A3 sheets, each headed with an issue

2: Choosing an image

Introduction
● Explain to the class that they will be planning and writing their own story with an issue of their choice as its basis. Today they will be considering various issues to help them make their decision.

Group work
● Organise the class into groups of 3–4 and give each a sheet of paper on which you have written one of the issues identified by the children in lesson 1. Select those most likely to produce interesting stories.
● Ask the children to think of ideas that could go with the issue on their sheet and write down the best three. The sheets will then be passed around, so that every group has the chance to add their ideas to all the lists. This will obviously become more difficult towards the end, so reassure the children not to worry if their ideas have already been used earlier.
● Collect in the completed sheets and pin them up around the room, so that the children can read all the ideas.

Review
● Bring the class together and ask the children to think of two or three ideas from the lists that they would like to use as the theme for their stories. Invite the children to share their selections, explaining why they have chosen them. Tell them they will have overnight thinking time to make their final selection.

Curriculum objectives
● To discuss writing similar to that which they are planning to write in order to understand and learn from its structure, grammar and vocabulary.
● To assess the effectiveness of their own and others' writing and suggest improvements.
● To propose changes to grammar and vocabulary to improve consistency.

Resources
A3 sheets from the previous lesson

3: Planning the story

Introduction
● Remind the children about the plot structure of Jacqueline Wilson's novels – after an introduction, the stories begin with a problem, the problem develops further and is finally resolved. Can they summarise *The Suitcase Kid* and *Cliffhanger* under these headings?
● Explain to them that they must bear this structure in mind when planning and drafting their stories.

Independent work
● Allow time for the children to plan their issues-based stories, choosing from the ideas they selected in the previous lesson.
● Ask them to structure their stories as previously discussed, making brief outlines of their characters, noting the sequence of events and working out how the problem they create will be resolved. They should include paragraphing in their planning.

Paired work
● Invite the children to use their plans to tell their story outline to a partner, giving and receiving comments on each other's work.

Differentiation
● Story structuring and sequencing can be guided by offering children the choice of using a storyboard approach, which they have used previously. They can add notes to each picture, which then become the paragraphing structure for the finished piece.

Review
● Discuss with the class the process they have gone through in their planning. Have they considered how they will let the reader know about their characters' feelings? Have they thought about how they will use dialogue? Will they write in the first person?

4: Show, not tell

Introduction

- Read the following to the class: *As she walked into the house, Mrs Craig smiled.* Ask the children how Mrs Craig was feeling. How do they know, even though they weren't actually told?
- Give another example: *Alex thumped the table. 'How dare you!' he shouted.* How is Alex feeling? How do we know?
- Explain that the examples are *showing* us how the characters are feeling, rather than *telling* us, for example *Mrs Craig was happy*, or *Alex was angry*. Ask which the children think is the better way (which way is more interesting for the reader). Remind them that these inferential sentences are what they have been used to working out in their reading, particularly in *The Suitcase Kid* and *Cliffhanger*.

Independent work

- Hand out photocopiable page 175 'Showing, not telling' and work through the first two examples with them.
- Invite them to complete the sheet individually. They may offer slightly differing interpretations, but that is fine as long as they fit the sentences.

Review

- With the class, use starter activity 11 'Show, don't tell'.

Curriculum objectives
- To discuss writing similar to that which they are planning to write in order to understand and learn from its structure, grammar and vocabulary.
- To identify how language, structure, and presentation contribute to meaning.

Resources
Photocopiable page 175 'Showing, not telling'

5: The final issue

Introduction

- Inform the class that today they will write the stories they planned earlier in the week. Explain that they must consider their use of language alongside telling the story. Spend a few minutes recalling the grammatical conventions the children have worked on during the year, listing them on the board. The list should include *fronted adverbials*, *pronouns*, *prepositions*, *conjunctions*, *the perfect form of verbs*, *clauses* and *subordinate clauses*. What do these add to the quality of their writing?
- Remind the children that while they must tell us about the events of the story and the actions of the characters, they should also try to use the 'showing, not telling' technique they worked on in lesson 4 in order to convey information about their characters' feelings. This can include dialogue, as what characters say can give us insight into what they are thinking.

Independent work

- Provide time for the children to use their plans to write their issues-based stories, bearing the previous points in mind. They should check through their writing as they go, editing as necessary.

Review

- Encourage partners to swap stories, reading each others' work and commenting on how well the stories have been told. Ask them to also note where grammatical conventions have been used well, or where they might have been used to improve the work.

Curriculum objectives
- In narratives, to create settings, characters and plot.
- To proofread for spelling and punctuation errors.
- To use and understand the grammatical terminology in Appendix 2 accurately and appropriately when discussing their writing and reading.

Resources
Children's plans (from lesson 3)

Expected outcomes
● All children can identify the main theme of the poem, draw a picture of the character, interpret inferential language at a basic level, and write a haiku.
● Most children can cite evidence in the text for their interpretations, spell adverbs with the suffix '-ly' and write more than one haiku.
● Some children can include inference in their own haiku.

Curriculum objectives
● To identify themes and conventions in a wide range of books.
● To draw inferences such as inferring characters' feelings, thoughts and motives from their actions, and justify inferences with evidence.

Resources
Photocopiable page 'Timothy Winters' from the CD-ROM; audio of 'Timothy Winters' by Charles Causley (on the internet)

Week 6 lesson plans

The theme of issues is this week approached through the medium of poetry. The children will study Charles Causley's poem 'Timothy Winters' to work on inference to determine the character's feelings. They will also work on interpreting unfamiliar vocabulary by looking at the context. They will discuss how we can ask questions of poetry. They will read several haiku and write their own on chosen issues. The completed poems will be displayed on a 'poet tree'. They will practise reading the poem in groups before performing it as a class. The children will learn to spell words where the suffix '-ly' is added to root words to form adverbs.

1: 'Timothy Winters'

Introduction
● Play the class the audio of Charles Causley reading his poem 'Timothy Winters' (on the internet) or read it aloud to the class.
● Ask for their reactions to the poem. What is it about? Is Timothy Winters a happy child? How can they tell? What are their feelings towards Timothy?

Whole-class work
● Hand out the photocopiable page 'Timothy Winters' from the CD-ROM, for the children to read the poem themselves. As they read, invite them to underline any words with which they are unfamiliar.
● Play the recording again, so the children can follow the poem as it is being read. Ask them to see if hearing it read aloud helps them to work out what some of the unfamiliar words mean.
● Discuss the words they didn't know – which were they, and which do they have some understanding of after hearing the poem again? Explain that it was written not long after World War II, and some of the references are linked to that (such as *bombs*, *blitz*). Can they work out what a **bomb**ardier is?

Independent work
● Ask the children to read the first four verses to themselves. Can they conjure up a picture in their mind of what Timothy looks like? Is he fat or thin, tall or short, fair or dark-haired? What sort of clothes does he wear? Ask for evidence from the poem to support their descriptions, such as: he is probably thin, as he *licks the pattern off his plate*, suggesting he is very hungry; he is probably dark-haired as exclamation marks are usually printed in black.
● Invite the children to draw a picture of Timothy Winters, based on what the poem tells us about him. Explain that Charles Causley has used similes to describe him, for example his ears don't actually look like real bombs, and his hair isn't exactly the same as an exclamation mark – these are well-chosen, poetic forms of language to get the picture across.

Differentiation
● Similes, metaphors and analogies can prove confusing for some children, so they may find difficulty in interpreting poetry that is not purely descriptive. Try showing them images or objects and asking if they remind them of other things to help them understand this abstract concept, using the terms *like* and *as* (such as *the night sky is **like** a huge blanket*, or *I was **as** cold as ice*).

Review
● Pin the finished drawings on the wall, producing a Timothy Winters gallery for the children to browse, noting the different ways they have interpreted the poem. Discuss the results. Did drawing Timothy help them understand the poem better?

Curriculum objectives
● To draw inferences such as inferring characters' feelings, thoughts and motives from their actions, and justify inferences with evidence.
● To discuss and record ideas.

Resources
Photocopiable page 'Timothy Winters' from the CD-ROM; whiteboards and pens

2: What does it actually say?

Introduction
● Encourage the children to first re-read the poem 'Timothy Winters' on the photocopiable sheet. Remind them of the work they did last week on 'showing, not telling'. Ask how this approach fits with the poem. For example, how did they work out how to portray Timothy in their drawings? They weren't told exactly what he looked like, but they all ended up with a drawing of how he seemed to them.
● Invite them to explain where their images came from, referring to the text. How did they decide what expression to put on his face?

Paired work
● In pairs, invite the children to use the poem to build up a picture of Timothy's life and how he feels about it. Working together, they should look at each verse and discuss what they can deduce about Timothy from it. Advise them to make notes on whiteboards as they go through the poem.

Review
● Ask the children for their observations on Timothy. What sort of life does he lead and how does this make him feel? They should refer to the text to support and explain their deductions. Ask what opinions the adults mentioned in the poem have about Timothy – his parents and grandmother, the teacher and the welfare worker. Do they all feel the same about him? How do we know? Why does Timothy shout 'Amen' (I agree) at the end?

Curriculum objectives
● To use further prefixes and suffixes and understand how to add them (Appendix 1).
● To spell words that are often misspelled (Appendix 1).
● To write from memory simple sentences dictated by the teacher, that include words and punctuation taught so far.

Resources
Individual whiteboards and pens; interactive activity 'Absolutely lovely!' on the CD-ROM; computer access

3: The suffix '-ly'

Introduction
● Write on the board the following words: *actually, recently, regularly*.
● Ask the children what the spellings have in common and what type of words they are (they have '-ly' endings and are adverbs). Ask what job adverbs do, and ensure they know they provide more information about verbs. Remind them that not all adverbs end in '-ly', and that not all words with the '-ly' ending use it as a suffix.
● Ask the class what happens to the words on the board if the '-ly' ending is removed, agreeing that they create complete words, correctly spelled.
● Use interactive activity 'Absolutely lovely!' on the CD-ROM, ask the children to select the words that are root words with the '-ly' suffix added.

Whole-class work
● Invite the children to write the following words, one at a time, each time showing you the results: *strangely, extremely, famously, naturally*. After each word, write the correct spelling on the board in this way: *strange + ly*, so the children can check for themselves. Reinforce the fact that they are root words with the '-ly' suffix added.
● Ask for examples of simple sentences that include these words, such as *He was acting strangely* or *They went swimming regularly*.

Independent work
● Show the children the following words on the board: *accidental, occasional, particular, peculiar, separate*.
● Encourage them to practise spelling each word + '-ly' on their whiteboards.

Review
● Dictate sentences including these words for the children to write. Try relating the sentences to this week's poem, for example *Timothy didn't particularly like school. He was extremely hungry.*

Curriculum objectives
● To ask questions to improve their understanding of a text.
● To recognise different forms of poetry.
● To listen to and discuss a wide range of fiction, poetry, plays, non-fiction and reference books or textbooks.

Resources
Photocopiable page 'Some haiku' from the CD-ROM; individual whiteboards; leaf-shaped pieces of paper; large twigs (to represent a tree), placed in a solid base, on which the leaves are hung; thread or string; scissors

4: The poet tree

Introduction

● Remind the children that they have been working as reading detectives to read between the lines of stories and poems to discover characters' feelings and motivations.
● Ask why they think some writers put their stories into poems rather than novels. Can we ask more questions of poems? Why do they think this might be? What do they think makes a good poem?

Paired work

● Hand out photocopiable page 'Some haiku' from the CD-ROM and invite pairs to read and discuss the five poems.
● Provide time for them to talk together about what might be going on behind these short verses. What feelings are inferred? Could they tell a whole story based on each haiku?

Independent work

● Remind the children that a haiku has the form 5-7-5 syllables. Invite them to write several haiku on any of the issues identified last week. They should try to stick to the traditional syllable count, but it's OK if they go over a little.
● Encourage them to draft their haiku on whiteboards, crafting the poem until they are happy with it, before writing each one on a leaf-shaped piece of paper and attaching it to the 'poet tree'.

Review

● With the class, enjoy sharing many of the haiku on the poet tree.

Curriculum objectives
● To prepare a poem to perform, showing understanding through intonation, tone, volume and action.

Resources
Photocopiable page 'Timothy Winters' from the CD-ROM; audio of 'Timothy Winters' by Charles Causley (on the internet)

5: Performing 'Timothy Winters'

Introduction

● Again, read aloud the poem or play the audio of 'Timothy Winters' by Charles Causley.
● Explain to the children that they will work in groups to rehearse the poem, in preparation for performing it together.
● Ask them to remind you of the criteria they will need to work to, in order to perform the poem effectively, particularly those relating to tone, volume, intonation and pace. Encourage them to include suitable actions or facial expressions.

Group work

● There are eight verses in the poem, so organise the class into appropriate groups to accommodate this. For instance, you could have six groups each allocated one verse from verses 2–7 to read, so the whole class reads the first and last verses together. Appoint group leaders if you think this would be helpful.
● Allow time for the groups to decide how they will read and perform their part of the poem, before practising it.

Review

● Arrange the groups in the order in which they will perform, and let them enjoy giving their performance. If possible, they could perform to another class, or in an assembly. Encourage them to evaluate their performances against the criteria they initially listed.

Curriculum objectives
● To use the present perfect form of verbs in contrast to the past tense.

Resources
Photocopiable page 'Perfect verbs (2)' from the CD-ROM

Grammar and punctuation: Perfect form of verbs

Revise
● Use starter activity 12 'The perfect verb'.
● Remind the children that this is used in the past tense, that we use the verb 'to have' before the past participle of the verb to create the perfect tense.
● Invite the children to do a print hunt, looking for examples of the perfect tense being used in books from the classroom shelves, and in their own writing.

Assess
● Hand out photocopiable page 'Perfect verbs (2)' from the CD-ROM. Go through the instructions and example with the children, ensuring they understand what they must do. If they seem unsure, provide some more examples on the board to work through with them, before allowing them to complete the sheet independently.

Further practice
● Play a quick-fire game of 'Perfect verb tennis'. Call out, or 'serve', any of the following forms of the verb 'to have': *have, has, has been, had, had been* or *have been*. Encourage the children to return with an appropriate verb to match it (such as *talked, thrown, remembered*).

Curriculum objectives
● To use further prefixes and suffixes and understand how to add them (Appendix 1).
● To spell words which are often misspelled (Appendix 1).

Resources
Photocopiable page 'Choose the spelling' from the CD-ROM; individual whiteboards and pens

Spelling: The suffix '-ly'

Revise
● Use starter activities 4 'Suffix challenge' and 9 'Spellchecker'.
● Remind the children of the work they did when adding '-ly' to root words, making adverbs. Read out some of the words for them to write on whiteboards, showing you their results.
● As well as those they have worked on previously, give other words that fit the same pattern, such as *independently, scarcely, roughly*. Write the correct spellings on the board for them to check against their own.

Assess
● Hand out photocopiable page 'Choose the spelling' from the CD-ROM. Ensure the children understand what they have to do before they complete the sheet independently.

Further practice
● Develop the children's spelling knowledge by adding root words whose spelling changes when '-ly' is added. For instance, root words which end in 'le', where the 'e' is dropped before '-ly' is added, such as *gently, simply, humbly*. Alternatively, words ending in 'y' where the 'y' is changed to an 'i' before adding the suffix, such as *heavily, angrily, cosily*.
● Dictate short sentences containing the target words for the children to write either on whiteboards for a quick response, or on paper if you wish to make further full assessments.

Curriculum objectives
● To draw inferences such as inferring characters' feelings, thoughts and motives from their actions and justifying inferences with evidence.
● To identify ideas drawn from more than one paragraph and summarise these.

Resources
The Suitcase Kid by Jacqueline Wilson

Reading: Stories dealing with issues

Revise

● Ask the children to recall the story of *The Suitcase Kid*. Who were the main characters and what relationships did they have with Andy? Can they remember how Andy felt about each of them? Select a few pages from the book to share with the children to act as reminders. Focus on Katie, Mum, Dad, Uncle Bill and Carrie.

● Remind the children that as the story is written in the first person, we see everything from Andy's point of view. Explain that now that they have done more work on inference and deduction, they will be able to use their reading detective skills to work out how the other characters might have been feeling about Andy, even though we don't hear directly from them. The things they do and say give us clues about what they might be thinking or how they might be feeling.

● Discuss with the class the following questions: When Carrie offered to make something else for Andy to eat because she didn't like the bean casserole she had cooked, what does that tell us about Carrie's feelings towards Andy? When both Mum and Dad wanted Andy to move to a school closer to where they lived, what signals is that giving us about their feelings for their daughter? What are Katie's feelings at having to share her bedroom and Bill's feelings when Andy kept fighting Katie?

Assess

● Invite the children to write a paragraph explaining what each of the main characters might have thought and how they might have felt, about Andy. Each paragraph needs to be headed with the character's name, making five paragraphs in total.

● Before writing their final piece, allow the children some time to think about each character in turn and make notes about each one. If possible, they should refer to particular incidents from the story to support their observations and opinions.

Further practice

● In guided reading sessions or when you are reading other books with the class, use opportunities to ask questions about characters' feelings, actions and what motivates them.

● Encourage the children to find examples of where writers have used the 'showing, not telling' technique, explaining what they have understood as readers when this has been used.

Curriculum objectives
● In narratives, to create settings, characters and plot.
● To compose and rehearse sentences orally (including dialogue), progressively building a varied and rich vocabulary and an increasing range of sentence structures (See Appendix 2).
● To punctuate direct speech.
● To assess the effectiveness of their own and others' writing and suggest improvements.
● To propose changes to grammar and vocabulary to improve consistency.
● To proofread for spelling and punctuation errors.

Resources
Photocopiable page 'Timothy Winters' from the CD-ROM

Writing: Stories dealing with issues

Revise

● Invite the children to read the poem 'Timothy Winters' to themselves, before performing it once more as a class.
● Ask the children to recall the impact the poem had on them and the impressions they gained about Timothy and the adults mentioned in the poem. What issues did they identify that the poem was about?

Assess

● Explain to the children that they will be writing Timothy's own story of a day in his life, as a first-person narrative, taking clues from the poem. This should be carried out over two days – the first for thinking, discussing and planning, the second for writing.
● Ask them to imagine a school day in Timothy's life. *What might he think as he woke up? What might other people in the house say to him before he left for school? How would he get to school and what might he be thinking about the day ahead? How might he be greeted when he gets into the school playground? Does he have any friends? Imagine some of his lessons, how he gets on in them and what the teachers might say to him. What happens to Timothy when he gets home? What might be his last thoughts before he goes to sleep?*
● After a general class discussion, give the children a short time to talk about the questions above with a partner before they plan their story.
● Provide the children with the following criteria against which you will be assessing their stories:
    ● they must be in the first person (as Timothy)
    ● they must include some 'showing, not telling'
    ● they must be a sequential story, told in the order in which things happen
    ● they must be written in paragraphs; they must include some direct speech.
● In addition, inform the class that you will be looking out for: fronted adverbials; correct punctuation; correct use of pronouns; good spelling; interesting vocabulary; a range of sentence structures.
● On the second day, allow time for the children to use their plans to write their stories.

Further practice

● It will be interesting for the children to read each others' versions of Timothy's day, comparing how they have told his story. Ask the class how they see Timothy's future. *What might he do to forge a better life for himself? Who might he turn to for help and what difference might that make? What might his life be like in twenty years' time?*
● Encourage the children to find more poems that could be retold as a narrative. Collect them and use them as a speaking and listening resource. Copy the poems onto card and store them in a box. Invite pairs of children to select a poem and use it to tell each other their version as a story.

Comparing characters

■ Complete this grid by comparing typical characters in different types of story.

	Type/Name of character	Main characteristics
Roald Dahl stories		
Myths		
Jacqueline Wilson stories		

I can identify and compare characters from different types of story.

How did you do?

Facts about Jacqueline Wilson

- Answer these questions about Jacqueline Wilson.

1. When and where was she born?

_____

2. Where did she spend her childhood?

_____

3. At what age did she write her first book?

_____

4. What was her job before she became a novelist?

_____

5. When was the first *Tracy Beaker* book published? _____

6. Who has illustrated many of her books? _____

7. Which three of her books have won awards?

   1. _____

   2. _____

   3. _____

8. How many of her books have been sold in the UK? _____

9. What award did she win in 2002? _____

10. What did she win the award for? _____

11. What job did she have between 2005 and 2007? _____

12. What is her title now? _____

I can find the answers to questions in a non-fiction text.

How did you do?

Theme matching

■ Cut out the boxes and arrange them under the headings 'Sadness', 'Jealousy', 'Divorce' and 'Friendship', according to which themes you think they best fit.

✂

Andy's parents don't want to be married any more.	Katie doesn't like sharing her bedroom with Andy and is mean to her.
Andy wishes she could still live at Mulberry Cottage with her mum and dad.	Andy locks herself in the bathroom to get away from the others.
Andy tells Radish how she feels.	At school, Andy's friend Aileen spends more time with Fiona now.
Andy's parents spend a lot of time arguing.	Andy spends half of her time with Mum and half with Dad.
Andy decided she would call the new baby Ethel, as it was a name she didn't like.	Andy hated seeing Katie snuggled up to un-Uncle Bill, eating chocolates he had bought for her.
Mum, Dad and Andy had to meet with a family counsellor.	Mum and Dad each want Andy to move to a school near where they live.
Andy's teachers complain that she isn't concentrating at school.	Andy is mad at Carrie, her dad's new wife.
Andy thinks Katie is not a sugar mouse but a king-size rat.	Andy is pleased that Dad doesn't like Katie.

Pronouns please!

- Underline the nouns that need changing into pronouns and write the correct pronoun above.

Jacqueline Wilson tells us Andrea's story of what happened to Andrea

when Andrea's mum and dad got divorced. Andrea is Andrea's full

name but Andrea is usually known as Andy. Andy decides to live with

Andy's mum one week and Andy's dad the next week. Andy's mum's

new partner Bill also lives at Andy's mum's house, as well as his three

children, Katie, Paula and Graham. Katie doesn't like Andy and Andy

doesn't like Katie. Katie is mean to Andy while Andy always seems to be

fighting with Katie.

When Andy goes to Andy's dad's house, Andy has more new people to

learn to live with. There's Andy's dad's partner Carrie and Carrie's twins,

Crystal and Zen. Andy seems to get on quite well with Crystal, which

may be because Crystal is younger than Andy and doesn't annoy Andy

like Katie does.

I can identify where pronouns are needed and improve a piece
of writing by using them correctly.

How did you do?

All about Tim

■ Write down how each character would describe Tim.

Mum says:

Dad says:

Tim says:

Kelly says:

Giles says:

I can describe how characters feel about each other from inferential clues.

How did you do?

PHOTOCOPIABLE

Because it happened yesterday...

- Here are examples of common conjunctions, adverbs and prepositions.

Conjunctions of time

before	Look both ways <u>before</u> you cross the road.
until	Wait here <u>until</u> I come back.
when	It was a beautiful day <u>when</u> we had our picnic.

Conjunctions of cause

because	The heating was on high <u>because</u> it was snowy.
but	He was short <u>but</u> he was very strong.
as	<u>As</u> it was raining, we stayed indoors.

Adverbs of time

yesterday	Cinderella went to the ball <u>yesterday</u>.
later	<u>Later</u> she left in a hurry.
never	She <u>never</u> imagined she would marry the prince.

Adverbs of cause

because	He did well <u>because</u> he had worked hard.
since	She left early <u>since</u> her plane left at 3pm.
as	<u>As</u> it's so hot, you'd better take a bottle of water.

Prepositions of time

at	The moon shines <u>at</u> night
after	I'll meet you <u>after</u> school.
during	We went swimming a lot <u>during</u> the holidays.

Prepositions of cause

for	He succeeded <u>for</u> many reasons.
from	You won't succeed <u>from</u> luck alone.
through	He came first <u>through</u> sheer determination.

Postcards from Tim

- Examine the four postcards below.

Dear Mum and Dad

I am at the Adventure Centre. Well.
You know that. You took me here.

   I have only been here
half an hour. I am not
enjoying it so far.
Not one bit.

With love from Tim
xxxxxxxx to Mum
x to Dad

Dear Mum and Dad

I promised to write you lots of postcards.
So I am. I keep my promises.
Not like some people.

   Maybe this will be the last postcard you will
get though. Because we are going abseiling
today. It is very dangerous. I could easily
fall to my death. But if you'd only come and
collected me last night you'd still have your
only son alive and well.

From Tim

Dear Mum and Dad

I went abseiling!!!
I didn't like it. (Understatement of the century.)
I let go of the rope and
was in MORTAL DANGER.
But I managed to grab
it again. I survived. Just.

With love from Tim

P.S. It's canoeing today.
I could still drown.

Dear Mum and Dad

Guess what! We won the bucket race!!! And
it was all because I sussed out how to do it.
Honest. The other Tigers all think I'm Mega-
Brilliant. Even Giles. Wonders will never cease.

   I can think of another Wonder. I'm quite
enjoying my adventure holiday now. In fact
I almost wish we weren't going home tomorrow!

With love from Tim
xxxxx to Mum
xxxxx to Dad

Showing, not telling

■ Be a reading detective! Next to each sentence, write how this might have been written if the author was simply telling us how the characters felt. Two examples are given.

"It's not fair!" complained Joe, stamping his foot.	Joe was annoyed.
Zara sat quietly in the corner, staring at the floor.	Zara felt unhappy.
The smile on Max's face could have lit up the night sky.	
Sanjit felt himself shaking and his heart began to pound.	
"I'm not sure if I can do that," said Luis, biting his lip.	
Suki eyed the huge slice of cake. "Mmm," she said, "Can I have two?"	
Mrs Watts looked again at the clock. She had already been waiting over an hour. How much longer would it be?	
As Kai watched the sun rising over the clear blue sea, he smiled to himself, knowing that from now on everything was going to be OK.	

I can understand what characters are feeling when a writer shows instead of tells me.

How did you do?

Rainforest

It would be ideal if this half-term's work on the rainforest coincided with studying the Amazon in geography and animals in science. The children will research the subject in books and online, using what they learn as the basis for writing a travel guide. They will consider issues of the rainforest to create a web page and poster for a 'save the rainforest' campaign. In looking at the people of the rainforest, they will write a diary entry in role for a day spent there. After reading two Brazilian stories, the children will write their own rainforest-based story in a genre of their choice. Animal poems are to be read and written in the final week. Grammar, punctuation and spelling that was covered earlier in the year will be consolidated in this unit.

Expected prior learning
- Can research a subject.
- Can use a dictionary.
- Can use pronouns, the perfect form of verbs, connectives and fronted adverbials.
- Can understand short stories as a genre.
- Can understand poems in different forms.
- Can understand and use a range of prefixes and suffixes.
- Can organise work under headings and subheadings.
- Can use paragraphing.

Overview of progression
- The children will demonstrate their knowledge and understanding of all aspects of grammar and punctuation covered in the year, extending their understanding of pronouns to use the possessive form.
- Their drafting and editing skills will be further used, including reviewing writing as they work.
- By reading a wide range of texts, the children will further develop their ability to combine factual and fictional writing. In researching the rainforest, they will use note-taking to aid them in summarising what they read. By planning, rehearsing and presenting poems to the class, the children will enhance their delivery of texts.

Creative context
- Much rich art work can be linked to the rainforest theme and can form a backdrop to a display of the children's writing.
- Rhythms and sounds of the rainforest can be used in music, while animal movement can be interpreted in dance.
- Habitats, deforestation issues and animals can all be studied in detail in science,
- The physical and human aspects can be studied in geography.

Preparation
Familiarise yourself with an overview of the Amazon rainforest from geographical, scientific and social perspectives. Find out which animals are found there, and which are not.

You will also need:
Internet access; range of books about the rainforest; selection of travel guides; individual whiteboards and pens; dictionaries; A3 paper; selection of posters and images of posters; felt-tipped pens; sticky notes; images of people and homes of the Amazon; *Diary of a Wimpy Kid* by Jeff Kinney; a selection of musical instruments; images of the rainforest including animals.

On the CD-ROM you will find:
Media resources 'Rainforest animals', 'Rainforest sounds'; interactive activities 'Editors needed', 'Possession'; photocopiable pages 'Deer and Jaguar: a Brazilian folk tale', 'Pronoun check', 'Rainforest survivor'

Chapter at a glance

An overview of the chapter. For curriculum objective codes, please see pages 8–10.

Week	Lesson	Curriculum objectives	Summary of activities	Outcomes
1	1	RC: 1, 2, 15	Introduce rainforest – what do you know? Watch rainforest videos. Begin 'KWL grid'. Browse books and internet to plan research.	• Can partly complete 'KWL grids'.
	2	RC: 1, 2 WC: 1	Look at online and hard copy versions of travel guides, noting writing style and information included. List headings for later use.	• Can recognise what is included in travel guides and language styles used.
	3	RWR: 1 RC: 3, 13, 15 WC: 2	Watch short video. Decide areas of Amazon rainforest to research for travel guide. Groups research one area and summarise for class.	• Can identify main areas of research and information gathered in groups and make notes ready for writing up.
	4	RC: 9, 13 WT: 5 WC: 2, 6	Groups divide research area into sections to be written in drafts. Writing style agreed. Drafts written, shared and edited.	• Can write draft paragraphs and make any necessary changes.
	5	WC: 6	Individuals share well-written sentences. Final drafts written and shared. Illustrations or maps added. Work evaluated.	• Can complete final version of the travel guide, with illustrations added and discuss and evaluate their work.
2	1	RC: 15	Recap rainforest information. Watch videos and discuss deforestation and other issues. Groups discuss problems and feedback to class.	• Can summarise previous research, understand and discuss new information and form opinions based on this.
	2	RC: 14 WC: 1	Working as conservation campaigners, the children plan a web page on the rainforest after investigating how pages are constructed.	• Can complete, share and explain web page plans.
	3	WC: 6	Discuss layout of web pages. Use plan to create web page on paper or on screen. Choose idea for poster.	• Can complete web pages with headings, subheadings and illustrations and select content for poster.
	4	WT: 5 WC: 6	Look at posters to identify key features. Draft and make rainforest campaign posters. Display for class to give positive comments to favourites.	• Can complete effective campaign posters and share with class for evaluative comments.
	5	RC: 16 WC: 10	Vote on whether to save rainforests. Groups discuss, in role, different opinions before whole-class debate. Vote again.	• Can use research to discuss points from various perspectives, listening to others and taking part themselves.
3	1	WC: 1, 2	View images of rainforest people and houses. Discuss differences. Complete 'How can I live without them?' sheet. Share ideas and discuss.	• Can use researched knowledge to compare rainforest and western lifestyles.
	2	WC: 2	Children choose persona for in-role writing. Use thinking sheet to note ideas under given headings. Discuss structure with partner.	• Can make notes on areas for inclusion in diary entries and use to outline a day in their rainforest life with partner.
	3	WC: 3, 11, 12, 13, 15, 17	Listen to extract from Diary of a Wimpy Kid, identify key features of a diary entry. Use plans to write first draft.	• Can complete drafts, covering required criteria, accurate use of pronouns and a range of conjunctions.
	4	WC: 7, 8, 9	Discuss marking criteria. Use starter activity 14 'Edit it'. Children review and edit drafts of diaries. Discuss progress in editing process.	• Can review and edit draft diary entries and discuss editing process.
	5	WT: 7, 8	Discuss criteria for good handwriting. Final drafts of rainforest diaries. Consider what rainforest people would make of western lifestyles.	• Can write final drafts of rainforest diaries in clear joined handwriting.
4	1	RC: 1, 2, 4, 10, 11, 12	Listen to 'Legend of the Mafumeira', making predictions. Discuss characters' feelings. Act scene in threes, hot-seat characters. Discuss tension in the story.	• Can demonstrate understanding of characters' motivations through prediction, discussion and acting.
	2	RC: 2, 7 WC: 11, 14	Identify differences between short story and novel. Read and discuss 'Deer and Jaguar', noting sentence structure and suggesting changes.	• Can identify short story conventions, discuss story and sentence structure and make suggestions for further use of conjunctions.
	3	WC: 16, 18, 20	Revise pronouns. Introduce possessive pronouns, with examples. Write dictated sentences from memory containing possessive pronouns.	• Can show understanding of possessive pronouns by accurate completion of sheet and writing dictated sentences on whiteboards.
	4	RC: 3, 4, 9, 13	Discuss story summaries. Read 'Deer and Jaguar' and complete summary. Compare with partner; retell using partner's summary.	• Can summarise a story in short sentences and retell using partner's summary.
	5	WC: 12, 13, 15, 17, 19	Use starter activity 7 'Fronted adverbials'. Rewrite sections of 'Deer and Jaguar' using fronted adverbials. Compare results.	• Can demonstrate through writing how to use fronted adverbials, with commas after them.

Chapter at a glance

Week	Lesson	Curriculum objectives	Summary of activities	Outcomes
5	1	WC: 1, 2	Complete 'KWL grids'. Think-pair-share. Groups suggest ideas for rainforest stories under given headings.	• Can compile lists of possible story ideas under story-type headings and begin to think about their stories, ready to plan.
	2	WC: 3, 4, 5	Share story ideas already chosen. Use planning sheet to plan characters, setting and plot of short stories. Outline to partner.	• Can compile and share orally their plans for rainforest short stories.
	3	WC: 11, 12, 13, 14, 15, 17, 18, 19, 20	Use starter activities appropriate for the class. Children complete 'What a lot I've learned' sheet. Further starters activities used to consolidate.	• Can demonstrate understanding of grammar, punctuation and spelling by taking part in starter activities and completing sheets.
	4	WC: 3, 4	Reminders about what should be included in drafts of rainforest stories. Children write first drafts, revising as they go.	• Can complete drafts of rainforest stories, including all necessary elements and discuss their writing.
	5	WC: 7, 8, 9	Partners read and comment upon each other's stories, offering suggestions for improvement. Final drafts written. Selected sections shared with class.	• Can write completed rainforest stories in best handwriting, showing children's best work of the year.
6	1	RC: 1, 7, 8 WC: 1	List rainforest animals. Read and discuss the three poems on the 'Animal poems' sheet. Think about animals for their own poems.	• Can analyse poems, discussing rhythm, rhyme, structure and word choice.
	2	RC: 6	Listen to rainforest sounds. Groups practise and perform one of the three animal poems, with musical and sound accompaniment.	• Can work together to practise and perform a given poem, adding sounds to create atmosphere.
	3	RWR: 1 RC: 7 WT: 1, 2, 3	Use starter activity 9 'Spellchecker'. List words ending in '-ous' and '-ly'. for animal description. Pairs compose descriptive phrases. Dictate phrases for spelling.	• Can compose descriptive phrases and correctly spell words with taught suffixes.
	4	WC: 3	Recap on earlier work. Share ideas for animal poem with partner. Write poem and some are read aloud to the class.	• Can write animal poems in chosen form, maintaining rhythm, and rhyme where appropriate.
	5	RC: 6	Hear audio and watch rainforest images. Plan and read aloud poems to a partner and a group. Discuss writing process.	• Can plan, rehearse and perform a reading of their own animal poems to a group.

Background knowledge

Alliteration: Words starting with the same sounds, used for poetic effect or to add emphasis.

Assonance: Words with rhyming sounds in the middle, such as *deep, believe, freeze*.

Possessive pronoun: A pronoun is a word that replaces a noun in a sentence. Possessive pronouns are pronouns that demonstrate ownership.

Week 1 lesson plans

To begin their half-term's work on rainforests, the children will first consider what they already know about rainforests and what they want to learn, by completing a KWL grid. They will use this to guide research in books and online. After looking at a variety of travel guides, they will combine their research with their understanding of what a guide contains and the varied writing styles used to create them, to work in groups to produce a class guide to the Amazon rainforest.

1: Let's go to the rainforest!

Introduction

● Ask the children what they know about rainforests. What and where are they? What might they expect to find there?
● Explain that they will be working this half-term on rainforests and show the two short BBC videos which give an introductory overview of the Amazon rainforest www.bbc.co.uk (search for 'Rainforest videos', then find clips 'Amazon wildlife' and 'Amazon rainforest'.)

Independent work

● Hand out photocopiable page 136 'KWL grid' and ask the children to complete the first column, writing what they already Know about rainforests, bullet-pointing each separate fact.
● Next, invite them to complete the middle column, again using bullet points to write down What they want to learn about rainforests. What are they curious or puzzled about? What particular aspects of the rainforest would they be interested in learning more about? Encourage them to think about different areas, such as location, plants, animals, habitats, geographical features, people of the rainforest, problems associated with rainforests and so on.
● Explain that they will use these questions to guide the research they will be doing.

Group work

● Organise the children into groups of 4–6 and give each group several rainforest books and a computer with access to the internet. A good resource is Dorling Kindersley's *Jungle*, which is in their 'Eyewitness' series. Allow them time to browse through the books and start online searches to gather insight into the areas they will be researching later. (Two sites which they may find useful are: www.rainforest-alliance.org/kids and www.sciencekids.co.nz/sciencefacts/earth/rainforests.html)
● Encourage the groups to make rough notes such as website addresses, books and page numbers to save time when they begin their more detailed research.
● Remind them to bear in mind the questions on their KWL grids to guide their reading and to complete the L section where they can note what they have already Learned.

> **Differentiation**
> ● If you have any children in the class with personal experience of, or a particular interest in rainforests, invite them to share their knowledge with the class.

Review

● Question the class on what they identified as areas they wanted to discover more about. Were there any common threads? What useful websites have been discovered, and which books have they found to be potentially helpful? Share interesting facts they have already discovered through their browsing.

Expected outcomes
● All children can identify what they know about rainforests, discuss and plan writing with a group, research basic facts and contribute towards a non-fiction text.
● Most children can recognise different writing styles and apply this knowledge to their writing.
● Some children can summarise their research in an efficient and engaging way.

Curriculum objectives
● To retrieve and record information from non-fiction.
● To read books that are structured in different ways and reading for a range of purposes.
● To listen to and discuss a wide range of fiction, poetry, plays, non-fiction and reference books or textbooks.

Resources
Internet access; photocopiable page 136 'KWL grid'; a range of books about the rainforest

Curriculum objectives
● To read books that are structured in different ways and read for a range of purposes.
● To listen to and discuss a wide range of fiction, poetry, plays, non-fiction and reference books or textbooks.
● To discuss writing similar to that which they are planning to write in order to understand and learn from its structure, grammar and vocabulary.

Resources
A selection of travel guides; individual whiteboards and pens; internet access

2: Travel guides

Introduction

● Explain to the class that later in the week, when they have done the research they began planning in lesson 1, they will write a travel guide to the Amazon rainforest. Today they will be exploring travel guides to help them plan their own.
● Choose destinations from travel guide websites, such as www.lonelyplanet.com and www.roughguides.com. Select guides which use language differently to describe destinations, and which offer different information about them. For example, the *Lonely Planet* guides use informal language which speaks directly to the reader, addressing them as 'you'. Lavish descriptions include many adjectives and interesting verbs. *Rough Guides*, on the other hand, are more formal in tone and more information-centred, but also make extensive use of adjectives.
● Read a few guides with the class and discuss the similarities and differences between them. Do they have a preferred style, and why?

Group work

● Provide groups of 4–6 with a selection of travel guides and allow them access to online versions, too. Ask them to browse through the guides, noting the sort of information which they contain and the styles in which they have been written.

Review

● Ask what areas of information the travel guides cover, and write them on the board, such as *weather, climate, sights, wildlife, currency, language* and *rivers*. Keep the list for use tomorrow.

Curriculum objectives
● To retrieve, and record information from non-fiction.
● To identify main ideas drawn from more than one paragraph and summarise these.
● To apply their growing knowledge of root words, prefixes and suffixes (etymology and morphology) as listed in Appendix 1, both to read aloud and to understand the meaning of new words they meet.
● To use dictionaries to check meanings of words that they have read.
● To discuss and record ideas.

Resources
Children's notes (from lessons 1 and 2); children's photocopiable page 136 'KWL grid' (from lesson 1); dictionaries; internet access; books on the rainforest

3: Researching the rainforest

Introduction

● Show the class the (2-and-a-half minute) BBC video of David Attenborough in the Amazonian rainforest at: http://www.bbc.co.uk/programmes/p00fdrh0
● Remind them that they will be carrying out their research on the Amazon rainforest using the work they did in previous lessons to guide them.
● Focus on the list from lesson 2. Discuss the headings and decide together on five or six that groups will research. Choose headings that allow for gathering plenty of information (for example *animals* is more wide-ranging than *language*). Can they suggest how some headings could be grouped together, so that smaller pieces of information are included? For example, travellers would want to know about language, currency and airports, which could be grouped under *Essential travel information*.

Group work

● Arrange the class into groups and assign one area of research from your list to each of the groups.
● Invite the children to use books and the internet to research their topic about the Amazon rainforest, making notes of the information they find. Encourage them to read and summarise where possible, not to copy out whole sections. They will need basic facts, but they will be writing it in their own words later in the week.
● Allow them to use dictionaries to check the meanings of unfamiliar words.

Review

● Ask the groups to summarise their findings for the rest of the class.

Curriculum objectives
- To discuss and record ideas.
- To check that the text makes sense to them, discussing their understanding and explaining the meaning of words in context.
- In non-narrative material, to use simple organisational devices.
- To identify main ideas from more than one paragraph and summarise these.
- To use the first two or three letters of a word to check its spelling in a dictionary.

Resources
Children's research notes (from lesson 3)

4: Planning the travel guide

Introduction
- Remind the children of the different writing styles in the travel guides they read at the start of the week. Explain that when they write their own travel guides, the groups must agree on the tone they will use.
- Inform them that today they will divide up the information they found in lesson 3 and write their first drafts. They must be sure they understand what they found, as they will be writing in their own words.
- Encourage the groups to work together, helping each other as necessary.

Group work
- Provide time for the children to decide in their groups who will write each part of the area they have researched. For example, those writing about animals could choose an animal each; climate and weather can be divided into seasons or weather types. Having made their decisions, encourage them to write first drafts of their parts of the travel guide, using the writing style they have all agreed on. Each child should write one paragraph. They should check spellings of words they are unsure of, using a dictionary.
- Ask the children to swap their drafts with others in their group, for comment and the opportunity to make changes. Have they explained things clearly and used interesting language?

Review
- Invite each group in turn to tell the class how they have divided up their own area of the guide, such as which animals or plants they chose.

Curriculum objectives
- In non-narrative material, to use simple organisational devices.

Resources
Children's drafts (from lesson 4)

5: Final travel guides

Introduction
- Invite the children to share with the class sentences from their draft travel guides that they feel work particularly well, either because they are very clear, well constructed or use excellent vocabulary.
- Remind the class that they will make final versions of their sections of the travel guide today, and that they should check through their drafts first, in order to make any final changes they think would improve their work.

Independent work
- Allow time for the children to write their final versions of the travel guides using clearly joined handwriting.

Whole-class work
- Ask the children if they can think of any additions they could make to the travel guides that readers would find extra helpful or interesting. So far they have not been asked to provide illustrations of any kind. They may also suggest including maps. There should be sufficient time left in the lesson for drawings to be made and added to the written information.

Review
- Ask the children to arrange their completed work on tables around the room for everyone to see what has been produced. Discuss the finished travel guides and decide on how they will be displayed, such as on a wall or collated into a book. Ask the children to evaluate their work.

Expected outcomes
● All children can research information and discuss what they find. They can create a basic web page and poster, using headings and subheadings.
● Most children can summarise information gained from a variety of sources and convey this to readers and listeners.
● Some children can engage actively in debate, using newly acquired information to inform opinion.

Curriculum objectives
● To retrieve and record information from non-fiction.

Resources
Computer and internet access; books about the rainforest; individual whiteboards and pens

Week 2 lesson plans

This week, the children will engage with the destruction of rainforests. They will research in books and online the perspectives of different interested groups. They will look at the structure and language of web pages and the key features of posters, in order to create their own as part of a 'saving the rainforest' campaign. Finally, they will use their new knowledge to engage in an in-role debate about the future of the rainforest. Note that children will need adequate keyboard skills to compose their writing online where this is an option, and also be competent in modifying text sizes and inserting pictures and downloaded images.

1: Rainforest destruction

Introduction
● In role, inform the children that you have heard they are experts on planning trips to the Amazon and you would like to go there. What advice can they give you? What should you not miss seeing? How should you prepare yourself for the trip? What should you expect to experience when you are there?
● Listen to the class's responses, which should be based on the research they did last week. Be prepared to ask questions to follow up their suggestions, requiring them to recall further information from their research.

Whole-class work
● Now come out of role and ask the class if they know of any threats to the rainforest. Did anyone find information last week about deforestation or threats to wildlife? What do they know of these issues?
● Show the class two short BBC videos about deforestation and the consequent threat to plants and animals of the rainforest at: www.bbc.co.uk (search for 'Rainforest videos', then find clips 'Rainforest destruction' and 'Deadly deforestation'.)
● Discuss the information in the videos. Did the children know about this? What are their reactions? Is there just one side to the story, or can they see arguments for both sides?
● Show the class the World Wildlife Fund web page about deforestation of the Amazon at www.wwf.org.uk (search for 'Amazon').
● Examine the web page and pick out several points to read and discuss with the children. Are there words they don't know, such as *species, natural resources, sustainable agriculture, logging*? Can they work out the meanings from the context?

Group work
● Working in groups of 3–5, ask the children to find out more about the issues raised. Offer them the headings: *local people, trees, animals* and *the wider world*, to guide their research. Encourage them to use books and online sources, making brief notes on whiteboards.
● Afterwards, invite them to talk together about what they have found. Suggest they formulate questions to talk about, starting with words such as *how, why, what if.*

Review
● Write on the board the headings you gave to the groups. Invite representatives from each group to summarise and report back to the class, the key points they discovered. What arguments did they raise? Did all groups come up with similar points or were there some differences? Ask if this extra knowledge would make them change or add anything to the travel guide they wrote last week.

Curriculum objectives
● To identify how language, structure, and presentation contribute to meaning.
● To discuss writing similar to that which they are planning to write in order to understand and learn from its structure, grammar and vocabulary.

Resources
Internet access; pre-selected child-friendly websites; photocopiable page 200 'My web-page plan'

2: Investigating web pages

Introduction
● Establish with the class that, from what they now know about deforestation, the loss of the world's rainforests is concerning. Explain that they will work as conservation campaigners, planning a campaign to save the rainforests.
● Invite suggestions for what they could do to get people's attention and give them information. Using the children's ideas, select web-based information and a poster campaign.

Whole-class work
● Inform the class that today they will plan a web page about the Amazon rainforest. They must decide whether it will be a home page, that covers several topics, or a page devoted to one aspect only.
● Select a web page they will enjoy, such as the Natural History Museum site at: www.nhm.ac.uk (click on 'Kids only' and then select 'Earth and Space'). Look at the differences between what is included on a homepage, and a page specific to a topic, listing these on the board.
● With the class, study the use of language. Notice how questions are used to engage the reader, often encouraging us to click on links to other pages.

Independent work
● Hand out photocopiable page 200 'My web-page plan'. Talk through it so that the children understand how to use the photocopiable sheet. Having decided on the focus for their web page, invite them to complete the sheet.
● If possible, allow the children time to find and print photographs or maps that they can use for their paper-based web pages.

Review
● Working in pairs, encourage the children to share their ideas, explaining what they plan to include and how they will arrange their web page.

Curriculum objectives
● In non-narrative material, to use simple organisational devices.

Resources
Children's web page plans (from lesson 2); A3 paper; computers (optional); printed illustrations (from lesson 2, if used)

3: Writing a web page

Introduction
● Invite the children to share their web-page ideas. Ask: *How will you organise the information and illustrations?* Remind them that they will need to think about font sizes for headings, subheadings and general text, as well as captions for the illustrations they plan to include.

Independent work
● Provide time for the children to use their plans to create their web pages. These can be written on A3 paper or on computers, where the images can be downloaded. Hand-written versions can include printed images that are pasted on, or drawings added afterwards.
● Remind them about their use of language, emphasising that they must inform and engage. How will they do this? Will they use questions or speak directly to the reader by using the pronoun *you*? What persuasive language could they use? Will they make use of facts to convince people of the need to support the campaign?

Review
● Explain to the class that they will be continuing their campaign tomorrow, by selecting information from their web pages to create a complementary poster. In pairs, invite the children to share their work, and then choose an idea for their poster.

Curriculum objectives
● In non-narrative material, to use simple organisational devices.
● To use the first two or three letters of a word to check its spelling in a dictionary.

Resources
Children's web pages (from lesson 3); individual whiteboards; selection of posters or images of posters; felt-tipped pens; dictionaries; sticky notes

4: Poster campaign

Introduction

● Show the class your selected posters – either actual examples or from an online image search. (Posters on the environment would be appropriate choices.) Remind the children of the 'Wanted' posters they created earlier in the year.
● Ask what are the important things to remember when making a poster. The children should mention clarity, such as using clear, bold writing and having uncluttered pictures. They should also recall that there must be varieties of font size for items of different importance.
● Remind the class that they will be using an idea from their web pages to make a complementary rainforest campaign poster. Invite suggestions for an engaging statement to act as a heading that will grab readers' attention. Will they use questions or make use of facts, perhaps using an exclamation mark?

Independent work

● Invite the children to first make a very rough draft of their posters on whiteboards. Encourage them to check their spellings in dictionaries before going on to make their final posters. They should consider how they will use colour on their finished posters.

Review

● Pin the finished posters onto the wall and allow the children to look at them. Give each child two or three sticky notes on which to write positive comments about their favourite posters, posting them underneath.

Curriculum objectives
● To participate in discussion about both books that are read to them and those they have read themselves, taking turns and listening to what others say.
● To read aloud their own writing, to a group or the whole class, using appropriate intonation and controlling the tone and volume so that the meaning is clear.

Resources
Individual whiteboards

5: Rainforest: the big issue

Introduction

● Ask the children to vote on the question: *Should we bother to save the rainforest?* It is likely they will vote yes.
● Pose the questions: *What do you think the people who work for the logging companies would say? Would they agree with you? What about the local people who need space to grow crops to feed their families?*
● Explain that there is often more than one side to an argument. Today they will consider the future of the rainforest from several perspectives and have a debate about it.

Group work

● Organise the class into four groups to represent the loggers, the local people, the conservationists and the tourists.
● Allow them time to talk together in role about their position in relation to the rainforest and what they think should be done with it. Explain that they must put themselves in the position of their particular group, even if they disagree.
● Ask them to keep notes on whiteboards.

Whole-class work

● When the groups have had time to consider the aspects of their argument, bring the class together to hold a debate.
● Ask for several representatives from each group to put forward their opinions about how the rainforest should be used, whether logging should be allowed and to what extent.

Review

● After the debate, invite the class to vote again. Has anyone changed their mind?

Week 3 lesson plans

The children will focus on the life of rainforest people this week, considering the differences between their everyday lives. They will discuss, list and use their observations, based on their previous research, to write a diary in role as someone living in the rainforest. They will identify key features of diary writing which they will use when writing their own diary entries. They will draft, review and edit their writing before writing a final version in their best joined handwriting. Their writing will include consistent use of personal pronouns and a range of interesting conjunctions.

1: Living in the rainforest

Introduction
● Show the class your prepared slide show of images of people and homes of the Amazon rainforest.
● Ask if any of them came across information about the people of the rainforest when they were doing their research. What did they learn?
● Using what they know about rainforests, carry out a class discussion about what it would be like to live there. Look at the houses on the slide show and talk about similarities and differences between them and the children's own homes. How would the climate and weather affect everyday life? What would they be unlikely to have that they are used to having in their everyday lives? What things would they have that are different from those they are used to?

Paired work
● Hand out photocopiable page 201 'How can I live without them?' which lists things we consider essential to our lives, but which they would be unlikely to have easily to hand in the rainforest. Encourage pairs to discuss each item on the list before recording their observations and ideas.
● Remind them that although there are things they would be without, they should think about those things that would be commonly used by native rainforest people, such as plants to make medicines; cultivated land to grow food crops and keep animals; fuel, plant and animal food from the forest and so on.

Whole-class work
● Bring the class together and pose further questions about everyday life in the rainforest. For example: *How would you tell the time? How would you cook food? What would children do about going to school? Where would you get clothes from? How would you manage without soap and toothpaste? How would adults earn money?*

Independent work
● Following the discussion, provide the children with some sticky notes to write down their ideas for how they would adapt to living in the rainforest, using the headings from the photocopiable sheet. Pin sheets of sugar paper to the wall with the same headings for the children to attach their ideas.

Review
● Summarise the class's comments from each of the sheets. Have they suggested manual methods of dealing with things we usually use electricity for, such as washing clothes? Have they thought of harnessing natural resources, such as rainwater? Has anyone thought of doing without something, such as television or computers? Ask the children what things they consider to be essential and which are luxuries that we have come to think of as essentials. How would they pass their time without TV, computers, books and ready-made toys?

Expected outcomes
● All children can discuss and write in the first person about life in the rainforest, based on their research. They can make some improvements to drafted work. They can use legible joined handwriting.
● Most children can use comparisons between their life and others to present a realistic view of another person's life. They can use pronouns, appropriate language and write consistently in the first person. They can review and edit their work making well-chosen improvements.
● Some children can use highly effective language when writing in role.

Curriculum objectives
● To discuss writing similar to that which they are planning to write in order to understand and learn from its structure, grammar and vocabulary.
● To discuss and record ideas.

Resources
Prepare a slideshow of images of people and homes of the Amazon; photocopiable page 201 'How can I live without them?'; sticky notes; large sheets of paper

Curriculum objectives
● To discuss and record ideas.

Resources
Photocopiable page 202 'My life in the rainforest'; children's work (from lesson 1)

2: A day in the life...

Introduction

● Describe to the class the start of your day. Ask them what differences there might have been if you had woken up in the rainforest instead.
● Explain that they will be writing a diary entry in role about a day in the life of a rainforest dweller. Ask them to decide if they will be a child or adult, male or female as this will affect how they spend their fictional day.

Independent work

● Hand out photocopiable page 202 'My life in the rainforest' to record their thoughts on the areas they will include in their diary writing. Talk the children through it, explaining that they can write their ideas in any order.
● Ask them to think about different times of day, for example what they hear in the morning and at night-time could be different.
● Remind them about yesterday's work, which they can refer to if they wish.

Paired work

● In pairs, ask the children to use their notes to talk about how they will structure their writing, starting at the beginning of the day and working through until bedtime.

Differentiation
● Some children may find it easier to write their diary entry in the third person.

Review

● Check that the children are clear about the structure of their day and are prepared for writing their first draft.

Curriculum objectives
● To compose and rehearse sentences orally (including dialogue), progressively building a varied and rich vocabulary and an increasing range of sentence structures (See Appendix 2).
● To extend the range of sentences with more than one clause by using a wider range of conjunctions.
● To choose nouns or pronouns appropriately for clarity and cohesion and to avoid repetition.
● To use the present perfect form of verbs in contrast to the past tense.
● To use fronted adverbials.
● To use commas after fronted adverbials.

Resources
Diary of a Wimpy Kid by Jeff Kinney; children's work (from lesson 2)

3: What's in a diary?

Introduction

● Choose a short section from Diary of a Wimpy Kid by Jeff Kinney to read aloud to the class, such as the first entry.
● Remind the children that they will be writing a diary entry and ask them what they notice about the language and writing style in the extract. Note these on the board, which should include: written in the past tense and first person; written after the events happened; uses a chatty style; is honestly and freely expressed; follows chronological order; is written just for the writer.

Independent work

● Allow time for the children to use their photocopiable sheets (from lesson 2) and recall their partner discussion in order to write a first draft of their in-role diary entry.
● Explain that they should use organisational language, such as this morning, later on, after that, next, finally to help structure their writing. They should use paragraphs to show changes of time or events. Also remind them to ensure they use pronouns, fronted adverbials, the perfect form of verbs, and an interesting range of conjunctions in creating sentences with more than one clause.

Review

● When their drafts are finished, invite the children to read them through quietly, making any first edits, before they do a full review and edit in the next lesson. They may wish to show you their drafts for feedback.

■SCHOLASTIC

Curriculum objectives
● To assess the effectiveness of their own and others' writing and suggest improvements.
● To propose changes to grammar and vocabulary to improve consistency.
● To proofread for spelling and punctuation errors.

Resources
Children's drafts of their diary writing (from lesson 3); interactive activity 'Editors needed' on the CD-ROM; computer access; dictionaries

4: Editing the diaries

Introduction
● Invite the children to imagine they are the teachers. If they were marking the class's writing, what sorts of thing would they be looking out for?
● Begin by using starter activity 14 'Edit it'.
● Next, work with the class on the interactive activity 'Editors needed' on the CD-ROM, asking them to spot the errors and to offer improvements.

Independent work
● Invite the children to bear the edits in mind as they re-read their own work from the previous lesson, editing and making changes as necessary.
● Allow time for the children to re-read their work, looking for ways in which it can be improved and noting these on their drafts.
● Encourage them to use dictionaries to check spellings they are unsure about.

Differentiation
● Some of the children can be reluctant to change their original work, or find the task too daunting. Remind them that all writers edit and redraft their writing, often several times, in order to achieve the best result they can. Break down the process into segments, looking for one thing at a time, such as just spellings, punctuation, pronoun agreement or where words can be changed to improve clarity or vocabulary.

Review
● Discuss with the class how they are improving in their editing and revising skills. What are they finding easier the more they do it? What do they find most difficult? Do any of them have any useful tips for how they work that they would like to share with the others?

Curriculum objectives
● To use the diagonal and horizontal strokes that are needed to join letters and understand which letters, when adjacent to one another, are best left unjoined.
● To increase the legibility, consistency and quality of their handwriting.

Resources
Children's edited drafts (from lesson 4)

5: Final diary drafts

Introduction
● Ask the children if they have ever written something for themselves that later they found difficult to read. Explain that when we jot things down quickly, we don't always use our best handwriting, as it isn't important at the time. In the case of a personal diary, we are usually writing down things that are important to us, to note events or to record our feelings about people and things, so it would be necessary to write neatly for us to read them in the future – sometimes long in the future.
● Explain that today they will write their final versions of their rainforest diaries, incorporating the amendments they made when editing their work, and using their best handwriting.
● Recap on what makes good, legible handwriting. This should include evenly-sized and spaced letters and words, keeping joining strokes, ascenders and descenders parallel, and remembering which letters should not be joined. Remind the children about sitting correctly and angling their paper according to whether they are left- or right-handed.

Independent work
● Invite the children to work quietly, making final versions of their diaries.

Differentiation
● Remind left-handers particularly to use a correct pencil grip, so they don't put undue pressure on their hand and arm.

Review
● Ask the children to consider how rainforest people would find living in our western lifestyle. What might they miss about the rainforest?

Week 4 lesson plans

This week, the rainforest theme continues with two Brazilian stories for the children to read and study. They will identify the features of a short story, comparing it with those of the novel, act in role as characters from one of the stories, question children in role in the hot seat, and summarise events in the second story. They will look at language use in the second story and suggest how it could be changed with the use of conjunctions and fronted adverbials. They will increase their knowledge of pronouns by being introduced to possessive pronouns, noting the lack of apostrophes in these important words.

1: A short story

Introduction
● Explain to the class that they will be starting work on stories set in the rainforest. Read them the story 'The Legend of the Mafumeira' at www.worldstories.org.uk (click on 'Stories', 'Portuguese', 'The Legend of the Mafumeria').
● As you read, pause at the following three places and ask the children to predict what they think will happen next in the story. Firstly, read to: *We could earn ourselves a great deal of money if we cut down more trees.* Secondly, read to: *…I am here to protect and preserve the trees and the animals.* Finally read to: *…nothing will change my mind!*
● At the end of the story, invite the children to give their reactions. How would they sum up the three characters? What would Adao's companions have thought when the wind destroyed everything? What might they have told people when they got back home? What might Adao have thought about the same incident?
● Ask what the children notice about truth and fiction in the story. They should notice the facts about deforestation from their research, and the elements of myth or legend associated with the spirit of the forest. Can they suggest reasons why people might believe in the forest spirits?

Group work
● In groups of three, instruct the children to act out a scene between the three characters, discussing the decision by Adao's friends to cut down more trees.
● Although this is an argument, encourage them to use persuasive language to try and win each other over to their point of view, explaining their reasons for their planned actions.

Whole-class work
● Invite volunteers to sit in the hot seat, alternating between Adao and one of his friends.
● Ask the rest of the class to question the children in role as the characters, about their motivations for their plans and actions, and how they felt at different points in the story. For example, at the start when they were friends who were in agreement, later when they disagreed and then after the wind destroyed things.

Review
● Discuss with the class the tensions in the story. Would it have been as interesting and effective if the original plan had gone ahead, without the two friends' change of mind and the consequent disagreement? What other stories can they think of where there is a disagreement or problem in the middle that is sorted out or solved? Can they think of any stories where there is no tension in the middle? Why do they think this is?

2: What's in a story?

Introduction

- Remind the children about yesterday's story. Ask them how it links to their previous weeks' work (the setting is the same and it includes deforestation issues).
- Invite partners to talk for a couple of minutes, about differences between a short story and a full-length novel.
- Ask the class for their ideas, noting them on the board. They should include: length, short stories usually focus on one main character and event or plot-line, one problem which is usually solved, and are usually set in one place or time-frame.

Whole-class work

- Hand out photocopiable page 'Deer and Jaguar: a Brazilian folk tale' from the CD-ROM. Read them the opening section up to *Deer went on into the forest*. Ask what they notice about the writing style. They should mention different sentence lengths and use of repetition for effect.
- Let the children finish reading the story to themselves, then ask for their reactions. Did they anticipate the ending? How does this match the features of a short story listed earlier? Ask: *What did you notice about the sentence construction?* They should note that sentences are mostly short, with few conjunctions, other than *and*. Why do they think this style has been chosen?
- Ask them to look for examples of all the other grammatical and sentence construction features they have worked on this year.

Paired work

- Invite pairs of children to suggest where conjunctions might be used, noting them on their copies of the story.

Review

- Ask what changes the children suggest and compare ideas with the class.

Curriculum objectives

- To read books that are structured in different ways and read for a range of purposes.
- To discuss words and phrases that capture the reader's interest and imagination.
- To use conjunctions, adverbs and prepositions to express time and cause.
- To extend the range of sentences with more than one clause by using a wider range of conjunctions.

Resources

Photocopiable page 'Deer and Jaguar: a Brazilian folk tale' from the CD-ROM

3: Possessive pronouns

Introduction

- Ask the class for examples of pronouns and write them on the board. Do they know what pronouns are and when and why they are used?
- Highlight, or add the following pronouns to the list: *ours, whose, theirs, mine, his, hers*. Ask if the children can work out what they have in common. Agree that they indicate possession, so they are known as possessive pronouns.
- Provide examples to show the difference between personal pronouns and possessive pronouns, such as *When Ella woke up, **she** noticed it was snowing. The car in the drive was **theirs**.*
- Ask the children to give examples of both and write them on the board.

Independent work

- Hand out photocopiable page 203 'Possessive pronouns'. Draw attention to the pronouns *its, hers, theirs, yours,* and the fact that they do not contain apostrophes, even though they are conveying possession.
- Encourage the children to complete the photocopiable sheet independently.

> **Differentiation**
> - Invite early finishers to write their own sentences containing possessive pronouns. Revise the use of apostrophes for omission, (for example *it's,* and possession by using starter activity 6 'One or more?'

Review

- With the class work through the interactive activity 'Possession' on the CD-ROM, asking for their suggestions as to which pronoun best fits the sentences.

Curriculum objectives

- To indicate possession by using the possessive apostrophe with plural nouns.
- To learn the grammar for Year 4 in Appendix 2.
- To use and understand the grammatical terminology in Appendix 2 accurately and appropriately when discussing their writing and reading.

Resources

Photocopiable page 203 'Possessive pronouns'; interactive activity 'Possession' on the CD-ROM; computer access; individual whiteboards

Curriculum objectives
● To identify main ideas drawn from more than one paragraph and summarise these.
● To increase their familiarity with a wide range of books, including fairy stories, myths and legends, and retell some of these orally.
● To use dictionaries to check the meaning of words that they have read.
● To check that the text makes sense to them, discussing their understanding and explaining the meaning of words in context.

Resources
Photocopiable page 'Deer and Jaguar: a Brazilian folk tale' from the CD-ROM; photocopiable page 204 'Deer and Jaguar: bite-size'; dictionaries

4: Bite-size stories

Introduction
● Write the following on the board: *The bears' porridge was too hot so they went out. Goldilocks went into their house and found the porridge. It was still too hot. She broke a stool and went to sleep in Little Bear's bed. The bears came home, found her and she ran away.*
● Explain to the class that this is a summary of the main events in the story of Goldilocks, and remind them of the story of 'Deer and Jaguar' that they read earlier in the week. Tell them that today they will be writing a similar type of summary for that particular story.

Whole-class work
● Hand out photocopiable page 'Deer and Jaguar: a Brazilian folk tale' (from the CD-ROM) and photocopiable page 204 'Deer and Jaguar: bite-size'. Ask the children to read through the first part of the story, matching the summaries on the photocopiable sheet to the relevant part of the story.
● Talk with the class about how the summaries have been achieved. What has been missed out? Notice that the summaries include just the key events.

Independent work
● Allow time for the children to continue reading the story, and to write their summaries on photocopiable page 204 'Deer and Jaguar: bite-size'.
● Provide dictionaries for them to check the meanings of any unfamiliar words.

Review
● Invite the children to swap their summaries with a partner, and to compare their work. Then encourage each child to use the other's summary to retell the story orally to the class.

Curriculum objectives
● To use fronted adverbials.
● To use commas after fronted adverbials.
● To use and punctuate direct speech.
● To use the present perfect form of verbs in contrast to the past tense.
● To choose nouns or pronouns appropriately for clarity and cohesion and to avoid repetition.

Resources
Photocopiable page 'Deer and Jaguar: a Brazilian folk tale' from the CD-ROM

5: Revising fronted adverbials

Introduction
● With the class, use starter activity 7 'Fronted adverbials'.

Whole-class work
● Explain to the children that they will be selecting parts of the story 'Deer and Jaguar: a Brazilian folk tale' (from the CD-ROM) to rewrite using fronted adverbials. Ask them to read to themselves the first short paragraph of the story.
● Show them the sentence: *By the river in the forest, Deer walked.* Ask them to identify the adverbial and note the use of the comma after it.
● Then show them the sentence: *Using his fine antlers, Deer cleared the trees.* Ask the children to find the part of the story this sentence has been reworked from.

Independent work
● Explain to the children that they need to read through the story and select sections to rewrite in a similar way as in the whole-class task. Remind them to use fronted adverbials and to use commas after them.

Differentiation
● Some of the children may need adult guidance in selecting the sections to rewrite. Advise them to read two or three consecutive sentences at a time to see if they can reconfigure them.

Review
● Invite several of the children to share their reworked sentences with the class. Did people select similar sections to rewrite? Did they do it in similar ways?

Week 5 lesson plans

This week, the children will draw together the knowledge and understanding they have gained about the rainforest and about short stories, to plan, draft, write and edit their own short story based in the rainforest. They will choose a genre from those covered this year. After revising the grammar, punctuation and spelling covered in the year, the children will aim to include as much of these elements as possible in their stories. This writing week is the culmination of the narrative writing the children have worked on this year, and so should be their best piece.

1: Revising the rainforest

Introduction
- Ask the children to complete the 'L' section of photocopiable page 136 'KWL grid', which they started at the beginning of this unit, writing what they have Learned about the rainforest over the last few weeks.
- When their sheets are completed, invite the children to share their information with a partner, comparing and discussing similarities and differences. If the discussion reminds them of things they had forgotten, they may add these to their list, writing on the back of the sheet if necessary.
- Then encourage pairs to join to form small groups, making further comparisons.

Whole-class work
- Inform the children that they will now begin to use their knowledge to plan and write their own rainforest short story. They won't be able to use everything they know, so in choosing the theme for their story they should select appropriate background information. Explain that writers need to know more than they tell their readers in order to make their writing plausible and effective.
- Recap with the children the key features of short stories from last week. Tell them they should plan their stories to fit these criteria, ensuring they have a clear beginning, middle and end, focusing on one main event with only two or three characters.
- Explain that today they will share ideas for their stories. Remind the class of some story types they know: *legends, myths, adventures, stories with issues, creative non-fiction*. Show the class five large sheets of paper with the same headings, and pin them to the wall.

Group work
- In their groups of five, ask the children to come up with possible ideas for stories based in the rainforest for each of the five headings.
- When they have formulated a basic idea, invite them to write it briefly on a sticky note and post it on to the appropriate sheet. They should think of as many ideas as they can.

Review
- Read out to the class some of the story ideas from the sheets. Ask whose ideas they were and invite them to offer further explanation for the stories they had in mind. Tell the children they should be thinking of which story they will choose to write this week – it doesn't have to be one they thought of themselves, but can be from any of the shared suggestions. They should start to think about whether their story will be humorous or serious, and who or what their characters might be. They will have overnight thinking time to mull over their ideas, ready to start planning tomorrow.

Expected outcomes
- All children can discuss what they have read. They can use what they have learned to plan, draft and write a short story, including examples of most grammar and punctuation covered in the year.
- Most children can include examples of all grammar and punctuation covered in the year.
- Some children can also include examples of spellings covered in the year.

Curriculum objectives
- To discuss writing similar to that which they are planning to write in order to understand and learn from its structure, grammar and vocabulary.
- To discuss and record ideas.

Resources
Sticky notes; photocopiable page 136 'KWL grid'; large sheets of paper with the headings: *legends, myths, adventures, stories with issues, creative non-fiction*

Curriculum objectives
• In narratives, to create settings, characters and plot.
• To organise paragraphs around a theme.
• To compose and rehearse sentences orally (including dialogue), progressively building a varied and rich vocabulary and an increasing range of sentence structures (See Appendix 2).

Resources
Five ideas sheets on the wall (from lesson 1); photocopiable page 205 'My rainforest story plan'

2: Planning a rainforest story

Introduction
• Remind the children that today they will plan their stories set in the rainforest.
• Ask who has a good idea of what their story will be about, and invite some of the children to share these briefly.
• Remind the class that they will be writing in the genre of their choice, so they should remember the key features as they plan and write.

Independent work
• Hand out photocopiable page 205 'My rainforest story plan', talking through it with the children. Explain that the top line is for them to write the genre of their story, such as adventure or legend. If they have more than two characters, they may outline a third on the back, but they should not have more than three characters.
• Remind the children that as these are to be short stories, they should not have complicated plots. Reinforce this by referring to the stories they read last week.

Paired work
• When their plans are complete, encourage the children to use them as a guide to outline their story orally to a partner. Then invite them to make any changes to the plan which may be suggested or occur to them during the discussion.

Review
• Invite the children to share summaries of their partner's story with the class.

Curriculum objectives
• To use and understand the grammatical terminology in Appendix 2 accurately and appropriately when discussing their writing and reading.
• To extend the range of sentences with more than one clause by using a wider range of conjunctions.
• To use the present perfect form of verbs in contrast to the past tense.
• To choose nouns or pronouns appropriately for clarity and cohesion and to avoid repetition.
• To use conjunctions, adverbs and prepositions to express time and cause.
• To use fronted adverbials.
• To use commas after fronted adverbials.
• To indicate possession by using the possessive apostrophe with plural nouns.
• To use and punctuate direct speech.

Resources
Photocopiable page 206 'What a lot I've learned!'

3: Revision of grammar, punctuation and spelling

Introduction
• Remind the children of the grammar, punctuation and spelling they have learned and worked on during the year.
• Explain that they will be using as many of these as they can when they write their rainforest stories in order to produce an excellent piece of writing and to demonstrate how well they have learned them.

Whole-class work
• Choose a selection of starter activities to use, relating to the elements of grammar, punctuation and spelling that you feel would most benefit your class.

Independent work
• Hand out photocopiable page 206 'What a lot I've learned!' and talk through it with the class. Ask for a few examples of sentences that could be used for some of the headings. Encourage the children to create sentences that might be useful in their rainforest stories.
• Invite the children to complete the photocopiable sheet on their own. Fast finishers can write further examples on the back of the sheet.

> **Differentiation**
> • As the children are working on the photocopiable sheet, note those individuals who are unsure of particular concepts and plan for further work with them. Also, note any areas which seem to be most troublesome across the class, to feed into the review at the end of the lesson.

Review
• With the class, use appropriate starter activities based on the most common areas of difficulty that you noticed while the children were working.

4: Rainforest stories: first draft

Curriculum objectives
● To draft and write by composing and rehearsing sentences orally (including dialogue), progressively building a varied and rich vocabulary and an increasing range of sentence structures (See Appendix 2).
● To organise paragraphs around a theme.

Resources
Children's planning sheets (from earlier in the week)

Introduction
● Explain to the class that this will be the last story they will write this year, so they must aim to make it the very best they can. Remind them to include as many as they can of the grammar, punctuation and spelling elements they have worked on over the year and which they revised in lesson 3.
● Point out that as they write their drafts they should remember to write in paragraphs, pausing after each one to re-read it and making any immediate changes they feel would improve their work. They must also consider characterisation – remind them about 'showing, not telling' and how what a character says and does should tell us about their personality. Also, encourage them to use some similes in the descriptive parts of their writing to engage the reader.

Independent work
● Allow the children to spend the majority of the lesson using their plans to write the first drafts of their rainforest stories, revising as they go along.

Review
● Talk with the class about the writing process and how their understanding of it has developed over the year. Ask what they do differently now to how they worked then. How do they feel about the planning, drafting and editing process? How does this help them to produce better pieces of writing? Can they identify what their next steps might be?

5: Completing the stories

Curriculum objectives
● To assess the effectiveness of their own and others' writing, suggesting improvements.
● To propose changes to grammar and vocabulary to improve consistency.
● To proofread for spelling and punctuation errors.

Resources
Children's drafts (from lesson 4)

Introduction
● Ask the children to work in pairs to read and comment upon each other's draft stories. They should provide positive comments as well as pointing out any spelling and punctuation errors, suggesting improvements either to the grammar, vocabulary or sentence structure.

Independent work
● Provide enough time for the children to write final versions of their rainforest stories, incorporating any of their partner's changes they agree with, or have identified for themselves. Ensure they use their best joined handwriting.

> **Differentiation**
> ● If there are any children who remain uncomfortable about receiving comments on their work from a partner, encourage them to first read through their own writing critically, noting anything they are unsure about. They can then ask their partner for comments on those specific things, rather than leaving themselves open to comments on any aspect of their work. This approach may help to build their confidence.

Review
● Ask the children to read through their final versions silently, choosing a section that they feel particularly pleased with. Invite them to share these sections with a partner and the class. Ask the children how well they feel their stories fit their chosen genre. Final drafts can be displayed, perhaps with appropriate illustrations, or collated into a class book of rainforest tales.

Week 6 lesson plans

The poetry week focuses on creatures of the rainforest, with three short poems for the children to read, discuss and perform in groups with their own planned musical and sound accompaniment. In order to write their own rainforest animal poems, they will revisit spelling the suffixes '-ous' and '-ly' to consider descriptive words and phrases that they can use. In writing their own poems they must consider content, style and structure as well as vocabulary. They will then work with a partner to plan a reading of their poem, which they will deliver to a group.

1: Poetic animals of the rainforest

Introduction
● Ask the children to name animals of the rainforest that they remember from their research. List them on the board. Spend a little time talking about those animals which they know the most about.

Whole-class work
● Hand out photocopiable page 207 'Animal poems', allowing time for the children to read the poems to themselves.
● Then select three children to read one poem each aloud to the class.
● Ask the children for brief initial comments on each of the poems.

Paired work
● Working with a reading partner, encourage the children to discuss the poems together.
● Invite them to think about the content, tone and language used as well as the structure of the poems.

Whole-class work
● Draw the class together, and discuss each poem in turn, starting with 'Honey Bear'. Begin by asking for the children's observations and comments. Ask them to tap out the rhythm of the poem. Draw attention to the use of adverbs to end each stanza, and which form the rhyme. Why do they think there is an ellipsis in the penultimate line? Can they find alliteration? Notice how the final word ends the poem creating a different rhythm. How would they describe the 'feel' of the poem (such as gentle)?
● Display the photograph of the kinkajou on screen 1 of 'Rainforest animals' on the CD-ROM, and talk about how the writing style reflects the animal.
● Next look at the poem 'River Wolf'. Again, begin by asking for the children's comments. Why do they think the poem isn't called 'Giant Otter'? Discuss the structure of the poem, noting the single-word lines. How does this device add to the strength of the poem? What verbs can the children identify?
● Show photograph of the giant otter screen 2 of 'Rainforest animals' on the CD-ROM. How well do they think the poem paints a picture of the animal?
● Finally, read 'Pain forest'. After discussing the children's observations, ask why they think this title was chosen. What sort of image does the poem give of the rainforest? How does it make them feel? Which senses have been used to describe it? Note the rhythm and rhyme. Point out the assonance in the words *between* and *trees*.

Review
● Explain to the class that later in the week they will be writing their own rainforest animal poems and refer them back to the list made at the beginning of the lesson. Encourage them to start to think of which animal or animals they may write their poems about and what sort of poem they might compose. They will have some thinking time to gather ideas together about rhythm, style and vocabulary.

Expected outcomes
● All children can discuss poems, noting key structural features. They can perform their own and others' poems. They can spell some words with '-ous' and '-ly' suffixes.
● Most children can demonstrate understanding of rhythm and rhyme in the poems and use volume, tone, pace and intonation in their performance. They can spell most words with the chosen suffixes.
● Some children can demonstrate a deeper understanding of poems they read and perform very effectively, using their voice to convey atmosphere. They can spell all of the words with the chosen suffixes.

Curriculum objectives
● To listen to and discuss a wide range of fiction, poetry, plays, non-fiction and reference books or textbooks.
● To discuss writing similar to that which they are planning to write in order to understand and learn from its structure, grammar and vocabulary.
● To recognise some different forms of poetry.
● To discuss words and phrases that capture the reader's interest and imagination.

Resources
Photocopiable page 207 'Animal poems'; media resource 'Rainforest animals' on the CD-ROM

Curriculum objectives
● To prepare poems to read aloud and to perform, showing understanding through intonation, tone, volume and action.

Resources
Photocopiable page 207 'Animal poems'; a selection of musical instruments, such as claves, swannee whistles, tambours, tambourines, snare drums, triangles, recorders, xylophones, glockenspiels; media resource 'Rainforest sounds' on the CD-ROM

2: Poetry performance

Introduction
● Play the class audio 'Rainforest sounds' on the CD-ROM. Talk about what they heard, how the sounds provide an atmosphere of the rainforest and how many of the sounds they could identify.
● Explain to the children that they will be working out, rehearsing and performing one of the animal poems. As well as reading the poem, they will be using musical instruments, or mouth and body sounds, to add a rainforest atmosphere to the poem.
● Ask them what key aspects they will need to bear in mind for their performance. They should ensure that the sound effects do not interfere with their reading of the poem itself. Suggest that they could be quiet accompaniments to the reading, or be used in between verses.

Group work
● Divide the class into three groups, giving one of the poems to each group. You may wish to appoint group leaders.
● Through discussion, ask the groups to agree on how they will read and perform the poem.
● Allow them time to select any instruments they wish to use and to practise their performance.

Review
● After rehearsing, each group will perform their poem for the rest of the class. After each performance, ask the listeners for comments, both positive and with suggestions for how it might have been improved.

Curriculum objectives
● To discuss words and phrases that capture the reader's interest and imagination.
● To apply their growing knowledge of root words, prefixes and suffixes (etymology and morphology) as listed in Appendix 1, both to read aloud and to understand the meaning of new words they meet.
● To use further prefixes and suffixes and understand how to add them (Appendix 1).
● To spell words that are often misspelled (Appendix 1).
● To spell further homophones.

Resources
Individual whiteboards

3: Choosing the best words

Introduction
● With the class, use starter activity 9 'Spellchecker'.

Whole-class work
● Explain to the children that to prepare for writing animal poems tomorrow, they will be thinking about descriptive vocabulary they might use. Remind the class of their work from earlier in the year on the suffix '-ous' and ask them to think of words with that suffix that might be used to describe rainforest animals. Encourage them to write them, one at a time, on their whiteboards, to show you.
● Select several of the words and write them on the board, such as *vicious, fabulous, poisonous, adventurous, dangerous.*
● Next, ask for adverbs ending in '-ly' which could describe how the animals move or behave, such as *carefully, noisily, confidently, rapidly.* Also, write these on the board.

Paired work
● Provide time for the children to work together, selecting words from those listed on the board, to write descriptive phrases for rainforest animals of their choice.
● Encourage them to use alliteration or assonance where they can, for example *adventurous anaconda, cautiously and carefully creeping, enormous jaws.* They should write their phrases on their whiteboards.

Review
● Invite the children to share some of their phrases with the class who should then suggest, where appropriate, animals the descriptions could be used for. Dictate some of the children's phrases for them to write on their whiteboards, and to show you.

Curriculum objectives
● To compose and rehearse sentences orally (including dialogue), progressively building a varied and rich vocabulary and an increasing range of sentence structures (See Appendix 2).

Resources
Media resource 'Rainforest sounds' on the CD-ROM; individual whiteboards

4: Writing rainforest poems

Introduction

● Play again the audio 'Rainforest sounds' on the CD-ROM, to create an atmosphere.
● Remind the class of the poems they read earlier in the week, and the words they worked on yesterday. Explain that today they will be writing their own rainforest animal poem. They should already have some ideas for their poems, so ask which animals they have chosen.

Paired work

● Invite the children to work with a partner to discuss their ideas. They must choose animals they know enough about for the poem to work. As well as being able to describe the animals, they should know how they move, their habitat and behaviours.
● During their discussion, encourage them to begin to note words and phrases for their poems. They should be aware of homophones they might use such as *deer/dear*, *herd/heard*, *high/hi*, *rain/rein/reign*, *sun/son*, *wood/would*.

Independent work

● Before the children begin to write their poems, ensure they decide on the form they will use, which includes the rhythm and rhyme, if there is one.
● Briefly remind them of the points discussed earlier in the week when they read the three animal poems. Remind them about the importance of punctuation in poetry. Then provide time for them to write their poems.

> **Differentiation**
> ● To help with form and rhythm, some children may find it useful to choose and use a rhythm from the poems they read earlier in the week.

Review

● Ask which animals were chosen. Invite the children to read their completed poems aloud to the rest of the class.

Curriculum objectives
● To prepare poems and playscripts to read aloud and to perform, showing understanding through intonation, tone, volume and action.

Resources
Children's poems (from lesson 4); prepare a slideshow of rainforest images, including animals; media resource 'Rainforest sounds' on the CD-ROM

5: Perform-a-poem

Introduction

● Set the scene by playing the audio 'Rainforest sounds' on the CD-ROM, while showing your prepared slideshow of rainforest images.
● Explain to the children that they will be working with a partner to prepare a reading of the poems they wrote yesterday. Recap on the features of a good performance.

Paired work

● In pairs, invite the children to help each other to prepare and rehearse readings of their own poems. They must consider the pace, volume, tone and intonation of their delivery. It may help for the children to read each others' poems aloud so the writer can hear what they sound like.

Group work

● Encourage pairs to join to form groups and then perform their poems to each other, offering comments for each reading.

Review

● Talk about the writing process. How did the children select their animal? How easy was it to decide on the focus of their poem? How well do they think they have managed to maintain rhythm and rhyme? Invite the children to perform what they feel is the most effective part of their poem for the class.

Curriculum objectives
● To choose nouns or pronouns appropriately for clarity and cohesion and to avoid repetition.
● To use and understand the grammatical terminology in Appendix 2 accurately and appropriately when discussing their writing and reading.

Resources
Photocopiable page 'Pronoun check' from the CD-ROM

Grammar and punctuation: Possessive pronouns

Revise
● Invite the children to define what a pronoun is. Ask: *What is the difference between a personal pronoun and a possessive pronoun?* Remind them that possessive pronouns ending with the letter 's' do not have apostrophes, even though they are indicating possession, because they are pronouns, not nouns.
● Encourage the children to suggest pronouns, writing them on the board. Invite them to say sentences containing a pronoun of their choice. Ask for some sentences which begin with the pronoun and others that don't.

Assess
● Hand out photocopiable page 'Pronoun check' from the CD-ROM. Go over the instructions with the class, ensuring they understand what they have to do before they complete the sheet independently.
● After they have completed the tasks, review their answers as a class before collecting them in.

Further practice
● Using a selection of both fiction and non-fiction books, ask the children to open the books at random, and keep a tally of the pronouns on one or two pages. For instance, note the pronoun when it first occurs, then keep a tally against it as the two pages are read.
● Ask them whether there is any difference in usage between fiction and non-fiction texts. Can they suggest why this might be? Does it make a difference what the non-fiction book is about?

Curriculum objectives
● To use further prefixes and suffixes and understand how to add them (Appendix 1).
● To write from memory simple sentences, dictated by the teacher, that include words and punctuation taught so far.

Spelling: The suffixes '-ous' and '-ly' together

Revise
● Invite the children to suggest words that end in '-ous-'. What sort of words are they? (adjectives). Ask for examples of phrases about rainforest animals with descriptive words ending in '-ous', such as *dangerous jaguar, curious monkey*.
● Encourage the class to list words ending in the suffix '-ly'. What type of words are these, often? (adverbs). Ask for phrases or sentences with examples, again relating to the rainforest, such as *deforestation is particularly problematic, some animals can be extremely dangerous*.
● Write on the board the words *fabulously, previously, continuously*. Ask what the children notice about the words. They should mention that they have both '-ous' and '-ly' endings, thus combining the two suffixes. Can they suggest any more?

Assess
● Dictate the following short sentences for the children to write: *The jaguar was dangerously close; He thought seriously about the problem; Obviously, he would have to go home; The monkey sniffed curiously at the fruit; The explorer trod cautiously through the forest; The python is tremendously strong; The rain fell continuously for days; The loggers were acting suspiciously; He looked nervously around; Many animals have mysteriously disappeared.*
● Collect in the children's work and check their spelling.

Further practice
● Challenge the class to see how many words ending with '-ously' they can collect.

Curriculum objectives
● To ask questions to improve their understanding of a text.
● To draw inferences such as inferring characters' feelings, thoughts and motives from their actions, and justify inferences with evidence.

Resources
Photocopiable page 'Deer and Jaguar: a Brazilian folk tale' from the CD-ROM; photocopiable page 'Rainforest survivor' from the CD-ROM; individual whiteboards

Reading: Rainforests

Revise

● Remind the children of the work they did on the two stories from Brazil – 'Deer and Jaguar: a Brazilian folk tale' and 'The Legend of the Mafumeira'. What can they remember of how they used inference to work out and understand the feelings of the various characters in the stories?

● Remind them about the work they did previously on 'showing, not telling' where we know as readers how a character is feeling because of what the writer gives them to say and do, and how their words and actions are described.

● Hand out photocopiable page 'Deer and Jaguar: a Brazilian folk tale' from the CD-ROM, for the children to re-read to themselves, to refresh their memories about the story. Let them work in pairs to frame comprehension questions about the story.

● Encourage them to devise both straightforward questions that can be answered with direct reference to the text, and questions which relate to inference. They should note their questions on whiteboards, and be sure they know their answers.

● Invite the pairs to then join together, asking each other the questions they have devised, and provide the answers if they are not correct.

● Bring the class together to discuss the question-and-answer activity. Which type of question did the children find easiest to write and to answer? How much did they refer to the text in both writing and answering the questions? What words and phrases did they use to begin their questions – was there any difference between the two question types? Did anyone use phrases like *How do we know...?* or *What tells us that...?*

Assess

● Explain to the class that the assessment requires them to read a story opening for which they will write their own comprehension questions, along with answers.

● Hand out photocopiable page 'Rainforest survivor' from the CD-ROM and allow time for the children to read it through to themselves.

● Explain that they will be writing their own comprehension questions about the piece. They must include both straightforward questions that can be answered by direct reference to the text, and questions which use inference, where the answer has to be worked out from clues in the text. As well as writing the questions, they must also provide the answers they would expect. Explain that, where appropriate, they should refer directly to evidence from the text to support their answers.

● Allow the children time to complete the assessment task. You may wish to suggest the number of questions and answers to be written, differentiating according to children's experience.

Further practice

● Answering and asking comprehension questions from a wide range of texts is one way of gauging children's understanding of what they have read. Provide them with both – ready-prepared comprehension questions to answer both orally and in written form, as well as a variety of texts for them to write their own questions for. This is a good activity to use as part of guided reading, where you are in a position to support the children in their understanding of a text, and where both questions and answers can be discussed in the group.

● Use class sets of books, where the children can confer on their reading and create a bank of comprehension questions for others in the class to answer when they read the books for themselves.

Curriculum objectives

- To plan their writing by discussing writing similar to that which they are planning to write in order to understand and learn from its structure, grammar and vocabulary.
- To discuss and record ideas.
- To write, building a varied and rich vocabulary and a range of sentence structures.
- In narratives, to create settings, characters and plot.
- To assess the effectiveness of their own and others' writing and suggest improvements.
- To proofread for spelling and punctuation errors.

Resources

Photocopiable page 'Rainforest survivor' from the CD-ROM; whiteboards and pens; sticky notes; large sheet of paper

Writing: Rainforests

Revise

- Ask the children what they consider to be the essential ingredients for a good story. Let them work with a partner to come up with ideas, listing them on whiteboards. If possible, they should try to choose their top five. When the lists are complete, invite the children to write them onto sticky notes and post them onto a large sheet of paper which has been pinned to the wall.
- Talk over the children's suggestions, summarising the ideas, and finding those which many have chosen as being important. As you read through them, look out for any areas which the children have missed, and add them yourself. For example, have they thought of including tension, atmosphere, different types of character, well-chosen vocabulary and the inclusion of 'showing, not telling'?
- Ask the class to give examples of stories they have particularly enjoyed, explaining which of the criteria they've discussed are included in the story.

Assess

- Hand out photocopiable page 'Rainforest survivor' from the CD-ROM, which the children know from their reading assessment. Ask what part of the story they think this comes from, agreeing that it is a story opening or preface to the story itself. Talk together about what is included and what is missing. For example, we are not told what the expedition was for, how many or who the other people were. We don't hear any details about their experiences apart from them losing their gear in the flood. Also, we don't know how they managed to survive, or indeed if all of them did or only the narrator.
- Invite the class to choose one part of the story to tell. They might choose a section from the beginning, an event from the middle, or the conclusion when we discover how they survived. Encourage them to assume the character of the narrator and write their version of events in diary form. Ask them for the key features of a diary entry, referring to the rainforest dweller's diary entry, which they recently wrote.
- Allow the children time to think about and plan their diary story, before writing it, re-reading it and editing as they go along.

Further practice

- For the children to write effectively, they should read widely from a wide range of texts, discuss these in an open forum, and apply what they learn about the structure in their own writing. To that end, a class book club could be formed, with the children choosing their own personal reading as a focus for discussion, where they explain what they liked and didn't like about the book. Moving on from here, encourage the children to write in the same style as that of the book they are reading, or to continue the story after the book has ended, again using the same writing style.

My web-page plan

- What will you include on your web page?

Main heading	
Subheading 1 and what it will cover	
Subheading 2 and what it will cover	
Subheading 3 and what it will cover	
Illustrations and how they will be used	
Links	
Other ideas	

I can use what I know about web pages to plan my own.

How did you do?

Name: _____   Date: _____

How can I live without them?

- Next to each item in the grid below, list what you use it for and how you could adapt to life without it.

What I use	How I use it	How I could adapt
Electricity		
Running water		
Cars and buses		
Shops		
Roads and railways		
Doctors and hospitals		

I can discuss and record information.

How did you do?

My life in the rainforest

■ Use this thinking sheet to note ideas for your writing.

I hear

I eat

I can smell

I feel

I can see

Today I will

I can use information from my reading and discussions to record my ideas for a piece of writing.

How did you do?

Possessive pronouns

■ Choose a possessive pronoun from those listed in the box, to complete the following sentences. See how many different ones you can use.

my	mine	our	ours	its	his	her	hers
	their	theirs	your	yours	whose		

I'm sorry, it was _____ fault.

The dog went into _____ kennel.

She said the hat was _____ .

He knew it was _____ only chance.

It isn't _____ so it must be _____ .

_____ keys are these?

Which one is _____ house?

Hey! That chair's _____ , not _____ !

The boys took _____ place in the line-up.

The car was rusty and _____ windows were broken.

I can use possessive pronouns.

How did you do?

Deer and Jaguar: bite-size

■ Read the story of 'Deer and Jaguar', and summarise it in short, bite-size sentences. A start has been made here for you.

- Deer and Jaguar both need somewhere to live.

- Deer cleared a place to build a house.

- Jaguar found Deer's clearing and decided to build his home there.

- _____

- _____

- _____

- _____

- _____

- _____

- _____

- _____

- _____

- _____

- _____

- _____

I can summarise a story.

How did you do?

PHOTOCOPIABLE   ■SCHOLASTIC
www.scholastic.co.uk

My rainforest story plan

- Create your story plan below.

My story is a _____

My characters:

Name:	Name:
Description:	Description:

My setting: (Which part of the rainforest is the story set in?)

What can be seen? _____

_____

What can be heard? _____

_____

My plot:

Opening: _____

_____

Main events: _____

_____

Ending: _____

_____

I can plan a story, creating characters, setting and plot.

How did you do?

What a lot I've learned!

■ Write a sentence to show an example for each of the things you have learned this year.

Possessive apostrophes _____

_____

Fronted adverbials with commas _____

_____

Possessive pronouns _____

_____

Direct speech _____

_____

Prepositions of time or cause _____

_____

The perfect form of verbs _____

_____

Homophones_____

_____

Conjunctions joining clauses _____

_____

Prefixes and suffixes _____

_____

I can demonstrate what I have learned in grammar, punctuation and spelling.

How did you do?

PHOTOCOPIABLE

■SCHOLASTIC
www.scholastic.co.uk

Animal poems

Honey Bear

Snug inside its hollow tree,
Honey Bear waits out the day,
sleepily.

Safe in shadows, now night falls,
Honey Bear eats fruit and leaves,
noisily.

Honey Bear, Honey Bear, you
have two names; whisper it,
quietly…

Kinkajou.

River Wolf

Quicker than thinking.
a Giant Otter hunting,
turns on a fish tail…

Bites.

Wolf of the river.
catch in its paws
sprawls on the Amazon shore…

Eats.

Belly full,
whiskers clean,
it cuddles its brothers
in a mud-cooled den…

Sleeps.

Pain Forest

There's hundreds
of eyes over there
in the dark, between
those invisible trees.

There's howlers,
there's growlers,
there's shriekers,
there's barks.
There's something that's
munching my ear.

The rainforest's great,
nature served on a plate.

But please,
pretty please,
before it's too late,
Get me out of here!

by Nick Dowson